The Rent Restrictions Acts : with a supplement bringing the work down to July 31, 1924, and including the Prevention of Eviction Act, 1924.

Theodore John Sophian

The Rent Restrictions Acts : with a supplement bringing the work down to July 31, 1924, and including the Prevention of Eviction Act, 1924.

Sophian, Theodore John

collection ID CTRG98-B2880

Reproduction from Yale Law School Library

Supplement to the Rent Restrictions Acts, 1920, 1923" has separate t.p. Includes legislation. Includes indexes.

London : Stevens and Sons, 1924.

xxvii, 280, xi, 28 p. : forms ; 22 cm

The Making of Modern Law collection of legal archives constitutes a genuine revolution in historical legal research because it opens up a wealth of rare and previously inaccessible sources in legal, constitutional, administrative, political, cultural, intellectual, and social history. This unique collection consists of three extensive archives that provide insight into more than 300 years of American and British history. These collections include:

Legal Treatises, 1800-1926: over 20,000 legal treatises provide a comprehensive collection in legal history, business and economics, politics and government.

Trials, 1600-1926: nearly 10,000 titles reveal the drama of famous, infamous, and obscure courtroom cases in America and the British Empire across three centuries.

Primary Sources, 1620-1926: includes reports, statutes and regulations in American history, including early state codes, municipal ordinances, constitutional conventions and compilations, and law dictionaries.

These archives provide a unique research tool for tracking the development of our modern legal system and how it has affected our culture, government, business – nearly every aspect of our everyday life. For the first time, these high-quality digital scans of original works are available via print-on-demand, making them readily accessible to libraries, students, independent scholars, and readers of all ages.

The BiblioLife Network

This project was made possible in part by the BiblioLife Network (BLN), a project aimed at addressing some of the huge challenges facing book preservationists around the world. The BLN includes libraries, library networks, archives, subject matter experts, online communities and library service providers. We believe every book ever published should be available as a high-quality print reproduction; printed on-demand anywhere in the world. This insures the ongoing accessibility of the content and helps generate sustainable revenue for the libraries and organizations that work to preserve these important materials.

The following book is in the "public domain" and represents an authentic reproduction of the text as printed by the original publisher. While we have attempted to accurately maintain the integrity of the original work, there are sometimes problems with the original work or the micro-film from which the books were digitized. This can result in minor errors in reproduction. Possible imperfections include missing and blurred pages, poor pictures, markings and other reproduction issues beyond our control. Because this work is culturally important, we have made it available as part of our commitment to protecting, preserving, and promoting the world's literature.

GUIDE TO FOLD-OUTS MAPS and OVERSIZED IMAGES

The book you are reading was digitized from microfilm captured over the past thirty to forty years. Years after the creation of the original microfilm, the book was converted to digital files and made available in an online database.

In an online database, page images do not need to conform to the size restrictions found in a printed book. When converting these images back into a printed bound book, the page sizes are standardized in ways that maintain the detail of the original. For large images, such as fold-out maps, the original page image is split into two or more pages

Guidelines used to determine how to split the page image follows:

• Some images are split vertically; large images require vertical and horizontal splits.
• For horizontal splits, the content is split left to right.
• For vertical splits, the content is split from top to bottom.
• For both vertical and horizontal splits, the image is processed from top left to bottom right.

THE RENT RESTRICTIONS ACTS

WITH A SUPPLEMENT

Bringing the work down to July 31, 1924,
and including the Prevention of Eviction Act, 1924.

BY

THEODORE JOHN SOPHIAN, B.A. (Oxon.),

OF WADHAM COLLEGE, OXFORD THE INNER TEMPLE, AND SOUTH-EASTERN CIRCUIT,
BARRISTER-AT-LAW, PROFUMO PRIZEMAN, YARBOROUGH-ANDERSON SCHOLAR,
AND AUTHOR OF THE "RENT RESTRICTIONS (NOTICES OF INCREASE) ACT, 1923."

LONDON·
STEVENS AND SONS, LIMITED,
119 & 120, CHANCERY LANE,
Law Publishers.
1924.

PRINTED IN GREAT BRITAIN BY
C. F. ROWORTH, 88, FETTER LANE, LONDON, E.C.

PREFACE.

———◆———

No piece of legislation perhaps has ever given rise to such a number of problems or has led to such acute controversy both among lawyers and laymen as the Rent Restrictions Acts. At the present time with the addition of the supplementary legislation contained in the Notices of Increase Act and the 1923 Act together with the steadily accumulating and sometimes contrary decisions on the Acts themselves the position appears to have become more chaotic than ever.

I have accordingly made a serious endeavour in this work to set out as clearly and as completely as possible, in a concise and comprehensive form, the law as it is to be found at the present time in the Acts themselves and in the numerous decisions thereon.

In the preparation of this book I have carefully read and examined all the cases dealing with the subject and contained in all the English Scotch and Irish Reports nor have I overlooked the decisions in the County Courts and, as regards Scotland, the Sheriff Courts. I have carefully noted every decision in its appropriate place, and I have further made use of any *obiter dicta* in the judgments which tend to throw light on the meaning of other portions of the Acts.

Any variation in the application of the Acts to Scotland has been indicated in the text or in footnotes, and attention has been drawn where necessary to the Rules made under the Acts

In dealing with the Notices of Increase Act, 1923 and the 1923 Act especially, I have examined the problems that are likely to arise on a construction of these Acts and I have given my carefully considered views thereon

In the Appendices will be found the text of the Acts and of the Rules made thereunder including the 1923 Rules and also the text of the repealed Acts

A special Index in addition has been prepared to facilitate references to the various sections of the Acts

The kind and gratifying reception already accorded to my pamphlet on the Rent Restrictions (Notices of Increase) Act 1923 leads me to hope that this book will prove of even greater service

In conclusion, I should like to record my thanks for the kindly advice and encouragement held out to me by Sir Hugh Fraser, to whom in no small measure the publication of this work is due. Last, but not least I must thank my wife for the assistance she has given me in correcting and revising the proofs and in preparing this book for the press

THEO J SOPHIAN

3 Prowdes Buildings
TEMPLE,
15th August 1923

(v)

CONTENTS.

———◆———

CHAPTER I

———

CHAPTER II

STANDARD RENT—RATEABLE VALUE—APPORTIONMENT

———

CHAPTER III

APPLICATION OF THE ACTS

———

CHAPTER IV

PERMITTED INCREASES OF RENT

CHAPTER X

APPENDICES

APPENDIX I

APPENDIX II

TEXT OF THE RULES

APPENDIX III

TEXT OF THE REPEALED ACTS

APPENDIX IV

INDEX TO THE SECTIONS OF THE ACT.

—◆—

II —THE RENT RESTRICTIONS (NOTICES OF INCREASE) ACT, 1923

III.—THE RENT AND MORTGAGE INTEREST
RESTRICTIONS ACT 1923

Part I

(xv)

TABLE OF CASES.

W

THE RENT RESTRICTIONS ACTS, 1920, 1923.

CHAPTER 1

INTRODUCTORY.

THE aim of the Rent Acts has been to confer protection against excessive increases of rent as well as continuity of tenure on tenants of houses let at rentals below certain specified limits At the same time the Legislature has safeguarded the interests of the owners themselves by curtailing the ordinary rights and powers of mortgagees in respect of such property

The principal Act is the Act of 1920 (10 & 11 Geo 5, c 17), which came into operation on the 2nd July, 1920 and was originally intended (*a*) to expire except as regards Scotland (*b*), on the 24th June 1923 This Act also applied to business premises, but its provisions so far as they relate to business premises expired on the 24th June 1921 (*c*) The Act further applied, with certain modifications to Scotland (*d*) and Ireland (*e*) as well The principal Act—and in this book the Act of 1920 will be referred to as the principal Act" or ' the Act," and the Act shall mean the Act of 1920 except when the context otherwise requires (*f*)—was further extended together

(*a*) Sect 19 (2)   (*b*) Sect 18 (1) (a)
(*c*) Sect 13 (3)   (*d*) Sect 18 (1)
(*e*) Sect 18 (2)

(*f*) References to sections simply will in this book refer to sections of the Act of 1920 unless the context otherwise requires

1

with the Notices of Increase Act 1923 (13 & 14 Geo 5 c 13)
until the 31st July 1923 by the Continuance Act 1923 (13 &
14 Geo 5, c 7) but the last mentioned Act excludes Northern
Ireland from its provisions and the Notices of Increase Act
1923 does not extend to Ireland (g) The principal Act of 1920
has been amended firstly by the Notices of Increase Act of
1923 which was passed in order to meet the difficult situation
created by the decision of the House of Lords in *Kerr v Bryde*
and secondly by the Rent and Mortgage Interest Restrictions
Act 1923 (13 & 14 Geo 5 c 32) which may be conveniently
called and will hereinafter be referred to as the Amendment
Act or the 1923 Act This Act like the Notices of Increase
Act does not apply to Ireland but it applies to Scotland with
certain modifications (h)

As regards the Legislation previous to 1920 the principal Act
of 1920 repealed *in toto* the Increase of Rent and Mortgage
Interest (War Restrictions) Act 1915 (5 & 6 Geo 5 c 97) the
Increase of Rent and Mortgage Interest (Restrictions) Act 1919
(9 Geo 5 c 7) and the Increase of Rent &c (Amendment)
Act 1919 (9 & 10 Geo 5 c 90) It also repealed sects 1 5
and 7 of the Courts (Emergency Powers) Act 1917 (7 & 8
Geo 5 c 25)

Besides the three Rent Acts mentioned above there was a
further Act the Increase of Rent &c (Amendment) Act 1918
8 Geo 5 c 7 which was repealed by the Amendment Act of
1919 (i)

At present therefore the Acts to be considered are the principal Act of 1920 as amended by the Notices of Increase Act
1923 and by the Amendment Act of 1923 It should further
be remembered that the Act of 1920 now applies and the
Notices of Increase Act and the Amendment Act of 1923 apply
only to England Wales and Scotland

By the Amendment Act the principal Act of 1920 as modified
by the provisions in Part I and Part III of the former Act

(g) Sect 4 of Notices of Increase Act 1923
(h) Sect 19
(i) 9 & 10 Geo 5 c 90

continues in force until the 24th June 1923 (k) except as
regards Scotland in which case it continues in force until the
28th May 1925 (l). After the expiry of the principal Act on
those dates in England and Scotland, respectively Part II of the
Amendment Act comes into force and provides some measure of
control for another five years though Part II may be repealed
by His Majesty in Council at an earlier date if a resolution to
that effect is passed by both Houses of Parliament (Sect 17).
The law as it will be after the expiry of the principal Act will
be found considered in Chapter XII (m).

The scope of the Rent Acts has gradually been extended so as
to bring within the ambit of their provisions dwelling-houses of
a higher standard rent and rateable value. The first Act of 1915
applied to houses where *either* the standard rent or rateable value
did not exceed (a) in the metropolitan police district including
the City of London 35l (b) in Scotland 30l and (c) elsewhere 26l. Sect 2 (2).

The Act of 1919 (n) extended the provisions of the principal
Act to houses where *both* the standard rent and the rateable
value were in the case of houses situated in the metropolitan
police district including the City of London between the limits
of 35l - 70l in the case of houses situated in Scotland, between
the limits of 30l —60l and in the case of houses situated elsewhere between the limits of 26l —52l (Sect 4).

The Act of 1920 reverts to the method adopted by the Act
of 1915, and applies to houses where *either* the standard rent
or the rateable value does not exceed—(a) in the metropolitan
police district including the City of London 105l (b) in Scotland 90l and (c) elsewhere 78l (Sect 12 (2)). This Act
further made a new departure by including business premises
within its provisions though at the present time once again
only dwelling-houses are within the Act (Sect 13).

(k) Sect 1
(l) Sect 19 (1)
(m) Infra p 161
(n) 9 Geo 5 c 7
(o) See infra p 23

The Act is not limited to governing the relations between the original lessor and lessee or the original mortgagor and mortgagee. By sect. 12 (1) (p) except where the context otherwise requires the expressions "landlord" "tenant" "mortgagee" and "mortgagor" include any person from time to time deriving title under the original landlord tenant mortgagee or mortgagor. Thus a landlord who is also a sub-tenant but has subsequently acquired the head interest in the whole of the premises is entitled to the benefit of the Act, and his rights and remedies as against the tenant (his immediate landlord and now his own tenant) are to be regarded as no greater and, at the same time, no less than the rights of his predecessor in title (*Rock* v. *Burke*, 56 I. L. T. p. 24). The expression "landlord" further includes in relation to any dwelling-house (except where the context otherwise requires) any person other than the tenant who is or would but for the Act be entitled to possession (p). Thus if a lease is void owing to some defect of title in the lessor, the tenant will nevertheless be protected. In *Martin* v. *Walton* a lease by a mortgagor was void as against the mortgagee but the tenant was nevertheless held entitled to the protection of the Act. Moreover the terms "tenant" and "tenancy" will include sub-tenant and sub-tenancy and the expression "let" will include sub-let, except where the context otherwise requires (q) but no sub-tenant will be entitled to the protection of the Act if the premises have not been lawfully sub-let to him, and before proceedings for recovery of possession or ejectment have been commenced (r) though where a breach of covenant has been committed in subletting the premises the sub-tenant may be entitled to rely on the provisions of the Conveyancing Act 1892 (s).

The Act prevents increase of rent or of mortgage interest beyond a certain amount and requires the fulfilment of certain conditions before the landlord can increase the rent but it is not all such increases that are forbidden. The words of sect. 1 are

(p) Sect. 12 (1) (g)
(q) Sect. 12 (1) (g)
(r) Sect. 5 (5)
(s) *Reid* v. *Jacques*, *Murphy* v. *Porte*

very important to bear in mind and are open to more than one construction. It is unfortunate that the very opening sentences of the Act should give rise to an ambiguity. Sect. 1 provides that where the rent or mortgage interest, in cases to which the Act applies, '*has been since the 25th March* 1920 *or is hereafter increased*, then if the increased rent or the increased rate of interest exceeds by more than the amount permitted under the Act the standard rent or standard rate of interest, the amount of such excess shall, notwithstanding any agreement to the contrary, be irrecoverable from the tenant or the mortgagor. The words that occasion the difficulty are the words 'has been increased since the 25th March 1920.' In all probability what is meant is an increase above the standard rent or the standard rate, as the case may be. But a further difficulty arises as to the correct interpretation of the word 'increased.' Is 'increased' to be construed as an isolated or as a continuous act? It is submitted that inasmuch as this is a provision of a penal character the word is to be construed more leniently in favour of the landlord and mortgagee. If this construction is adopted, the section would mean that where the increased rent or interest had accrued due prior (*t*) to the 25th March 1920 then such increased rent or interest could legally be recoverable by the landlord or mortgagee even subsequent to that date, and even though such rent or interest was beyond the limits prescribed by the Act. It might further be urged in favour of the above view that it has been judicially held that the Act is quite otiose as regards a current tenancy at an agreed rent (*u*), and the policy of the Act is not to affect agreements made prior to the Act and at a time when the parties to the agreement could not fairly have had the Act in contemplation (*x*). Moreover, it may be said that the whole of the arguments and decisions in the cases of *Goldsmith* v. *Orr* and *Raikes* v. *Ogle* were impliedly founded on the view that an increase before the material date would not be affected. At any rate the view taken above is in

(*t*) *Goldsmith* v. *Orr*, *Raikes* v. *Ogle*, *Kerr* & *Orr* v. *Bryde*.
(*u*) Per Lord Dunedin in *Kerr* v. *Bryde*.
(*x*) *Sackso* v. *Powell*, but see *Woodhead* v. *Putnam*.

accordance with the dicta of Atkin L.J., in *Sinclair v Powell* (y) The decision of Astbury J., however in *Hollands v Cooper* z results in the adoption of the other interpretation of the word increased. In that case the learned judge held that a mortgagee was not entitled to an increased rate of interest beyond the limits permitted by the Act although the rate had been increased prior to the 25th March 1920 It is doubtful whether this decision can be supported (a)

When however rent or mortgage interest has been increased prior to the 25th March 1920 but such rent or interest has already been affected by the previous Acts then no increase prior to the 25th March 1920 will escape the provisions of the present Act This it is submitted is practically the combined effect of sect 19 3 of the Act and sect 38 of the Interpretation Act 1889

In this connection should also be noted that the rent even of furnished houses cannot be increased beyond certain limits But in these cases the Act adopts a different method for fixing the maximum amount of rent The rent of such houses is not to be increased so as to yield to the lessor an amount beyond 25 per cent of the normal profit which might have reasonably been expected from a similar letting in the year ending the 3rd August 1914 (1) It might incidentally be observed that this is the only respect in which furnished houses are affected by the Act

The Act enables the tenant of premises to which it applies to retain possession even though the tenancy has expired or been duly determined the tenant thereupon becomes a 'statutory' tenant retaining possession solely by virtue of the Act and against the will of his landlord At the same time, however there is nothing to prevent an agreement from being arrived at between the landlord and statutory tenant but such agreement must not contain any conditions which are contrary to the

(y) (1922) 1 K. B. at p. 405
(z) See infra p. 334
(a) See *Sinclair v Powell* (1922) 1 K. B. at pp. 402 405
(b) Sect 9

provisions of the Act Even a sub-tenant may become a statutory tenant of the original lessor Where the interest of a tenant of a house within the Act is determined whether as the result of an order or judgment for possession or ejectment or for any other reason (as, for example by surrender but not by notice to quit) (c) any sub-tenant to whom the premises or any part thereof have been *lawfully* (d) sub-let will *subject to the provisions of the Act,* be deemed to become the tenant of the landlord Such a tenancy however will be on the same terms on which the sub-tenant would have held from the tenant if the tenancy had continued (e)

Where a tenant is a statutory tenant the Act provides that the tenant shall observe and be entitled to the benefit of all the terms and conditions of the original contract of tenancy. so far as the same are consistent with the provisions of the Act (f) The statutory tenant, further, will be entitled to give up possession of the dwelling-house only on giving such notice as would have been required under the original contract of tenancy or if no notice would have been so required on giving not less than three months' notice (g)

It is further made a condition of the tenancy (whether statutory or not) of any dwelling-house to which the Act applies that the tenant shall afford to the landlord access to the premises and all reasonable facilities for executing therein any repairs which the landlord is entitled to execute (h)

The conditions, therefore under which a statutory tenancy is held will have to be determined by the conditions in the original agreement But any such condition which is contrary to the provisions of the Act must be disregarded Thus the usual condition to give up possession at some agreed date must necessarily be neglected since a landlord is not entitled to possession of premises under the Act unless he can bring himself within the provisions of sect 5 (i)

(a) *Hunter v Hunt* see *ante* p 101
(b) See sect 5 (5)
(c) Sect 15 (1)
(d) Sect 16 (2
(e) Sect 15 (3)
(f) *Ibid*
(g) See *ante* p 15

It has been held that an option to renew if it was a term contained in the original contractual tenancy is to be considered a term of the statutory tenancy the position in the case of a statutory tenant being the same as that in the case of a tenant holding over with the consent of the landlord (*k*)

It has further been held that a statutory tenant has the right to assign or to sub-let if he enjoyed such rights under the original contract of tenancy (*Keeves* v *Dean Nunn* v *Pellegrini*)

To prevent the statutory tenant from making a profit out of his position, the Act forbids him to take a fine or premium from anyone else except his landlord, as a condition of giving up possession of the premises (*l*) On the other hand, the Act absolutely forbids the taking of any fine or premium by a lessor in consideration of the grant, renewal or continuance of a tenancy of any dwelling-house to which the Act applies (*m*) The Amendment Act of 1923, however, makes an exception to this rule in cases where a landlord after the passing of the Act grants a lease of not less than two years for a term expiring at some date after the 24th June, 1925 or enters into an agreement for a tenancy for such a term (Sect 2 (2)) That Act, by sect 9, further prevents any evasion of the provisions with regard to the taking of fines and premiums by enacting that where an excessive charge is made for furniture or other articles which are required to be taken over, the excess is to be regarded as a fine or premium

The landlord is only entitled to possession of premises within the Act in the cases enunciated in sect 5, as amended by the Amendment Act of 1923 but he will in any case have to show that he is entitled to possession, irrespective of the Act, before he can avail himself of the provisions of sect 5

A notice to quit by the landlord will be of no effect in itself and in such a case the landlord will not be even entitled to

---

(*k*) *Mellroy (William) Ltd* v *Clements* Qu whether an option to purchase can be regarded also as a condition of the statutory tenancy, see *Bradbury* v *Grimble & Co*, *Rider* v *Ford*

(*l*) Sect 15 (2)

(*m*) *Infra* p 91

recover double value under the Landlord and Tenant Act 1730 nor will the tenant be liable to an action for use and occupation (n) On the other hand, even where the tenant himself gives notice terminating the tenancy the landlord will not be entitled to possession by reason only of such notice but if in such a case the tenant holds over he will be liable to double rent double rent being considered rather as a penalty than as rent (o)

In the case of mortgages, the Act only applies to certain classes of mortgages, but in any case the Act will not apply unless the mortgaged property itself is within the Act

The maximum rate of interest that the Act allows is $6\frac{1}{2}$, an increase of 1 per cent is at present the maximum total increase allowed over the standard rate Any agreement to pay a higher rate of interest is absolutely unenforceable The Act does not deal very clearly with the question of the increase of mortgage interest. It is uncertain whether the interest can be increased irrespectively of any consent on the part of the mortgagor, other doubts arise as to the time from when the interest can be legally increased, and as to the personal liability of the mortgagor for such increase The view taken in this book is that the interest can be increased irrespectively of any consent on the part of the mortgagor that before an increase will be recoverable a notice of increase must be given by the mortgagee that the increase will be recoverable as from the date fixed for redemption in cases where a notice has been given prior to such date but that if the mortgagee allows the date of redemption to pass such increase will only be recoverable as from the date of the expiry of a period of time after the giving of the notice of increase equal in length to that of a notice to call in the mortgage required under the agreement to be given by the mortgagee Where such increased interest is legally recoverable, it is further submitted that the position will be the same as if the mortgagor had consented to the increase (p)

(n) *Ciccl* v *Whitbread* *Lipsohn* v *Macfarlane*
(o) *Flannagan* *Shaw*
(p) *Infra* p 136

The mortgagee is further restricted with certain exceptions (q) from calling in his mortgage or taking any steps for realising his security so long as (a) the interest permitted under the Act is paid and is not more than twenty-one days in arrear, and (b) the covenants by the mortgagor (excepting the covenant for the repayment of the principal money) are performed and observed, and (c) the mortgagor keeps the property in a proper state of repair and pays all interest and instalments of principal recoverable under any prior encumbrance (r). Special provisions are made for mortgages of leasehold property (s).

There are various other miscellaneous and penal provisions contained in the Acts, all of which will be considered in detail in the succeeding chapters.

(q) Sect. 7 (2).   (r) Sect. 7.   (s) Sect. 7 (4).

CHAPTER II

STANDARD RENT—RATEABLE VALUE—APPORTIONMENT

Sect. 1.—Standard Rent

This Act provides for each house or part (a) of a house or rooms (b), to which it applies a fixed standard rent to be calculated in the manner indicated in sect. 12 (1) (a) of the Act.

It is necessary to understand how the standard rent is arrived at, as this is an important factor to be considered in determining whether the house comes within the Act. Moreover, the standard rent is made the basis on which the increases of rent are to be calculated.

The *standard rent* is defined (c), as being—

(1) Where the house (d) was let on 3rd August 1914—the rent at that date.

(2) Where the house (d) was not let on 3rd August 1914, then—

    (a) If it was let before 3rd August 1914—the rent at which it was *last* let before 3rd August, 1914.

    (b) If it was *first* let after 3rd August 1914—the rent at which it was *first* let.

(3) Where the rent is progressive (e)—the maximum rent payable.

(a) Sect. 12 (2). (b) Sect. 12 (8).

(c) This definition is not qualified by the words "except where the context otherwise requires" in sect. 12 (Marchbank v. Campbell and Snell, per Salter J.).

(d) Or part of a house or rooms.

(e) A progressive rent is a rent which is periodically increased. Where an agreement provides that the rent is to be increased once only for a certain period such rent is not a progressive rent (Gill v. O. (1920) 36 T. L. R. 281, Pond v. Baker).

4 Where at the date by reference to which the standard
rent is to be calculated (i.e. either on before or after
3rd August 1914, the rent was less than the rateable value—the rateable value at such date (Sect
12 1) (a) :

In arriving at the standard rent, the rent to be considered is
the rent that is actually paid by the occupying tenant, whether
the rent is inclusive or exclusive of rates and taxes

Where a sub-tenant in occupation of a public-house was paying
a tied-house rent of 24l in August, 1914 though his 'landlord,'
i.e. the tenant was paying his own landlord a rent of 130l
(which was a free-house' rent), the Court held that the rent
to be considered was the actual rent paid, viz 24l, and as the
rateable value of the premises at that date (August 1914) was
48l and therefore more than the rent (24l) the standard rent
was the amount of such rateable value viz 48l (*Glossop v
Ashley*)

Where the lessor agrees to pay the rates the amount of the
rates is not to be deducted from the rent for the purpose of com-
puting the standard rent (*Westminster and General Properties
Investments Co v Summons* (f)

So again, where the lessee pays the rates and taxes such rates
and taxes are not to be taken into consideration in arriving at
the standard rent

Where A prior to August, 1914, was the lessee of a house
at a rent of 19l per annum, and subsequently (but at a date
prior to August 1914) purchased the house, still occupying it
himself, and then subsequently to August, 1914, let it to B at a
rent of 34l the Court refused to hold that the words "not let
in sect 12 (1) (a) of the Act were equivalent to ' unoccupied,
and accordingly held that the standard rent was not 24l, but
19l the rent at which the house was last let prior to August
1914 (*O Neill v Duncan*)

(f) See also *Isaacs v Lethbridge* *Lawrie v Woods*, *Mackworth v Hedland*

A question of difficulty arises in cases where there is more than one tenancy of premises existing at the material date. The landlord may have let the premises at one rent, his tenant at another, the tenant's sub-tenant or assignee at another and so on. It is submitted that in such a case the standard rent is the rent actually paid by the person who was in actual occupation of the premises at the date at which the standard rent is to be calculated. The case of *Glossop* v. *Ashley* appears to be an authority for this proposition, indeed McCardie J. expressly said in that case that the "rent to be considered in each case must be the rent paid by the occupying tenant at the material date." (g) Reference may also be made to the recent case of *Veale* v. *Cabelas*. In that case one Black was assignee of a ninety years ground lease of a house at a ground rent of 12*l*. 12*s*. per year. In August, 1914, the house was let in separate tenements on weekly tenancies at rents aggregating in all to 1*l*. 4*s*. 6*d*. per week. The house was subsequently let for the first time *as a whole* at 1*l*. 3*s*. per week. The Court held that although there might be cases in which the ground rent might be the standard rent, yet in this case the standard rent was neither the ground rent of 12*l*. 12*s*. nor the rent of 1*l*. 4*s*. 6*d*. per week, but inasmuch as the tenancy before the Court was a single tenancy of the whole house, the standard rent would be the rent at which the house had been first let in one letting as a whole (*i.e.* in this case 1*l*. 3*s*. per week).

Care must be taken in fixing the correct date with reference to which the standard rent or the rateable value is to be calculated. If for instance a house subsequently to August, 1914, is pulled down and rebuilt, undoubtedly the material date will be the date at which it is first let after being so rebuilt. Or again, if a house is converted and the effect of such conversion is that there is no longer any unity of character between the old and the new building, then the standard rent will be the rent at which the building as converted is first let (*Phillips* v. *Barnet*; *Sinclair* v. *Powell*. Complete reconstruction however, is not necessary. The question is one of mixed fact and law (h) and will depend on the nature and extent of the structural alterations (Marchbank v. Campbell; Woodhead v. Putnam (i)).

Where a house not previously within any of the Acts is subsequently let off into suites at rentals within the statutory limits then the standard rent of each suite will be the rent at which it was first let, and it would also appear that should there be a reshuffling of the rooms and a letting of different suites thereby created by reason of such reshuffling then the new suites so created will have a separate rent, and no question of any apportionment will arise although some of the rooms comprised in the new suite happened to have formed part of any of the old suites (Priest and Kirkpatrick v. Bromfill).

By sect. 11 (1) of the Amendment Act the County Court has jurisdiction now, on the application of either the landlord or the tenant, to determine summarily any question as to the standard rent, a power which it was formerly held it did not possess (Broomhall v. Property Agents and Owners, Ltd., 38 T. L. R. 56).

Furthermore by sect. 11 the tenant of any dwelling-house within the Act is entitled to a statement in writing from the landlord as to what is the standard rent on making a request in writing to that effect.

Sect. 2.—Rateable Value

In the Act the words "rateable value" (k) mean the *net rateable value* (Waller v. Thomas, 37 T. L. R. 325).

Rateable value is defined as being :—

(1) The rateable value on the 3rd August 1914

(h) *Darrell v. Whitaker* (per McCardie J.), *contra*, Lush J. (Qy. whether there is any appeal from judge's finding (b), 39 T. L. R. at p. 448.

(i) See also *Hart v. Martin; Darrell v. Whitaker.*

(k) As regards the law of rating it has been held by the House of Lords that the Rent Act does not affect the rateable value of the premises to which it applies, and that the maximum gross value is not to be limited to the standard rent plus the additions permitted by the Rent Act (*Poplar Assessment Committee v. Roberts*).

(2) In the case of a dwelling-house or part of a dwelling-house first assessed after 3rd August 1914—the rateable value at which it was first assessed (Sect. 12 (1) (e)).

As regards *Scotland*, rateable value means yearly value according to the valuation roll and rateable value of the 3rd August 1914 means yearly value according to the valuation roll for the year ending 15th May 1915 (Sect. 18 (1) (a)). In *Anderson v. Assessor for Peebles*, it was held that the actual rent must be entered in the roll in the absence of evidence that the landlord could have successfully exacted the higher rent to which he was entitled under the Act.

In *Naismith v. Assessor for Renfrew*, the Court allowed an increase of 25 per cent. on the value of a house which was occupied by the owner, in the absence of proof that the house in question had not participated in the general rise of values which was a matter of common knowledge.

Again, in *M'Garrity v. Assessor for Lanarkshire*, it was held that the assessor had power to increase the valuation notwithstanding the failure of the owner to give due statutory notice before increasing the rent (l).

Sect. 3.—*Apportionment*

Where it is shown that a dwelling-house (m) the subject of the tenancy between the parties is within the Act and that it is necessary for the purpose of determining the standard rent or the rateable value of that dwelling-house, to apportion the rent at the date in relation to which the standard rent is to be fixed or the rateable value of the property in which that dwelling-house is comprised the County Court is given, by sect. 12 (3), power to make such apportionment (n) on the application (o) of either party

(l) See also *Smith v. Assessor for Edinburgh*; *M'candless v. Trustees v. Assessor for Ayrshire*.

(m) The dwelling-house may only be part of a house or even consist of rooms. (Sect. 12 (2).)

(n) For form of certificate see Appendix Form 6

(o) For form of summons see Appendix Form 5. The application

The County Court, moreover, has power to entertain an application for apportionment, even though there are no other proceedings pending between the parties in which the question of the standard rent or the rateable value of the premises arises(p). By Rule 7 of the Increase of Rent (&c.) Rules 1920 applications are to be made to the registrar in the first instance. The registrar may, however, and must on the application of either party refer the matter to the judge. If the registrar has given his decision an application for variation or rescission of any determination or order made by the registrar may be made to the judge in the manner prescribed in Rule 7c. Notice in writing must also be given in accordance with the County Court Rules as to interlocutory applications and such notice must be filed within four clear days from the date of the determination or order of the registrar. As to the costs of such applications, see Rule 16 of the Increase of Rent (&c.) Rules 1920. The decision of the County Court as to the amount to be apportioned is final and conclusive and there can be no appeal therefrom.

Apportionment will be necessary, for instance, when a house which was originally let as a whole at the material date has subsequently been let in separate portions. A house, however, which has been reconstructed by way of conversion into two or more separate and self-contained flats or tenements(q) since 2nd April, 1919, or was being so converted at that date is exempt from the operation of the Act (sect. 12 (9) (r)) and accordingly there can be no question of apportionment in such a case.

Even if the conversion took place prior to the 2nd April, 1919, there will be no question of apportionment if the effect of the conversion is such that the old building is no longer one and the same as the new. (*Phillips* v *Barnet*.)

---

must be made to the Court in the district of which the premises are situate (Rule 1 (b)). See Appendix.

(p) *Rex* v *Seully*. *Ex parte Boon*.

(q) Sect. 12 (9).

(r) The above provision was passed in order to encourage landlords to convert houses into flats.

Woodward v *Samuels* (s) was a case (under the previous Acts) in which apportionment was considered necessary. In that case the house had been let as a whole in August, 1914, at a rent of 45*l*. In 1919 it was converted into three flats which were let separately at rents amounting to 152*l*. It was held that for the purpose of arriving at the standard rent of each flat, the rent in 1914 of the undivided house had to be apportioned, and that the standard rent was not the rent at which each flat was first let, the work done in converting the house into flats apparently not being such as to destroy the identity of the house.

In *Sinclair* v *Powell*, a house had been converted prior to the 2nd April, 1919, into three flats. The original rent of the whole house in 1914 was 65*l*. so that the house was not, in any case, within the Rent Act of 1915. The tenant of one of the flats, which was let at 50*l*. which rent was apparently the rent at which the flat was let for the first time since the conversion, applied for apportionment. The Court held that there was no case made out for apportionment. It would seem that this decision is to be based on the grounds that the house had lost its original character, that the flat was to be regarded as a separate dwelling and, as such had been let for the first time, prior to the date at which the Act of 1920 had come into operation, at 50*l*. per annum, and that this sum represented the standard rent of the flat. The suggestion made by the Divisional Court that, since the house as a whole was not within any of the previous Rent Acts at the date when it was let off into portions, the landlord could, therefore demand any rent he pleased for such portions, seems to be correct, though it was expressly dissented from by the Divisional Court in the case of *Woodhead* v *Putnam* (t).

In *Ellen* v *Goldstein*, 89 L J Ch 586, which was a case under the previous Acts, it was held that where premises used partly as business premises and partly as a dwelling-house were

(s) Approved in *Sinclair* v *Powell* (1922) 1 K B at pp 400, 407 but see per Scrutton L J, at p 403

(t) It is to be noted, however, that the judgment of Scrutton, L J, in *Sinclair* v *Powell* was based on this ground see also *supra* p 5

2

demised together there was no machinery provided whereby the rent of that portion of the premises which was used as a dwelling could be apportioned

The view is submitted in this book that the true test in determining whether apportionment is necessary depends on whether the identity of the particular premises in respect of which apportionment is asked has been lost or not and for this purpose it is not necessary that there should be reconstruction into two or more self-contained flats or tenements.(*a*) Furthermore it is submitted that apportionment may be granted in respect of one portion of premises let as a whole at the material date though it may be refused in respect of another portion of the same premises. A house consisting of five floors for instance may have been let as a whole in August 1914 at a certain rental. Suppose that subsequently the two upper floors were cut off from the rest of the house and converted for the purpose of being let as a self-contained flat. It is true that the two upper floors are no longer substantially in the form in which they previously existed but the same cannot be said of the rest of the house if the other remaining floors have been left in the same state as they were in previously. In such a case if the three floors were let separately to a tenant it is submitted that an apportionment could be made though no apportionment may be possible in respect of the two upper converted floors.(*b*) If, however, the alterations effected in part of the premises are such as to benefit although indirectly other portions of the premises in which no alteration has been made then no apportionment can be made.(*c*)

When apportionment in respect of any premises is asked for the first question to be determined is when the premises were first let. If they were let as a whole on the 3rd August 1914 the rent payable then would be the standard rent. If however they were let as part of a whole in 1914, then the question of apportionment will arise if the premises have not lost their identity by structural

(*a*) See sect. 12 (9).
(*b*) See judgment of Scrutton L. J. in *Snelling* v. *Parrott* (1922) 1 K. B. at p. 406.
(*c*) *Snelling* v. *Parrott*.

alteration or otherwise at the time when the application for apportionment is made. Nevertheless if the part in respect of which apportionment is asked has at any time been let separately and further, if the whole house at the time of such letting was not within any of the Acts, it is submitted that no case for apportionment can be made out, the rent at which the part was so let being the standard rent of that part. (Cf. *Sinclair v Powell*.) If the premises were not let, whether as a whole or as part of a whole, on the 3rd August, 1914, then the question would depend on whether they were let as a whole or as part of a whole on the last day prior to the 3rd August, 1914, on which they were let.

If the premises were let for the first time subsequently to the 3rd August 1914—and it should be remembered that premises which were let on or previously to the 3rd August, 1914, might subsequently by reason of structural alteration or otherwise, have lost their identity so that they are to be regarded for the purposes of the Act as having been first let subsequently to the 3rd August 1914—then in such cases the question will depend on whether the premises in respect of which an application for apportionment is made were let as a whole or as part of the new premises so let for the first time subsequently to the 3rd August 1914.

It must be remembered, however, that the Act will not apply to houses erected after, or in course of erection on the 2nd April 1919 or to houses which were being on or have been since that date *bonâ fide* reconstructed into two or more separate and self-contained flats or tenements (z).

In considering whether the premises were let separately or as part of a whole at the material date it is submitted that the letting to the occupying (a) tenant or tenants must be considered. Thus A might be the lessee of the whole of a dwelling-house in August, 1914 but he may have sub-let the premises to various sub-tenants who happen to be in occupation in August 1914. It could not be said in such a case that the house was let as a whole, it must be regarded as being divided and let in separate parts, each of

(z) Sect. 12 (9).
(a) See *Glasson v Ashley, Lewis v Cubison* and *ante*, p. 13.

2 2

these parts constituting the subject-matter of a separate letting
for the purpose of the Act   The fact, however, that the sitting
tenant of the whole house has let a room furnished, e g , to a
lodger, does not apparently prevent the house from being regarded
as let as a whole (b)

As regards the apportionment of the rateable value of premises,
this may be necessary, for instance, where a house is rated as a
whole and a tenant of a portion of the house may require an
apportionment of the rateable value in order to determine for
what proportion of an increase in the rates he may be liable to
his landlord   or again, in order to determine whether the house
is or is not within the Act

Where a certificate of apportionment has been obtained the
apportionment will be binding between such persons who were
parties to the application and their privies according to the principles of the law of estoppel by record (c

The provisions of Rule 6 (1) should be noted, whereby the
summons is to be served on every person affected thereby

(b) Simpson v Zubrasky   As to the elements which should be considered
in making an apportionment reference might be made to Sutton v Fishman

(c) In Heardwood v Heddersley the Divisional Court differed on the point,
is to whether an order for apportionment made on a landlord would also be
binding on a prior owner of the premises in question

CHAPTER III

APPLICATION OF THE ACTS

Sect 1 —Houses to which the Act of 1920 applies

THE Act of 1920 originally applied both to a dwelling-house and to a house used for business purposes. The Act however no longer applies to business premises, the provisions of the Act, so far as they related to business premises (sect 13), having expired on the 24th day of June, 1921 (Sect 13 (3)). The Act therefore now applies to dwelling-houses only but the term "dwelling-house" is used in a particular sense in the Act, inasmuch as sect 12 (2) expressly provides that a dwelling-house is to be considered none the less a dwelling-house by reason only that part of it is used for business purposes (a). But on the other hand, business premises will not necessarily constitute a "dwelling-house" merely because some portion is used as a dwelling. The true test to be applied in any given case would seem to depend on the determination of the "dominant purpose and user" of the premises (per McCardie, J. in *Walker v Thomas*) (b) and also on a consideration of the purpose for which the premises were let (per Swift, J. in *Greig v Francis and Campion, Ltd*), while another important factor would be whether the premises are used for being slept in. Per Scrutton L J in *Duke of Richmond and Others v Devon and Others* 38 T L R at p 152.

Thus in *Epsom Grand Stand Association Ltd v Clarke*, the Court held that a public-house, part of which was used for

---

(a) See also *Walker v Thomas*, *Laird v Graves* thus giving statutory confirmation to the decision in *Epsom Grand Stand Association v Clark*

(b) But see *Cohen v Benjamin* 38 T L R at p 11

residential purposes, was a dwelling-house In *Callaghan v Bristowe*, premises which consisted of a garage with living rooms above for the chauffeur and his family were held to have been let for a double purpose, viz., as a garage and as a dwelling-house, and to be accordingly within the Act These were decisions under the previous Acts, but they are of equal authority under the Act of 1920. However, in *Taylor v Eaves*, a boarding-house, and in *Tomphins v Rogers*, a lodging-house, were held to come under the description of business premises But in *Taylor v Eaves*, the question as to whether the premises were business premises was merely incidental, and in *Tomphins v Rogers* the premises were considered as business premises only for the purposes of sect 13 (1 (See *Duke of Richmond and Others v Dewar and Others*, 38 T L R per Bankes, L J , at p 152 If *Tomphins v Rogers* decided that a lodging-house is not a dwelling-house, then it is a decision which is not to be followed (See *Colls v Parnham* (c), 152 L. T 345, 346) In *Colls v Parnham*, the Court held that a flat which was used partly for taking in lodgers, the remainder of the rooms being reserved by the tenant as a residence for himself and his family, was a dwelling-house within the Act In the *Duke of Richmond's Case* (*supra*), the Court held that certain premises used by a hotel company as sleeping apartments for their staff constituted a dwelling-house within the Act

Every case however must be decided on its own facts It is quite possible that the Court may hold part of the premises in any given case to be a dwelling-house, and part to be business premises, if the two parts are distinct, and can be sufficiently segregated (*Murphy v Porter and Blaney* ,

Where, however, the Court decides that premises, the subject of a separate letting constitute a dwelling-house, although part is used for business purposes, the Court has no power to give the landlord possession of that part which is used for business purposes (*Ellen v Goldstein* (d))

As has been stated above, the provisions of the Act relating to business premises expired on 24th June, 1921, but apparently

(c) And see *Cohen v Benjamin*   (d) See also *Gates v Blau*.

no provision has been made for safeguarding rights which were *in memorio legis* by proceedings begun before or pending on 24th June, 1921 (*MacQuillan v Clinton*, 55 I. L. T. R. at p. 141.)

Besides the cases mentioned above, reference may also be usefully made to *Roberts v. Poplar Assessment Committee* (tied beer-house) and *Stephens v. Tatham* (school-house) for instances of premises which have been held by the Courts to constitute a dwelling-house within the Act (*e*)

The Act, according to the provisions of sect. 12 (2) and sect. 12 (8) will apply to—

(1) a dwelling-*house*
(2) *part* of a house let as a separate dwelling (see *Woodfield v. Bond*, 152 L. T. 310 *Greig v. Francis and Campion Ltd.*)
(3) any *rooms* in a dwelling-house subject to a separate letting wholly or partly, as a dwelling,

where *either* the annual amount of the standard rent (*f*) (of such house, part of a house, or rooms) or the rateable value (*g*) thereof does not exceed—

(a) in the Metropolitan Police District (*h*) including therein the City of London, 105*l*
(b) in Scotland, 90*l*
(c) elsewhere, 78*l*

The Act supplies two independent criteria and in this respect follows the Act of 1915 (*i*)

According to the Act, therefore, a house will be outside its provisions only where both the standard rent and the rateable value at the material time are beyond the prescribed limits. If either the standard rent or the rateable value (*k*) are within the specified limits the premises will be within the Act. Once a

See also *Rock v. Jools, Hind v. Potts*
(f) *Supra* p. 11 *sq*
(g) *Supra* pp. 14 15
(h) As regards what is the Metropolitan Police District see Note to this Chapter
(i) *Supra* p. 3
(k) *Hethe...*

dwelling-house comes within the Act, it will always be within the Act (l). Thus, suppose a house comes within the Act merely because its rateable value, though not its rent in 1911, was below 105l. If subsequently the rateable value exceeds 105l., the house will nevertheless be within the Act.

The Act will apply to the house, however, only so long as it continues to be the same house, but not if its whole character is altered so that it is no longer possible to say that it is the same house. (*Phillips* v. *Barnett*. The "new" house may, however, be within the Act by reason of some other provision, e.g., if it was built or converted prior to 2nd April, 1919, and otherwise comes within the Act. A house again, which comes within the Act by reason only that it is used for business purposes, will no longer be within the Act. (See *MacQuillan* v. *Clinton, supra.*)

The Act operates *in rem*, and not *in personam*, so that the Act will apply to every tenancy of a house coming within its provisions. (*King* v. *York*.)

If there is one single tenancy (e.g., a sub-tenancy) of a house at a rent within the limits of the Act, that house will be within the Act, at any rate with respect to such tenancy, even though the rateable value of the house and the rents of the other intermediate tenancies are above the prescribed limits.

The words 'let as a separate dwelling' in sect. 12 (2) of the Act govern the words "part of a house" only, so that a house will not be excluded from the operation of the Act merely because it does not happen to be 'let.' Thus in *Woodifield* v. *Bond* (152 L. T. 310), the Court held that the Act applied to a mortgage of a house which had been in the continuous occupation of the owner (mortgagor) since August, 1914, and previously thereto (m). It is therefore submitted that a house also which has been in the occupation of the owner continuously since its erection, will nevertheless be within the Act if its rateable value is within the prescribed limit. The owner, however, will be in

(l) Sect. 12 (6).

(m) See however, *Re Hogan* in Irish case where a contrary view was taken.

a position to demand any rent he pleases, though not a premium.
The rent that he is first paid will then become the standard rent,
and the Act will apply to such a house and every tenancy thereof.

Where there is one single letting of two or more houses or
portions of houses or flats, the aggregate rent and rateable value
must be considered. If such aggregate rent and rateable value
exceed the prescribed limits the Act will not apply, even though,
if the rent or rateable value of each flat were considered separately, each flat might be within the Act. *Rudes v. Rollitt*,
36 T. L. R. 687. If however each house, or portion of flat
was let separately at the material time at which the standard rent
or rateable value is to be calculated, the landlord will not be able
to evade the provisions of the Act by including several houses to
which the Act applies in one separate letting.

Sect. 2.—Houses to which the Act does not apply

1. The Act does not apply to a house where both the standard
rent and the rateable value at the material date (n) exceeded the
limits indicated in sect. 12 (2) of the Act.

2. The Act no longer applies to houses used solely for business purposes (Sect. 13 (3 o). The Act may however apply
to premises used partly for business purposes if such premises
nevertheless constitute a dwelling-house (p)

3.—(a) The Act does not apply at all to any dwelling-house
which has been erected after or was in course of erection on, the
2nd April, 1919. Sect. 12 (9).

(b) The Act does not apply at all to any dwelling-house which
has been since the 2nd April, 1919 or which was being at that
date *bonâ fide* reconstructed by way of conversion into two or
more separate and *self-contained* flats or tenements. *Ibid.* (q)

"Separate" in the above sub-section does not mean "separated
physically" as by means of a partition, but means "distinct"

(n) See sect. 12 (1) (a) and (e)
( ) Not even apparently if they are subsequently used as a dwelling-house
( ) *Bros. Houses 1911 Ltd. v. Rovers*
( ) As to what is a dwelling-house see *supra* pp. 21-23
( ) This provision meets the difficulty caused by *Headland v. N. . . .*

in the sense that the flat or tenement can be occupied as a separate and distinct dwelling-house (*), nor is it necessary, in order that a flat or tenement should be "self-contained" within the meaning of the above sub-section, that it should contain within itself and within its own ambit all the elements or all the accommodation necessary to make it a separate dwelling-house (*). A flat may be self-contained even though for instance its coal cellar and servants' quarters were outside the ambit of the flat itself or even though the tenant may have to use a lavatory and bathroom in common with the tenant of another flat (*).

A house which has been pulled down and rebuilt again at the material date 2nd April 1919 would be outside the Act, and so may a house which has only been partially altered on or since that date if the rent at which it was let after the alterations and the subsequent rateable value were beyond the limits set by the Act for sub-sect. 12 (9), is not exhaustive of the cases in which the structural alteration of a house will prevent the application of the Act. See *Phillips v. Barnett*, (1921) 2 K. B. at p. 806.) The true test would seem to be whether the identity of the old building has been lost in the new. Thus in *Phillips v. Barnett supra*, three adjoining houses were converted into a factory for which purpose the houses were gutted, the staircase being removed, and a new one built in its place, though the main walls and roofs were left untouched and the party walls only altered to the extent of having doorways cut through them on each floor to allow of internal communication, the Court held that the identity of the old buildings was entirely lost in the new (*

_____

See *v. Pram. see also Dowell v. Whitaker and Another*

Smith v. Prom

) In the case of "new" and "converted" houses as defined above the Act makes special provisions as regards their rating whereby, for the purpose of any enactment relating to rating, the gross estimated rental or gross value of any such house to which the Act would have applied if it had been erected or reconstructed before the 3rd August, 1914 and let at that date is not to exceed

i) If the house forms part of a housing scheme to which sect. 7 of the Housing, Town Planning &c. Act 1919 (whereby power is given to

(4) The Act does not apply to a dwelling-house where the house is let together with land other than the site of the house (Sect. 12 (2) (iii) of the Act of 1920).

At the same time when land (other than the site or premises are let together with a house the Act provides *ibid* that if the rateable value of such land or premises let separately would be less than one-quarter of the rateable value of the house then such land or premises are to be treated as part of the house and the house will therefore in such a case be within the Act if the other necessary conditions are satisfied. Even where a house is let with other land, the rateable value of which is more than one-quarter of the rateable value of the house the house it is submitted, may nevertheless be within the Act if it is sub-let separately, or with only part of the land included in the original tenancy, where the rateable value of such part is less than one-quarter of the rateable value of the house. The Act in such a case would not affect the original tenancy, but would only affect the sub-tenancy though the sub-tenant might also be protected against the original landlord (a). If this view is correct the effect of this provision is very similar to that of sect. 12 (7).

The above provision (sect. 12 (2) (iii)) is intended to deal only with the case of a protected house being let with unprotected land or premises. (*Read v Goater*, (1921) 1 K. B. at p. 612).

The main object of the above provision was to deal with agricultural holdings and to prevent a farmer who possesses on the one hand a dwelling-house and on the other hand a large acreage, from keeping possession of the dwelling-house, although he might be bound to give up the land. In the majority of agricultural holdings the possession of the dwelling-house and

the Local Government Board to give financial assistance to local authorities who have suffered loss in carrying out housing schemes), applies the rent (exclusive of rates) charged by the local authority in respect of that house and

b In any other case the rent (exclusive of rates) which would have been charged by the local authority in respect of a similar house forming part of such a scheme as aforesaid. (Sect. 12 (9).

(a) See sects. 15 (3), 5 (5).

See pp. 34–36.

farm buildings is essential to the proper working of the holding;
but undoubtedly clause (iii) may go beyond agricultural holdings. *Ibid.* at p. 614.)

The difficulty that arises in applying the provisions of sect.
12 2 (iii) to any particular case lies in accurately discriminating
between the "house," including its site, and the "land or other
premises" let together with it. Some light is thrown by a consideration of the respective proportions of the rateable values
referred to in the proviso. The fact that the rateable value of
the house is to be at least four times the rateable value of the land
goes to show that the land, to be included in the house, must not
be of any great extent (y).

It would seem that the word "house" includes, besides the
actual dwelling-house, the adjoining premises as well. Thus,
where a holding consisted of (1) a dwelling-house with an outhouse
detached, stable and small garden, and adjoining mill and granary,
both communicating with the house by connecting doors, and a
piece of water, and (2) a meadow, Lush, J. inclined to the view
that for the purposes of the above provision the term 'house'
included not only the dwelling-house, but also the stable, garden,
and adjoining buildings. *Wellesley* v. *White.*

It is important to note that the phraseology of the above provision is different from that of the corresponding provisions in
the Acts of 1915 (z) and 1919 (a). The words in the previous
Acts are as follows :— Where such letting does not include any
land other than the site of the dwelling-house, *and a garden or
other premises within the curtilage of the dwelling-house,* the
words in *italics* being omitted from the Act of 1920. An important case under the former Acts was the case of *Scott* v.
Austin ((1919) W. N. 85). In that case certain land had been
divided into building plots. A cottage had been built on one of
these plots and let to A. On one side of the cottage there were
several vacant plots forming a piece of open ground, and this

(y) *Tarbin* v. *Drummond and Another* (per Bailhache, J.)
(z) See sect. 2 (2) of the Act of 1915.
(a) See sect. 4 of the Act of 1919.

open ground was included in the letting. The cottage with its original ground and the adjoining ground was surrounded by a continuous fence, the whole of the ground forming an entire garden for the cottage. The Court held the adjoining land to be within the curtilage of the dwelling-house, inasmuch as the Court was of opinion that the words were intended to apply to ' premises domestically appurtenant to the dwelling-house.'

It would seem that the case of *Scott v. Austin* would be decided differently under the Act of 1920. The change in the phraseology of the Act of 1920 appears to have been intentional, and the meaning of the word "house" in the Act of 1920 is not so wide as it was in the Act of 1915, where in terms it included the curtilage (b). In that event the opinions of Lush and McCardie, JJ., in *Wellesley v. White* (supra), may well be open to doubt. It might be argued that in the latter case it appears as if the Court arrived at the conclusion that the adjoining premises were included in the dwelling-house because they were domestically appurtenant thereto, thus following, unconsciously perhaps, the reasoning of the Court in *Scott v. Austin*. If, however, the change in the phraseology of the Act of 1915 was occasioned by a consideration of the difficulty raised by *Scott v. Austin*, and by a desire to obviate that difficulty, it is submitted that *Scott v. Austin* would be decided differently now, and that the opinion of the Court in *Wellesley v. White* would not be upheld.

In *Early v. Drummond and Another* a public-house, a cottage, and land to the extent of seven acres and thirty-one poles were let under one lease. The rateable value of the house was 11*l*. per annum and of the land 10*l*. per annum, and the lease comprised a grant of the public-house separately from the land. It was held that the land did not form part of the house within the meaning of proviso iii of sect. 12 (2).

(5) Save as is expressly provided by sects. 9 and 10, the Act does not apply to a dwelling-house where the house is *bonâ fide* (c) let at a rent which *includes* payments in respect of board,

(b) *Early v. Drummond.*
(c) First introduced into the Act of 1920.

attendance, or use of furniture "* (Sect. 12 (2), of the Act of 1920. But a dwelling-house shall not be deemed to be *bona fide* let at a rent which includes payments in respect of attendance or the use of furniture—but not, apparently, of board —unless the amount of rent which is fairly attributable to the attendance or the use of furniture, regard being had to the value of the same to the tenant forms a substantial portion of the whole rent. Sect. 10 (1) of the Amendment Act.)

Two tests are to be applied in order to ascertain whether the letting is outside the Act, viz.: 1, the *bona fides* of the letting and 2, the fact that the rent *includes* payments in respect of board, attendance or use of furniture. The first test is a question of intention; the second is a question of fact and degree. In some cases the tests may run the one into the other, in others they may be entirely independent.

The first test will be satisfied provided there is an intention to include in the rent a *real* charge in respect of board, attendance or use of furniture, and if there is such a real charge, and genuine agreement with regard to it, it is immaterial that the tenant had no option but to pay such a charge for the board, attendance or furniture as the case may be. Similarly it is immaterial whether such a charge was included by the lessor in order to take the letting out of the provision of the Act, provided again that there was such an intention, and the charge was a real charge.

As regards the second test, it was previously held in *Wilkes v. Goodwin*, that any amount of board or attendance, or use of furniture would be sufficient to take the letting out of the Act provided the amount was not so small as to be excluded by the rule *de minimis*, but at the same time this rule was to be strongly applied in favour of the tenant. *Rummer v. Carson*. The law has now been altered in this respect by sect. 10 (1 of the Amendment Act of 1923, whereby it is necessary that the amount of rent which is fairly attributable to the attendance or the use of the furniture, regard being had to the value of the same to the tenant must form a substantial part of the whole rent.

* For the exceptions to this provision see sects. 9 and 10 *notes*, p. 7.

It is to be observed that no mention of board is made in this section
but that is probably because " board " in itself suggests sufficiency
(See per Younger, L J in *Wilkes v Goodwin*

The concluding words of sub-sect 1 of sect 10 of the Act of
1923 appear indirectly to support the view that the payments
in respect of board, attendance, or use of furniture must further
be *included* in the rent in order that the letting might be taken
out of the Act If on the other hand the rent is exclusive of
such payments in respect of board, attendance or use of furniture the tenancy will be within the Act

Whether the rent is " inclusive' or " exclusive " will depend on
the construction of the words used where there is a tenancy agreement in writing Where there is no such agreement it will be
a question of fact to be deduced from the words used by the parties
from their conduct, and from the other circumstances of the case

Where an agreement provided that the rent of certain premises
should be 100*l* per annum but that a weekly sum of 10s per week
should be paid for " service " it was held that the sum of 10s
per week was not to be considered as rent but that the rent of the
premises was 100*l* , and that such rent was exclusive of the above
payment for 'service' (*Wood v Wallace*

Where an agreement provided for a rent of 18*l* with an additional rent of 2s per week as the tenant's contribution toward
the expenses of a housekeeper for cleaning the premises such
additional rent to be recoverable by distress the Court held that
this sum of 2s was part of the rent, inasmuch as the parties had
agreed that the payment was to be regarded as rent and was
to be recoverable as rent *Woods & Co Ltd v City and West
End Properties Ltd* Again, in *Douglas v Beeching* (un-
reported, 25th Feb 1920 , Roche J , held that a payment for
service was part of the rent, inasmuch as the parties had stipulated
that the payment in question should be treated as rent

In *Ellen v Goldstein*, premises consisting of a shop and bake-
house with residential rooms above were let under an agreement
at 52*l* per annum By a supplemental agreement the tenant
agreed, in consideration of the tenancy agreement the goodwill
of the baker's business and the use of the landlord's fixtures to

pay during the term a further sum of 1*l*. per week ' to be recoverable as rent. The Court nevertheless held that this latter sum did not come within the description of rent, and that the rent of the premises was 52*l*., and not 104*l*. per annum.

The true test would seem to be whether the rent of the premises and the other charges for attendance, board or use of furniture, etc. reserved by the agreement as one aggregate rent or as separate rents. In the latter case the fact that the charge is treated as rent will not make any difference (*f*)

Board.—Although no mention of "board" is made in sect. 10 (1) of the Amendment Act, 1923, it is as well to note, as Younger L. J. pointed out in *Wilkes* v. *Goodwin*, that "board is different from food or 'drink' and that the word itself suggests 'sufficiency.' It would appear therefore, that merely the supply of an early morning cup of tea would not be sufficient to take the letting out of the Act, but on the other hand, that the provision of one substantial meal a day, as breakfast or dinner, would take the letting out of the Act, provided of course the other conditions required by the section were fulfilled.

Attendance.—In *Nye* v. *Davis* (*g*) a lease provided that the landlord should "keep the entrance hall and the general staircase and other common parts of the building clean and in good order, remove house refuse from the flat and carry coals once in every working day free of charge." The Court held that the services to be rendered by the landlord constituted ' attendance.'

In *King* v. *Millen*, however, the Court held that the cleaning of the hall and staircase did not amount to ' attendance ' within the section, inasmuch as the hall and staircase did not form part of the demise. Shearman J. considered that ' attendance ' implied something in the nature of personal service in the flat, just as 'board' and ' the use of furniture ' involved something in the flat itself.

(*e*) *Heal* v. *Soloman*
(*f*) *Ibid.* The whole question was left open in *Wilkes* v. *Goodwin*, see also *Dick* v. *Duncan*
(*g*) Followed in *Dick* v. *Duncan*, see also *Wilkes* v. *Goodwin*

In *Wood* v *Carwardine* it was held that the provision of a constant supply of hot water did not constitute attendance. It was considered essential that there should be some personal attendance by the servants of the landlord, and that such attendance should be rendered *within* the premises.

This case, moreover, is authority for the proposition that even if services are rendered which might constitute attendance, such services are not to be taken into consideration where the landlord has not agreed whether expressly or impliedly to perform these services. Accordingly, in the above case the fact that the caretaker had taken up coals and also removed refuse was ruled out of consideration since there was no covenant in the lease with regard to these services. The Court further held in the above case that the receipt and delivery of parcels and letters by the resident housekeeper formed so trivial a part of her duties that these services were ruled out of consideration by the principle *de minimis*.

Use of furniture. —As regards the amount of furniture that will be necessary in order that the house should be outside the scope of the Rent Acts, sect. 10 (1) of the Amendment Act, 1923, virtually overrules so much of the decision in *Wilkes* v *Goodwin* as was to the effect that any amount of furniture would be enough for that purpose provided that it was not so small as to be ruled out of consideration by the maxim *de minimis*, and restores the principle laid down in such cases as *Crane* v *Cox* and *Hocker* v *Solomon* that the amount of furniture must be substantial. This, it is submitted, is to be inferred from the language of sect. 10 (1), the material part of which states that the ' amount of rent which is fairly attributable to the use of the furniture ' must ' form a substantial portion of the whole rent.' At the same time the above provision leaves untouched the rule which was laid down in the Irish case of *Sloane* v *Cooke* (h) that the house need not be fully furnished in order to be taken out of the Act. Attention should also be paid to the words at the end of sect. 10 (1), "regard

---

(h) See also *Rimmer* v *Carson* where it was held that the words "use of furniture" did not import the letting of a furnished house.

3

being had to the value of the same to the tenant. A landlord is thus prevented from successfully maintaining that a house is not within the Rent Acts in such cases as, for instance, where the hall and common staircase of a house are furnished by the landlord.

In considering this question, furniture must be distinguished from fixtures and fittings, and the latter must not be taken into account (_i_). On the other hand, it must be remembered that articles attached slightly are not to be regarded as fixtures, but as furniture, _e.g._ a carpet which is nailed to the floor. Again, payments in respect of the use of tools, utensils, fixtures and fittings for use in a business would not be payments for the use of furniture within the meaning of the section (_k_).

Furniture means furniture in the popular sense of the word (_l_). In _Wilkes v. Goodwin_, fitted linoleum was considered to come within the description of furniture. This decision does not in any way overrule _Wallace v. Hardingham_ which decided that the linoleum in that case was not furniture. The latter case can be reconciled because the parties themselves treated the linoleum as fixtures (_m_).

(6) Where the rent payable is less than two-thirds of the rateable value the Act will not apply to that rent or tenancy nor to any mortgage by the landlord from whom the tenancy is held of his interest in the dwelling-house and the Act will apply in respect of such dwelling-house as if no such tenancy existed or ever had existed. Sect. 12 (7) of the Act of 1920.)

By the "rent payable" in this section is meant the actual rent paid by the tenant without any deduction for rates and taxes, although such are paid by the landlord, and not the net amount the landlord receives. Thus where the rent paid by the tenant was 30_l._ the landlord paying rates and taxes, which amounted to 31_l._ 8_s._, so that the landlord was actually suffering a loss of

(_i_) _Crane v. Lee Wallace v. Hardingham_ and see _Wilkes v. Goodwin_, 39 T. L. R. at p. 205

(_k_) _Cohen v. Benjamin_ 39 T. L. R. at p. 11

(_l_) _Wilkes v. Goodwin_

(_m_) _Ibid_ 39 T. L. R. at p. 265

11 8s., and the rateable value of the premises was 40l., the Court held that the tenancy was not excluded from the operation of the Act, inasmuch as the rent (30l.) was not less than two-thirds of the rateable value 40l. (*Mackworth v. Hilland*, (1921) 2 K. B. 755; *Whelan v. Worth*, 55 L. T. 111; *White v. Eastaugh*, L. T. C. C. R. vol. X, p. 11) (*n*)

Rateable value in this section means the net rateable value ascertained upon the footing that no part of the rates falls upon the landlord. As Lush, J., said in *Waller v. Thomas* ((1920) 1 K. B. at p. 54): "It seems to me impossible to suppose that the legislature used those words which occur so frequently in the Act to mean the gross value. For purposes of comparison, if the rent be one factor to be compared, it seems to me certain that the other factor would be the net value. A further fact which confirms this view is that the ordinary person is only acquainted with the net and not the gross value."

Where there is such a tenancy, the tenant will not be able to avail himself of the protection of the Act at all. The result will be that on the expiration of the tenancy whether by effluxion of time or due notice to quit, the landlord will be entitled to possession of the premises (*Whelan v. Worth*, *White v. Eastaugh*). The landlord of course, will also be entitled to demand any rent he pleases from any subsequent tenant, so long as the standard rent of the house has not become stereotyped. An illustration, perhaps will make this clearer. Take the instance of a house in town the rateable value of which is within the limits of the Act, say 50l. Suppose that the house was let in 1914 at 100l. per annum, but that in 1921 it was let at a rent less than two-thirds of its rateable value. On the expiration of the latter tenancy, the landlord will only be able to increase his rent by the amounts allowed by the Act over and above the standard rent which in this case is 100l. If, however, the premises have always been held under a tenancy falling under sect. 12 (7) then the standard rent will be the first rent which was more than

(*n*) See also *supra*, p. 12.

3 (2)

two-thirds of the rateable value of the house, and at which the house was so first let.

It is only the particular tenancy that will be affected. If the dwelling-house is one within the Act, then the operation of the Act will only be suspended pending such tenancy. Any further tenancy, and even any existing sub-tenancy where the rent is more than two-thirds of the rateable value, will be within the Act. (*Waller v. Thomas*, (1920) 1 K. B. at pp 548, 549)

Sect. 3.—*Who is a tenant within the Act*

It is not every occupier of premises within the Act who can claim its protection. It is essential that the occupier should be a tenant, and that there should be a legal "letting" of the premises in question. The Act will equally apply to a tenancy for a term certain as well as to a periodic or continuing tenancy (*Cruise v Terrell, Vernon Investment Assoc v Welch*).

But the Act will not apply in the case of a mere trespasser or squatter (see *Remon's Case*), nor in the case of a tenancy at will with no rent reserved (*Commissioners of H M Works v Hutchinson, Ecclesiastical Comms v Hilder, Brake v Wade*) (o), nor in the case of a tenant whose interest has been divested by law, e g bankruptcy, for the tenant has no longer any interest in the premises, and his position is no better than that of any passer-by in the street. So, where a trustee in bankruptcy disclaimed a lease, the landlord, in whom of course the interest in the property thereby revested, was held entitled to recover possession of the premises from the tenant in the absence of any evidence that a fresh agreement had been subsequently arrived at, whether by acceptance of rent or otherwise (*Reeves v Davies*). It is immaterial whether the tenant is in possession by virtue of a lease or an agreement, or merely by virtue of the protection afforded by the Rent Act to a statutory tenant, for a "statutory tenancy" is property within the meaning of sect 167 of the Bankruptcy Act, 1914. (*Parkinson v Noel*)

(o) Purchaser, let into possession pending completion of purchase, whose possession is that of tenant at will with no rent reserved

Again, a tenant against whom a closing order has been made under the Housing, Town Planning, &c. Acts, cannot avail himself of the protection of the Act, even though he may have retaken possession of the premises (*Blake v Smith*

Furthermore, the Act will not apply in the case of a servant who is allowed to occupy premises for the purpose of his employment merely, without a tenancy of any kind being created by such occupation. Whether the relation of landlord and tenant exists between the master and his servant depends on the following considerations 'Where it is necessary for the due performance of his duties that a person should occupy certain premises, or where he is required to occupy premises for the more satisfactory performance of his duties, although such residence is not necessary for that purpose, such person occupies in the capacity of servant but where a person is merely *permitted* to occupy premises, whether as a privilege or by way of remuneration or part payment for his services, he occupies as a tenant and not as a servant. A person cannot be said to occupy as a servant a house which is not that of his master, even though the master pays the rent. The circumstance that a person is allowed as part of his remuneration to carry on his own business in the premises he is required to occupy does not alter the character of his occupation into that of a tenant ' (p

Reference may usefully be made to the following cases under the Rent Acts for instances in which the Courts have held that a tenancy did not exist between the master and the servant —

National Steam Car Co, Ltd v Barham, where a servant was required to occupy a dwelling-house adjoining a garage, because it was his duty to take charge of the garage and lock it up at night. He lived there rent free, but the value of the accommodation was taken into consideration in fixing his remuneration

Ecclesiastical Commrs v Hilder, where a caretaker of premises

(p) See Halsbury's Laws of England Vol XX, p 69 Woodfell's Law of Landlord and Tenant 20th edit p 290 Smith on Master and Servant

occupied rooms on the premises without paying any rent, and without receiving any remuneration.

Marquis of Bute v *Prenderleith*, where a gamekeeper was in occupation of premises for the purposes of his employment, the value of the accommodation being taken into consideration in the payment of his remuneration.

Pollock v *Assessor for Inverness*, which was the case of a schoolmaster occupying, in virtue of his office, a house belonging to the Education authority.

On the other hand, the Act is not confined in its operation to cases where the premises are held with the consent of the landlord by virtue of a lease or agreement of some kind, as where the occupier is a yearly, or monthly or weekly tenant; the Act will also apply to cases where the tenant holds against the will of the landlord and even though his original tenancy has been duly determined. A tenant at sufferance has been held to be a tenant within the Act, and to be entitled to its protection. (*Dobson* v *Richards*).

In *Remon's Case* a tenant whose term had expired before the Rent Act of 1920 came into operation remained in possession wrongfully against the will of the landlords until the very day on which the Rent Act came into operation, 2nd July, 1920, when the landlords entered and regained possession of the premises. The Court however held that the tenant, who was not even a tenant at sufferance, was a statutory tenant, and was entitled to possession of the premises, and that, too, notwithstanding that the landlord had regained possession of the premises without the intervention of the Court *(q)*. Moreover, the premises in question were business premises, and were therefore not within any of the previous Rent Acts.

Even a tenant who himself gives notice to quit, but afterwards refuses to give up possession at the end of the term is a tenant within the Act. *Flannagan* v *Shaw*, *Hunt* v *Bliss*, *Artizans, Labourers and General Dwellings Co.* v *Whitaker*. He will

---

(q) The statutory tenancy is to be regarded as continuing until an order for possession is made by the Court; the tenant in the meantime is not a trespasser (*Remon* v *Lovell* (1922) 1 K. B. at p. 669).

be liable, however, to pay double rent to his landlord under sect. 18 of the Distress for Rent Act, 1737, the reason being that double rent is in the nature rather of a penalty than of rent. *Flannagan v Shaw; Northcott v Roche.*

A tenant holding over after notice to quit determining the tenancy has been given by the landlord will become a statutory tenant, and will be entitled to the protection of the Act, nor will he be liable to pay double value.

But a statutory tenant will be entitled to protection, at any rate against eviction, only in respect of premises of which he can be truly said to be in possession. In *Rushton v Magill*, the plaintiff, who was the lessee of certain premises, sub-let them to the defendant in breach of covenant. The superior landlord accordingly avoided the lease by way of forfeiture and subsequently let the premises to the under-tenant (the defendant). In an action for possession brought by the plaintiff against the defendant, the Court held that the plaintiff's interest in the premises had been completely determined, as the superior landlord had already obtained possession by giving it to the defendant.

Sub-tenants are expressly protected by the Act (s), but there must have been a previous legal letting to the original lessee and the under-tenancy must have been lawfully created (t). An interesting point arose in the case of *Brake v Ward*. In that case a purchaser let into possession pending the completion of the purchase, let the premises to a third person. The purchase was not completed through the default of the purchaser. The Court held that the purchaser was in the position of a tenant at will with no rent reserved, and had no power to create except as against himself any greater possessory interest than he himself had, and that accordingly the tenant was not a lawful sub-tenant within the meaning of sect. 15 (3) of the Act. With this case, however, should be contrasted the Irish case of *Martin v Watson*, where the Court was of opinion that a tenant holding

Northcott v Roche, supra, p. 9.
Sects. 12 (1) & (2), 15 (3), 5 (3).
Sect. 15 (3). *Brake v Ward, but see Martin v Watson, q. p. 1.*

under a lease granted by the mortgagor of the premises in question was nevertheless entitled to the protection of the Act, although the lease was void as against the mortgagee

Even where a tenancy is not within the Act a sub-tenancy may nevertheless be within the Act (*Cottell v. Baker*).

Whether the sub-tenant of a statutory tenant is entitled to rely on the Act would depend on whether the statutory tenant had the right of sub-letting by virtue of his original lease or agreement (*u*).

The common law rule that a tenancy vests in the executor or administrator of the deceased tenant is extended to statutory tenancies (*v*). On the death of a statutory tenant his interest will vest in his executor or administrator (*y*). Where however, there is no executor or administrator, it would appear that the provisions of sect. 12 (1) (g) will apply. Sect. 12 (1) (g) provides that where a tenant dies intestate the widow of the tenant if she was residing with him at the time of his death is to be considered as the tenant. But if the deceased tenant happens to have left no widow, or to have been a widow herself, some member of the tenant's family who was residing with the tenant at the time of his or her death is to be regarded as the tenant. If no agreement can be arrived at as to which member of the family should be regarded as the tenant, the question will have to be determined by the County Court (Sect. 12 (1) (g).)

As to the procedure to be adopted, reference should be made to Rule 19 of the Increase of Rent, &c. Rules, 1920

It would appear that persons not in actual occupation are not necessarily excluded from the Act (*z*). The Act expressly provides, in sect. 12 (1) (g), that 'tenant' includes any person deriving title from the tenant. Thus in *Collis v. Flower*, an executor of a tenant was held to be a tenant within the meaning of the previous Acts although he was not himself in occupa-

(u) See *Nunn v. Pellegrini, Keeves v. Deane*

(v) *Mellows v. Low*

(y) See sect. 12 (1) (t)

(z) *Collis v. Flower*, (1921) 1 K. B. at pp. 412, 413. *Reed v. Buck, Rountsway v. Holmes* (1922) Sc. L. T. (Sh. Ct. Rep.) at p. 24

tion (a) The same rule applies to an administrator (*Mellows v Low*)

Where possession is taken of any dwelling-house by a Government Department during the war under the Defence of the Realm Regulations for the purpose of housing workmen, the Act will apply to such houses as if the workmen in occupation thereof at the passing of the Act (2nd July, 1920) were in occupation as tenants of the landlords of such houses (Sect 12 (10))

The operation of the Act, it is interesting to observe, will not be excluded even though the landlord is a statutory body representing the Crown, and even though the landlord is the Crown itself (b)

Sect 4 —Decontrolled Houses

The Amendment Act of 1923 provides some measure of decontrol, and, on the happening of certain events enumerated in sects 2 and 3, a house may cease to be any longer subject to the operation of the Rent Restrictions Acts

1 —(a) Where the landlord is in possession of the whole of the dwelling-house at the date of the passing of the Amendment Act (31st July 1923), the dwelling-house is to be regarded as decontrolled as from that date (Sect 2 (1) of the Amendment Act, 1923)

(b) Where the landlord comes into possession of the whole of the dwelling-house at any time after the passing of the Amendment Act, the dwelling-house is to be regarded as decontrolled as from such later date (Sect 2 (1) *ibid*)

This provision was inserted in the Amendment Act in order to prevent landlords from keeping their houses empty while waiting for a purchaser The prejudice that a landlord might formerly have had against letting to a tenant who taking advantage of the Act, might refuse to give up possession at the end of the term and thus spoil the chances of the landlord to find a purchaser, has thus been obviated

(a) See also *Reed v Burke*
(b) *Prison Commissioners for Scotland v Donaldson*

As regards the nature of the possession which the landlord must have in order to be entitled to rely on the above provision, sect. 2 (3) of the Amendment Act requires such possession to be "actual possession or *de facto* possession." Furthermore the landlord is "not to be deemed to have come into possession by reason only of a change of tenancy made with his consent." On the other hand it is not necessary that the landlord should enter himself into occupation of the premises.

Possession however which has been obtained under an order or judgment made or given on the ground of non-payment of rent will not be sufficient for decontrol in cases where such order or judgment was made or given subsequent to the passing of the Amendment Act. (Cf. the second proviso to sect. 2 (1) of the Amendment Act.)

Where again, an order or judgment for possession has been obtained by the landlord after the 31st July, 1923, on any of the grounds specified in sect. 5 (1) (d) as amended by the Amendment Act, and it is subsequently made to appear to the Court that the order or judgment was obtained by misrepresentation or concealment of material facts, the Court, *inter alia*, is given a discretionary power of directing that the dwelling-house shall cease to be decontrolled notwithstanding the possession of the landlord, as from the date mentioned in such direction. (Sect. 5 (7), as in sect. 4 of the Amendment Act, 1923.)

The possession that the landlord must obtain must be of the "*whole*" of the "dwelling-house." What is meant is that the landlord must obtain possession of the whole subject of the letting in order that the *whole* subject may be decontrolled. It must be remembered that the Act of 1920 applies not only to a dwelling-house but also to "part of a house let as a separate dwelling" (sect. 12 (2) *Woodifield v. Bond*), and also to "rooms in a dwelling-house subject to a separate letting" (sect. 12 (8).) Such "part" and such "rooms," it is submitted, are to be regarded as dwelling-houses for the purposes of sect. 2 (1) of the Amendment Act.

The Amendment Act further provides, in the first proviso to sect. 2 (1), for the decontrol of part only of the original subject of the letting in cases where the landlord is or comes into possession of a part of the premises the remainder being in or coming into the possession of a sub-tenant from the original or other *mesne* lessee. In such cases the part in the possession of the landlord becomes decontrolled, the other part still remaining controlled. But in order that such other part should still remain controlled it is essential (c) in the first place, that such part should have been lawfully sub-let, and in this respect it is as well to remember that a statutory tenant may have the right of assigning or sub-letting (*Keeves v Deane Nunn v Pellegrini*, and in the second place such part must be a dwelling-house to which the principal Act applies (d (e g it must not consist of business or furnished premises)

A few illustrations may help to make the meaning of sect 2 (1) of the Amendment Act 1923 clearer

Illustrations

(1) On the 31st July, 1923, Blackacre is untenanted and unoccupied. Blackacre, *ceteris paribus* is decontrolled. It is not necessary that the landlord should be in occupation himself

(2) On the 31st July, 1923, the whole of Blackacre is in the occupation of A. A is not the original lessee, but T, the original tenant, lawfully sub-let the whole of the premises to A. T's interest has expired at some time prior to the 31st July, 1923, but A has nevertheless continued in occupation since then by virtue of the provisions of sect 5 (5) and sect 15 (3) of the Act of 1920, being in fact now a statutory tenant. Blackacre is not decontrolled

(3) On the 31st July, 1923, *part* of Blackacre is in the occupation of A. The facts are otherwise the same as in Illustration 2. The part in A's occupation is still controlled, the remainder, which is untenanted and unoccupied, is *ceteris paribus*, decontrolled

(4) On the 31st July, 1923, T is the lawful tenant of the whole of Blackacre. T's interest expires on the 25th March, 1924. On Sept 29th 1923, T lawfully sub-lets the whole of Blackacre to A. On the 25th March 1924, A still remains in possession as a statutory tenant. Blackacre is still controlled

(5) The facts are the same as in Illustration 4 except that T sub-lets only part of the premises to A. On the 25th March, 1924 the part still in the possession of A remains controlled. The remainder *ceteris paribus* becomes decontrolled

The Amendment Act 1923, does not define the meaning of

(c) First proviso of sect 2 1 of the Amendment Act
(d) Cf *supra* pp 21 36

landlord in sect 2 1, and questions of difficulty may arise in case where there happen to be several co-existing sub-tenancies Regarding the purpose (e) of the insertion of this clause in the Act it would appear that the term landlord is to be used in the popular acceptance of the term, as being the person who is the freeholder or in the case of ground leases or long terms the principal lessee

Illustration

On the 31st July, 1923, Blackacre is in the occupation of D D has previously to the 31st July, 1923 sub-let the whole of Blackacre to E E's interest having expired on the 25th June, 1923 D himself is a sub-tenant of C who is a sub-tenant of B, to whom A the freeholder has granted the ground lease of Blackacre It is submitted that Blackacre is not decontrolled That would only be the case if A or possibly B, were in possession

II Where, subsequently to the 31st July, 1923 the landlord grants a valid lease, or enters into a valid agreement for a tenancy of a dwelling-house (f), the dwelling-house which is the subject of the lease or agreement becomes decontrolled as from the commencement of the term, provided that not only must the lease or agreement have been respectively granted or entered into subsequently to the passing of the Amendment Act, but further, the term must be for a period of not less than two years, and must end at some date after the 24th June 1926 (g. Sect 2 (2 of the Amendment Act)

It is immaterial whether the tenant to whom the term is granted is in occupation under an existing lease or agreement, or as a statutory tenant by virtue of the Act Sect 2 (2 of the Amendment Act, however, would not apparently apply to cases where there was a letting to a new tenant not in occupation since by sub-sect 1 of sect 2 of that Act the house will have become decontrolled

A sub-tenant, however, is protected in certain cases By the

(e) supra p 41

(f) Which may also consist merely of a portion of a house or of rooms in a house see supra, p 23

(g) As regards Scotland, the 28th May 1926 is to be substituted for this date see 19 1 of the Amendment Act) proviso to sect 2 (2) of the Amendment Act, where part of the dwelling-house is lawfully sub-let at the commencement of the term, and is a dwelling-house to which the principal Act applies (*h*) (*e g* does not consist of furnished premises) such part shall notwithstanding remain controlled

Illustrations

(1) A subsequently to the 31st July 1923 remains in possession of Blackacre as statutory tenant, a portion of the house being in the possession of L, as A's sub-tenant. L, the landlord after the 31st July 1923 grants to A a lease of Blackacre for a term of more than two years, ending in December, 1926 The portion in the possession of L remains controlled, the remainder being decontrolled

(2) A subsequently to the 31st July 1923 grants T who is in occupation as a tenant, a valid lease of Blackacre as from the 29th September 1923 for a term of three years In the meanwhile T, sub-lets a portion of the house to S as from the 29th September 1923 the date of the commencement of the term The portion so sub-let, *ceteris paribus* still remains controlled Had the tenancy commenced on the 25th December, 1923 the portion comprised in the sub-tenancy would also have been decontrolled

III Where *prior to the 31st July*, 1923, the landlord of a dwelling-house (*i*) to which the principal Act applies has granted to the tenant a valid lease, or has entered into a valid agreement with the tenant for a tenancy of the dwelling-house for a term ending at some date after the 24th June, 1923 and the rent thereby reserved is at a rate which after but not before the 24th June, 1923 exceeds the standard rent and the increases permitted under the Act of 1920 or the Amendment Act of 1923, the landlord may determine the lease subject to certain conditions (See sect 3 of the Amendment Act, 1923)

Three essentials are required before sect 3 will apply —

   i The lease or agreement must have been respectively executed or made prior to the 31st July 1923 (date of the passing of the Amendment Act

   ii The term created must be one ending at some date after

(*h*) Cf *supra*, pp 21—36

(*i*) Or part of a dwelling-house, or rooms in a dwelling-house (See sect 12 (2) and 12 (8))

the 24th June, 1923 (original date of expiry of Act of 1920).

(iii.) The rent reserved must have been reserved at a rate which *after*, but *not before*, the 24th June, 1923, exceeds the statutory limits permitted by sect. 2 (1) of the Act of 1920 or sect. 7 of the Amendment Act, 1923.

This provision was inserted in order to meet the case where a landlord had provided that after the expiry of the principal Act in June, 1923, the tenant should pay him an increased rent, the amount of the rent being such as he was not entitled to demand while the Act was in force.

The landlord, therefore, is given the right to determine the lease or agreement. He must however first serve on the tenant a three months' notice in writing, expiring not earlier than the 21st December, 1923, and not later than the 31st March, 1924.

The tenant however is given the option of electing to abide by his agreement, or else of continuing in possession as a statutory tenant. In some cases, no doubt, the tenant would be wise in electing to abide by the lease or agreement, as for instance, when the term thereby created is for a considerable period, and the rent reserved is not outrageous.

If the tenant elects to abide by the lease or agreement he must give the landlord, within one month of the receipt of the above-mentioned notice from the landlord, a notice in writing to the effect that he elects to abide by the lease or agreement.

In such a case the lease or agreement will remain in full force and effect in every respect, including the amount of rent expressed to be reserved unaffected by the Act of 1920, or the Amendment Act. (Sect. 3 of the Amendment Act.)

NOTE TO CHAPTER III

THE METROPOLITAN POLICE DISTRICT (*h*)

THE Metropolitan Police District, as constituted by the Metropolitan Police Act, 1829 and by an Order in Council (3rd

(*h*) See the Metropolitan Police Guide (1922) p. 32.

January 1840) made under that Act, and the Metropolitan Police Act, 1839, comprises the following places —

(1) The county of London, exclusive of the City of London and its liberties

(2) The county of Middlesex

(3) In the county of Surrey the following parishes and places — Addington, Banstead, Barnes, Beddington, Carshalton Cheam Chenington, Coombe, Coulsdon, Cuddington, Epsom, Ewell (exclusive of Kingswood liberty), Farley, hamlet of Ham with Hatch, hamlet of Hook, Kew, Kingston-on-Thames, Long Ditton Malden (Old and New), Merton, Mitcham, Morden Mortlake Molesey (East and West), North Sheen, Petersham Richmond Sanderstead, Surbiton Sutton, Thames Ditton (comprising the hamlets of Claygate, Ember and Weston), Tolworth, hamlets of Wallington, Warlingham, Wimbledon and Woodmansterne

(4) The county borough of Croydon

(5) In the county of Herts, the following parishes and places — Aldenham (and hamlet of Theobald Street), Arkley, East Barnet, Barnet Vale, Bushey (urban and rural), Cheshunt Chipping Barnet, Elstree, Hadley, Monken Hadley, Northaw, Ridge, Shenley, South Mimms (urban) and Totteridge

(6) In the county of Essex, the following parishes and places — Barking, Buckhurst Hill Cann Hall, Chigwell, Chingford, Dagenham the borough of East Ham (including Little Ilford), Great Ilford, Loughton, Low Leyton, Waltham Abbey and Town (including the hamlets of Holyfield, Sewardstone and Upshire), Walthamstow, Wanstead and Woodford

(7) The county borough of West Ham

(8) In the county of Kent, the following parishes and places — Beckenham, Bexley, Bromley, Chislehurst, Crayford, Down, Erith, Farnborough, Foot's Cray, Hayes, Keston, hamlet of Mottingham, North Cray, Orpington, hamlet of Penge, St Mary's Cray, St Paul's Cray and Wickham (East and West)

CHAPTER IV

PERMITTED INCREASES OF RENT

Sect. 1.—General Observations

The principal Act of 1920 recognises the basic rule which appears to underlie the earlier repealed Acts as well, that a landlord cannot increase the rent merely by giving notice to the tenant that he requires an increased rent. The existing tenancy must first be determined (a). In the words of sect. 3 (1) of the Act of 1920 it is only in respect of a "period during which (but for the Act—(c) if it had not been passed)—the landlord would be entitled to obtain possession" (b) that the rent can be increased

---

(a) Kerr v. Bryde, Connelly v. Barclay, Glossop v. Ashley, Newell v. Carter, Cottage Soci. v. Parr, v. Lehmann, Phillips v. Rhymes. As regards Scotland notice to prevent tacit relocation must in the case of a small dwelling-house be in the form provided by the House Letting and Rating (Scotland) Act, 1911. The provisions of sect. 18 (1) (d) of the Act of 1920 should also be noted. This provision which applies to Scotland only, is the only exception to the rule contained in sect. 3 (1) that it is only after a tenancy has been duly determined that the landlord may be entitled to an increase of rent. The exception however (i) applies only to a specified class of tenancies viz. those arising from a yearly contract or from tacit relocation and ending at Whit-Sunday, 1921, and further (ii) it is limited to a particular period of time ending at Whitsun, 1921. The period after Whitsun 1921 therefore will not be a period "during which but for the Act the landlord would be entitled to obtain possession." Where therefore an increase of rent is legally recoverable under sect. 18 (1) (d) in respect of the period ending at Whit-Sunday, 1921, such increase will not be recoverable for any period subsequent to Whit-Sunday 1921 unless the landlord can show that the tenancy has been duly determined e.g., by notice to quit or that a new agreement for a tenancy has been made and that the tenant is not remaining in occupation under a contract extended by tacit relocation. (Molloy v. Thomson.)

(b) As to the meaning of these words see Kerr v. Bryde (H. L.), per Lord Sumner. Contrast judgment of Lord Atkinson and see also Holl v. Hasler,

The Act, however does not override agreements between a landlord and his tenant, so that the landlord is not entitled to increase the rent during the currency of an existing lease or agreement.

As to the manner in which a tenancy can be duly terminated a tenancy is determined in some cases by mere effluxion of time whereas in other cases a valid notice to quit (c) is necessary. Where such a notice was required i.e., where a tenancy was not determined by mere effluxion of time, it was essential (d) that the landlord should have served such a notice before he would be entitled to any increase of rent. Where however, the tenancy expired by mere effluxion of time, no notice to quit was held to be necessary in order to entitle the landlord to an increase of rent provided the tenant remained in possession as a statutory tenant (Felce v Hill, Newell's Case).

The law has now been altered by the Notices of Increase Act 1923 but the alteration is one more of form than of substance. The Notices of Increase Act 1923, still recognises the rule contained in sect 3 (1, of the Act of 1920, and its short effect (e) is merely to do away with the necessity of serving any notice to quit where such notice is necessary in order to terminate a tenancy and to make a notice of increase provided it is in conformity with sect 3 (2) of the Act of 1920 do double service by operating as a notice to terminate the tenancy (f). It will therefore, be observed that the principle contained in sect 3 (1) of the Act of 1920, that the tenancy must first have come to an end is still maintained, the Notices of Increase Act providing an artificial means for bringing about this result

---

(1921) 3 K B at pp 651, 652 As regards Scotland, see further sect 18 (1) (d) of the Act of 1920, and see sect 19 (b) of the Amendment Act, 1923

(c) As to the length of a notice to quit and the day on which it must expire see, inter alia Savory v Bayley and Queen's Club Garden Estates, Ltd v Bignell disapproving of Simmons v Crossley

(d) Newell's Case, Felce v Hill, Kerr v Bryde

(e) Sect 1 (1)

(f) For a detailed consideration of the fictitious effect given to a notice of increase by the Notices of Increase Act 1923 see infra pp 79—87

The Act of 1920 further requires the landlord to satisfy the "condition precedent" (g) in sect 3 (2), whereby he must serve on the tenant a valid notice (h) of increase of rent, which must be in writing and in the form (i) contained in the First Schedule of the Act. Such a notice of increase is essential even in the case of a new tenant (j) if the rent payable by him was above that paid by the former tenant.

Although it is no longer necessary to serve a notice to quit, if a notice of increase is served, it would be as well to examine some of the cases decided under the prior Act Under the prior Act the notice to quit had to be served before or contemporaneously with the notice of increase (*Hill* v. *Hasler*), though the point was left open in that case as to whether a notice of increase given before the notice to quit would be a good notice In view of the alteration of the law by the Notices of Increase Act (h) this ruling would now appear to be immaterial

Where a landlord had once served a valid notice to quit, it was held that there was no necessity for him to serve a further notice to quit in order to be entitled to a further increase while the **tenancy** was a statutory tenancy no agreement for a fresh **tenancy** having been made (*Shuter* v *Hersh*) This ruling also, for the reason mentioned above, would now appear to be immaterial But it should be observed that it was further held in that case that a valid notice of increase would be necessary each time the rent was increased (l). and this is still the law at the present time

It was further held under the Act of 1920 that where a notice to quit had been served, but the tenant still remained in possession, acceptance of rent for a period of even more than three

---

(g) *Worthy* v *Mann, Bridges* v *Chambers*

(h) As regards Scotland no such notice is necessary in the case of increased assessments under the House Letting, &c (Scotland) Act, 1911 See *Kennedy* v *Campbell*, and see sect 19 (b) of the Amendment Act, 1923

(i) *Infra* p 190

(j) *Schmit* v *Christy*

(k) Cf *infra*, pp 78 sq

(l) *Shuter* v *Hersh*, *Newell's Case*, (1922) 1 K B at p 660

months *m*, would not invalidate the notice and make a fresh notice necessary (*n*) and that the onus rested on the tenant to show that a fresh agreement of tenancy had been arrived at and that the tenant was not a statutory tenant, the mere acceptance of rent where the original tenancy had expired not affording conclusive evidence of the creation of a fresh agreement of tenancy (*o*)

Again it would appear that the Notices of Increase Act makes the above decision nugatory at the present time

In *Bridges v Chambers* and in *Michael v Phillips*, decided under the Act of 1920 it was held that the provisions of sect 3 of the Act of 1920, necessitating the determination of the tenancy and the service of a valid notice of increase, had a retrospective operation and it should be observed that by sect 3 (3) of that Act a notice served before the Act (2nd July 1920, of an intention to make any increase of rent, permissible only by virtue of the Act of 1920 is not to be deemed to be a valid notice for the purposes of sect 3 of that Act Now the Notices of Increase Act in sect 1 (1) speaks of a notice of intention to increase being served in conformity with sect 3 (2) of the Act of 1920 and, therefore refers of necessity to a notice served subsequently to the 2nd July 1920 It would seem therefore that the fictitious effect given to a notice of increase can only be given to it if it was served subsequently to the 2nd July, 1920, and that inasmuch as sect 3 of the Act of 1920 has a retrospective effect the landlord who has not complied with its provisions prior to the 2nd July 1920 will not be able to avail himself of the benefit of the Notices of Increase Act

Although the Act of 1920 gives no express power to the landlord to impose *in invitum* an increase of rent on the tenant who remains in possession by virtue of the Act it has nevertheless

Sect 16 (3)

Shanly v Hassan, Fair Rent Courts Decisions ...

Bridges v ... Michael v Phillips ... Series II, ... cases in which the Court held that a new agreement for a tenancy ...

been held that the landlord is entitled to the increases permitted by the Act even though the tenant in such a case does not assent thereto (p).

The Act appears to assume that although a landlord cannot raise the rent of a house above the standard rent plus the permitted increases, yet he may at any time raise to a standard rent a rent which previously had been below the standard rent provided of course the original tenancy has been duly determined (q). It is submitted that in such a case the rent can be raised not only to the standard rent but to the maximum rent, including the increases allowed by the Act. The clauses relating to the form of notice with respect to the permitted increases as for example for increased rates do not deal with such a case and it would appear that the Court could not and would not require a form of notice exactly in accordance with the form given in the First Schedule.

If the landlord is entitled by virtue of any other Act or statutory provision not affected by the Rent Act to increase the rent by a sum which is in excess of that permitted under sect. 2 the landlord will nevertheless be entitled to that increase. Thus in *Baker v. Wood* an agricultural labourer was in possession of a cottage the rent of which was one shilling per week. This sum was deducted by the landlord from his wages. Subsequently, by virtue of the Corn Production Act, 1917, and certain Orders under that Act a minimum wage of twenty-five shillings was fixed for agricultural labourers and from such wages the employer was authorised to deduct in this particular case, the sum of three shillings per week in respect of the occupation of the cottage. The effect of this was to raise the original rent of one shilling, which was also the standard rent by two shillings. The Divisional Court however held that the landlord was nevertheless entitled to this increase of two shillings per week.

It is only rent which has been increased since the 25th day of

(p) *Coal Improved Fuel and Co. v. Brien; Glossop v. Ashley* (1921) 2 K. B. at p. 456.

(q) *Glossop v. Ashley* (1921) 2 K. B. at pp. 458, 459.

(r) *Ibid.* at p. 459.

March, 1920 beyond the limits permitted by the Act that is made irrecoverable(s) from the tenant and that too notwithstanding any agreement to the contrary. In the Act of 1915 the material date was the 4th August, 1914, and in the Act of 1919 the 25th December, 1918, so that the combined effect of sect. 1 of the Act of 1915, sect. 4 proviso (i) of the Act of 1919 sects. 1 and 19 of the Act of 1920 and sect. 38 of the Interpretation Act 1889, may be briefly set out as follows, viz:—

No increase of rent is valid—

(a) In the case of 1915 houses if such rent was increased since the 4th August, 1914, and was in excess of the limits prescribed by the Act of 1915 (t).

(b) In the case of 1919 houses if such rent was increased since the 25th December, 1918, and was in excess of the limits prescribed by the Act of 1919.

(c) In the case of 1920 houses if such rent has been increased since 25th March, 1920, and is in excess of the limits prescribed by the Act of 1920.

In considering whether the rent has been increased since a given date, the material date is the date at which the rent begins to run and not the date of the agreement (*Goldsmith v. Orr*) nor *semble* the date when the rent becomes payable (u). Thus in *Goldsmith v. Orr*, a house was held under an agreement dated October, 1918 whereby the rent of the house was fixed at 50l. per year until the 25th March 1919 and after the expiration of that period the rent was to be increased to 65l. until the 25th March 1920. After the making of the agreement the Act of 1919 came into force, and the question arose whether the rent had been increased since the 25th December 1918. The Court held that the rent had been increased since that date 25th December 1918, the date on which the agreement was made (October, 1918) being considered immaterial.

As to when the rent "begins to run" will depend on the con-

s) As to recovery of sums made irrecoverable, see *infra* p. 145.

t) *Howards v. Coy.*, 152 L. T. 293.

u) See judgments of Bailhache and Sankey JJ. in the Divisional Court and of Bankes L. J. in the Court of Appeal in *Goldsmith v. Orr*.

struction of the agreement in question. In *Raikes v. Ogle* [r] the premises were let "from' 25th March, 1920, and the Court held that the rent accrued on 26th March, 1920. Acton, J., said that "the ordinary meaning . . . would be that the quarter day upon which the rent of a bygone quarter falls due and becomes payable is to be regarded as included in that quarter, and not in the quarter thereafter next ensuing, so that the 24th June, 1920, would be included in the first quarter of the defendant's tenancy, and the 25th March, 1920, consequently excluded.' (*Ibid.* at p 581.)

The result is that under the present Act of 1920 where the rent of a house has not been increased since the 25th March, 1920, assuming the house to be one to which none of the previous Acts applied, such increase is not at all affected by the Act [u]. The dwelling-house, however, will nevertheless be within the Act, and such of the other provisions of the Act as deal with recovery of possession, or ejectment, or distress, or the taking of a premium will not be excluded. There can be no difficulty in a case where the increased rent has accrued due on or before the 25th March, 1920, and where the same tenant is still in possession: in such a case the landlord will still be entitled to demand such rent from his tenant. As Lush, J., said in *Sinclair v Powell* (37 T. L. R. at p 744) (x) "When the Act of 1920 came into force, all that it did was to prevent subsequent increases after a specified date. How could it affect already existing rents? It did not make unlawful contracts with regard to rent which had been already made. How could it be argued that the landlord who had been acting perfectly lawfully in taking an increased rent was suddenly doing something wrong?'

But what would be the position on the termination of the tenancy? What would be the effect, for instance, if the landlord were to let the premises to another tenant subsequently to 25th March, 1920? Would the rent still be considered as not having

(r) Reference may also be made to *Holland v. Litten* and *Sidebotham v. Holland*, as explained by Peterson J. in *Meggeson v. Groves*.

(u) *Supra*, pp 5, 6

(x) But see *Woodhead v. Putnam*

been increased since 25th March 1920? There is no actual authority on the point, but it is submitted, on the natural and reasonable construction of sect. 1 of the Act, that if the rent has been increased prior to the material date, the landlord will be entitled to the same rent from any subsequent tenant.

In the case, however, of a house which was within the provisions of any of the Acts passed prior to 1920, the landlord will not be able to avail himself of the benefits conferred by sect. 1 merely because the rent has been increased prior to the 25th March 1920. If such increased rent was beyond the limits allowed by any of the previous Acts, the landlord will not be entitled to demand any the same rent, assuming of course that the rent is also beyond the limits permitted by the present Act.[1]

The Act further provides in sect. 2 (3) that any transfer to a tenant of any burden or liability previously borne by the landlord is to be treated as an *alteration of rent,* and that where as the result of such a transfer the terms on which the house is held are on the whole less favourable to the tenant, the rent shall be deemed to have been increased, whether the actual rent payable is increased or not.

If, however, any burden or liability previously borne by the tenant is transferred to the landlord, and the actual rent paid by the tenant is correspondingly increased, so that the terms on which the house is held are not on the whole less favourable to the tenant, then the rent shall not be deemed to have been increased.

At any rate, if the liability for rates is transferred from the landlord to the tenant, and a corresponding reduction is made in the rent, the rent shall not be deemed to have been increased.

Where there has been such a transfer of liability by mutual agreement, so that there is no disturbance of the pre-existing pecuniary obligations between the landlord and the tenant, no notices of increase or *semble* notices to quit are necessary, *Phillips v. Whymes.*

Any questions arising under sub-sects. 1, 2, or 3 of

[1] As regards recovery of sums made irrecoverable, see *infra* p. 115.
See *Hunter v. Cooper ? ? ? ?* p. 134.

sect 2, (a) as regards the increases of rent to which the landlord is entitled (sub-sect. 1), or whether increases under sect 2 (1) (c) and (d) should be suspended (sub-sect (2), or whether any transfer of a burden from the landlord to the tenant or *vice versâ* is permissible (sub-sect. 3), are to be decided by the County Court and the County Court alone (a) whose decision is to be final and conclusive (b). Application may be made by the landlord or the tenant, the landlord now including in relation to a sub-tenancy, not only the immediate landlord of the sub-tenant, but also the landlord of that person.—Sect 7 (3) of the Amendment Act 1923.

It is as well to remember that there is no possibility of contracting out of the Act. The words of sect 1 state clearly that any excess above the amount of rent permitted by the Act is to be irrecoverable from the tenant notwithstanding any agreement to the contrary, and if such excess is paid the tenant has a right to recover it (c). Even where a judgment was marked for an amount of rent in excess of that which was permitted the Act the Court made an order reducing the judgment.

The County Court has the power on the application of the landlord or the tenant to determine summarily any questions as to the amount of the rent or as to the increases (e) of rent permitted whether under the Act of 1920 or the Amendment Act, 1923.—Sect 11 (1) of the Amendment Act.)

Sect 2.—The Notice of Increase

As has been mentioned above (f), before a landlord will be entitled to recover from the tenant any of the increases (g) permitted by the Act the tenancy must first have been duly deter-

---

(a) See N Ross Ltd v Armitage
(b) Sect 2 (6). See also Lyon v Morris (1887), 19 Q B D 139
(c) See ante p 11.
(d) Tuxill v Acland
(e) Infra p 61 sq
(f) Supra pp 48—50
(g) A transfer of a burden or liability under sect 2 (3) may not be in certain cases an increase and in such cases a notice will not be necessary (Phillips v Rhone (1923) 1 I L 18

mined whether by effluxion of time, or by a proper notice to quit,
or by a notice of increase in conformity with sect 3 (2) of the
Act of 1920 (h) The landlord must also in any case satisfy
the condition precedent laid down by sect 3 (2) and serve on the
tenant a valid notice in writing of his intention to increase the
rent, except in the cases mentioned in sect 7 (1) of the Amendment
Act, which notice must be in the form (i) contained in the First
Schedule of the Act of 1920 or in a form substantially to the
same effect (h)

The increases, however, will not be recoverable until, or in
respect of any period prior to, the expiry of four clear (l) weeks
from the date of the service (m) of the notice except where the
increase is on account of an increase in rates, in which case a limit
of one clear week is to be substituted for that of four clear weeks

Thus, suppose T is a monthly tenant, and that on the 31st
March L the landlord, serves on him a notice to quit on the 30th
April, and also a notice of increase increasing the rent by 1l
per month under sects 2 (1) (c) and 2 (1) (d) (1) of the Act
The increased rent will accrue as from 1st May For the period
prior to the 1st May, L is only entitled to the former rent (n)

A notice of increase is essential not only where the rent of a
tenant already in occupation is to be increased, but also in the
case of a new tenancy, where the rent the new tenant is charged is
an increase above the rent formerly paid Thus in *Schmit* v
Christy a tenant had underlet a portion of a dwelling-house to
his sub-tenant at a rental of 35s per week the rent being in
excess of the standard rent of that portion, which was 21s per
week At the expiration of the tenant's tenancy, the sub-tenant
remained in possession as the tenant of the landlord at the same
rent of 35s No notice of any increase had been served on the

(h) See Notices of Increase Act
(i) See *infra* p 75
(k) As to the criminal liability of landlords in respect of false or misleading
statements and representations in the notice, see *infra* p 159
(l) *Ie* the first and last days of each period are to be excluded
(m) See sect 6 (2) of the Amendment Act
(n) The decision in *Saul* v *Mahoney*, that the increase will be recoverable
is from the date of the notice is no longer authoritative

undertenant or on any previous tenant of the landlord. The Court held that although this was a new tenancy the landlord could not recover more than the standard rent from the undertenant. In order to be entitled so to do, it was necessary that he should have first served a valid notice to quit and a valid notice of increase on the new tenant. By reason of the Notices of Increase Act the service of a notice to quit will no longer be essential in such a case.

Where, however, a notice of increase which at the time was valid has been served on any tenant the increase may be continued without any fresh notice on any subsequent tenant. Sect. 3 (2).

A notice served before the passing of the Act (2nd July, 1920) of an intention to make any increase of rent which is permissible *only* by virtue of the Act of 1910, will not be deemed a valid notice. Sect. 3 (3). A further notice to increase must be served. This provision, however, must be read with sect. 1 whereby only increases of rent since the 25th March 1920 are affected. Reference may also be made to *Bridges v. Chambers* o a case under the previous Acts where it was held that a notice to increase was necessary, even though the increase, which was on account of an increase of rates, had been made and actually paid before the Act of 1915 had come into operation.

H. Act states that the Notice of Increase must be substantially in the form contained in the First Schedule. But instances are possible where a departure from the above form may be necessary and in such a case the notice will nevertheless be valid. (See *Glossop v. Ashley*, 1921, 2 K. B. at pp. 458-459.)

A notice of increase will not be bad if it changes the incidence of the rates, provided the aggregate burden on the tenant will not be in excess of the statutory limit. (p)

Under the Act of 1920, it was held that a notice of increase might be quite valid although it was served along with or (q) during the currency of, the notice to quit by which the tenancy was determined provided the rent was not to be thereby increased before a date subsequent to the date of expiry of the notice to

(o) Followed in *Michael v. Phillips* and see *Samuel v. Christie*
(p) *Strange v. Henderson*
(q) *Holt v. Mason* and see *Sharpe v. Deacon*

quit (*Hill v Hasler*). This decision, however, owing to the Notices of Increase Act, has lost any importance that it might otherwise have had.

Prior to the change of law effected by the Notices of Increase Act, the notice of increase had to be preceded by or accompanied with a valid notice to quit, for the former, which was invalid, could not be rendered valid by a subsequent valid notice to quit. If, therefore, an invalid notice to quit had been given at the same time as the notice to increase, no increase was recoverable unless a further valid notice to quit as well as a further notice of increase had been given.

A notice of increase, to be valid, must state the correct standard rent, and the correct date as from which the landlord is entitled to the increase, since dates are matters of substance (t).

A notice of increase will be valid although longer periods than those prescribed by sect. 3 (2) of the Act are given before the increases are to become effective (u).

In *Penfold v Newman*, a notice of increase which claimed more than the fixed percentage permitted by sect. 2 (i) (c) of the Act, i.e., 15 per cent instead of 5 per cent, was held invalid.

Whether a mistake in the notice as to the amount of increase payable under sect. 2 (1) (a) (b) or (d), would invalidate the notice has not been expressly decided in the English Courts (v), although the Appeal Court of the Irish Free State has held in *Elliott v Ellis* that such a mistake would not invalidate the notice. This case further casts doubts on the correctness of the decision in *Penfold v Newman*, though at the same time it was distinguished from the latter case, inasmuch as the parties had arrived at a full agreement as to the rent properly payable. The Irish Court however seems to have lost sight of the words "notwithstanding any agreement to the contrary" at the beginning of sect. 3 (2) of the Act. Reference may further be made to two other cases

Price v Lekeman. Hill v Hasler (1921) 3 K.B. at p. 657
Imper v Holland
Lewis v Lekeman
Hill v Hasler, ibid at p. 653
See Penfold v Newman

which deal with the question of the validity of notices of increase

In the Irish case of *Conolly v. Whelan*, the Court was of opinion that a mistake in the notice of the increase as to the amount of the rates payable in 1914, and the amount payable at the date of notice as well as a mistake as to the date from which the increase was payable would not invalidate a notice. In *Steel v. Mahoney* it was held that it was immaterial that the notice of increase was inaccurate in form if the increase was reduced to the proper amount at the time when the claim was made. It is submitted however in view of the decisions in *Petzer v. Federman*, *Hill v. Hasler* and *Penfold v. Newman*, that the decisions in *Conolly v. Whelan* and *Steel v. Mahoney* are no longer to be considered authoritative. Moreover these cases were decided under the previous Acts.

It will be seen that the provisions with regard to notice of increase are very stringent. The notice must be correct not only in form but in substance; it must state accurately all material facts *e.g.* the amount of the increase, the date of its beginning, the correct standard rent and the correct net rent and generally the figures it contains must be accurate and correct (*q*).

A very equitable innovation, however, has been introduced by Sect. 6 (1) of the Amendment Act 1923. Formerly if the notice of increase was invalid the landlord was not entitled to the increase set out in the notice, but now, by the above provision, the County Court is given a discretionary power of amending a notice of increase, even where it has been served prior to the 31st July, 1923 if it is satisfied that any error or omission in the notice was due to a *bonâ fide* mistake on the part of the landlord. The County Court may amend the notice by correcting any errors or supplying any omissions in the notice, on such terms and conditions as respects arrears of rent or otherwise, as appear to the Court to be just and reasonable. The Court may further direct that the notice shall not only have effect as a valid notice in the future, but also that it shall be deemed to have had effect as a valid notice, presumably as from the date of the original service of the notice

---

(*q*) See *Penfold v. Newman* (1921) 1 K. B. at pp. 653-655

Where such latter direction is made, however, sect 8 (1) of the Amendment Act provides that no increase of rent which becomes payable by reason of the amendment of the notice shall be recoverable in respect of any " rental period " which ended more than six months before the date of the order It is the " rental period " which has to be considered so that the landlord may be entitled to recover the increase thus validated in respect of a period which may be more than six months before the date of the order On the other hand, if an increase validated by sect 6 (1) of the Amendment Act has already been paid, even in respect of a rental period ending more than six months before the date of the order, the tenant nevertheless will not be entitled to recover it from the landlord

A difficulty will arise in cases where the tenant has already paid the invalid increase and has subsequently recovered it from the landlord by an order or judgment of a competent Court It is submitted that in such a case, notwithstanding sect 8 (1 of the Amendment Act the landlord will not be entitled to recover the increase now validated from the tenant (z)

By Rule 3 of the new Rent Restrictions Rules, the Court may exercise the power of amending a notice of increase either on an original application (a) under the Act of 1923, which may be made by the landlord or the tenant, or where proceedings before the Court are pending in which the validity of any notice of increase is in question or material, on request by either party at any time in the course of those proceedings

Sect 3 —Permitted Increases of Rent in the case of Unfurnished Houses

The rent of a dwelling-house to which the Act applies is not to be increased so as to exceed the standard rent by more than

---

(z) As to the effect of an order or judgment in cases coming within the Notices of Increase Act see p 83

(a) The Increase of Rent Act Rules will apply to such applications As to the fees payable and as to the costs of such application, see Rule 2 of the Rent Restrictions Rules 1923

the amounts mentioned below. The increases, moreover, are cumulative.

> a. Increases on account of improvements or structural altera-
> tions (Sect. 2 (1 (a))
>
>   i. Where the landlord has incurred expenditure on
> improvements or structural alterations between the 4th
> August, 1914, and the 2nd July, 1920, the standard
> rent may be exceeded by an amount not exceeding 6 per
> cent. per annum on the amount expended.
>
>   ii. Where such expenditure has been incurred sub-
> sequently to the 2nd July, 1920, 8 per cent. on the
> amount so expended is allowed.

The amount of expenditure on which the increase is to be based is not only the amount actually paid in cash, but the amount of expense incurred and to be discharged by some legal mode of satisfaction (b).

It is, however, on account of improvements or structural altera-tions only that the landlord will be entitled to an increase, he will not be entitled to any increase of rent on account of expen-diture on decoration or repairs.

Whether the work carried out by the landlord amounts to an improvement or structural alteration would depend on whether the work has the effect of restoring the house to its original state or not. Thus, if a landlord expended money in fitting an electrical installation or in fixing up a boiler and the necessary pipes in order that the house may be supplied with constant hot water, this it is submitted would be an expenditure on an "improve-ment." It would seem, however, that where a landlord incurs expense on account of street improvements, e.g., paving and channelling, he will not be entitled to an increase on account of such expenditure nor, it seems, would he be entitled to an increase on account of decoration, even though such decoration might at the same time amount to an improvement.

The Act expressly provides that the tenant may apply to the County Court for an order suspending or reducing any increase

(b) See Nield v. Jackson 37 T. L. R. at p. 592.

under this sub-sect (a, on the ground that the expenditure is or was unnecessary in whole or in part. The decision of the County Court will be final and conclusive. (See sect. 2 (6).)

In this connection should also be remembered the provisions of sect. 15 (2) of the Act whereby it is to be deemed to be a condition of the tenancy of any dwelling-house to which the Act applies that the tenant shall afford the landlord access thereto and all reasonable facilities for executing therein any repairs which the landlord is entitled to execute.

(b) On account of increase of rates. (Sect. 2 (1) (b).)

In such a case the standard rent can be exceeded by an amount not exceeding any increase in the amount for the time being payable by the landlord in respect of rates over the corresponding amount paid in respect of the yearly half-yearly or other period which included the 3rd August, 1914.

If, however, the dwelling-house is one for which no rates were payable in respect of any period which included the 3rd August, 1914, then the standard rent can be exceeded by an amount not exceeding any increase in the amount for the time being payable in respect of rates over the corresponding amount paid in respect of the period which included the date on which the rates first became payable. (Sect. 2 (1) (b).)

As regards *Scotland*, no increase is permitted under this head in respect of any increase after the year ending Whit Sunday 1920, in the amount of rates payable by the landlord, other than rates for which he is responsible under the House Letting and Rating (Scotland) Act 1911. (Sect. 18 (1) (b).)

In this connection the provisions of sect. 1 (1) and (2) of the House Letting and Rating (Scotland) Act 1920, which was passed on the 20th May, 1920 should be observed. By sub-sect. (1) of sect. 1 of the above Act it is provided that the assessments imposed by any assessing authority in Scotland for the year to Whitsun 1920, and for any subsequent year which are imposed on any occupier of a small dwelling-house (c), and

(c) For definition of ' small dwelling-house ' see sect. 1 of House Letting

for which the owner is by law responsible shall subject to the provisions of this Act and to the extent (if any) to which the total of such assessments is in excess of the total of the assessments for the immediately preceding year, be deemed to have been and be a lawful addition to the rent for the whole of the year for which the increased assessments are imposed and shall be payable by the occupier or successive occupiers of the small dwelling-house during that year." Sub-sect. (2) provides that so much of the provisions of the Rent Act 1915 s. 1 (1) proviso (vi) as amended by sect. 5 (3) of the Rent Act 1919 (9 Geo. 5, c. 7) as provides that no increase of rent by the said Act of 1915 permitted shall be due or recoverable until or in respect of any period prior to the expiry of four clear weeks after the service of the notice in the said proviso mentioned, shall not apply to any addition to rent payable by an occupier to an owner under this Act.

For the purpose of clearing up doubts the Amending Act of 1923 provides in sect. 19 (b) that nothing in the Rent Act of 1920 affects the operation of the House Letting and Rating (Scotland) Act 1920 and that the reference in the above sub-sect. (2) of sect. 1 of the House Letting &c. Scotland Act set out above, to the above mentioned provisions in the Rent Acts of 1915 and 1919 (now repealed) shall be construed as a reference to the provision of sect. 3 of the Rent Act of 1920.

The House Letting (Scotland) Act 1920 provides in itself for the recovery of increased assessments (*Kennedy* v. *Campbell*) and any doubts on the matter have been removed by the above provision of the amending Rent Act of 1923.

Where the landlord has been paying the rates chargeable on the occupier of a dwelling-house and those rates are increased, there is no transfer of any burden or liability within the meaning of sect. 2 (3) of the Act if the landlord seeks to recover such increase from the tenant by virtue of the above sub-sect. 2 (1) (b). (*Connolly* v. *Whelan*, 54 I. L. T. R. 18, at p. 20.

and Rating (Scotland) Act 1911, and sect. 1 of the House Letting &c. (Scotland) Act 1920.

The Act does not state definitely what are the rates for increases in which the landlord can raise the rent. The previous Act of 1915 (sect 1 (1 (iv)) uses the words "rates chargeable on the occupier" and in the Irish case of *Cork Improved Dwellings Co v Barry* the Court held that certain rates levied under local Acts, inasmuch as they were not chargeable on the occupier were excluded from the provisions of the Act (of 1915). The words "chargeable on the occupier" are omitted from the present Act, and the definition section (12 (1) (d)) defines rates merely as including water rents and charges." Whether rates other than those expressly mentioned are excluded remains an open question, though it might be argued that the Act impliedly excludes them, according to the principle of construction *expressio unius*.

As regards *Scotland*, the Act defines rates as meaning rates "as defined in the House Letting and Rating (Scotland) Act, 1911" (See sect 18 (1) (a)). By sect 1 of that Act, "assessment" includes 'all rates, charges and assessments imposed, assessed or levied by an assessing authority, the proceeds of which are applicable to public local purposes, and which are leviable in respect of the yearly value of lands and heritages, and includes any sum which, though obtained in the first instance by a precept, certificate, or other instrument requiring payment from some authority or officer, is or can be ultimately raised out of an assessment'

A landlord is entitled to increase the rent by the amount of actual increase in the rates, whether the increase is due to an increase in the rates, or to an increase in the rateable value of the premises. (*Steel v Mahoney*) In a Scotch case, *Kennedy v Campbell*, where the landlord was responsible for having entered the house in the valuation roll at a rent in excess of that actually paid by the tenant it was held that the tenant had no redress against the landlord in respect of the extra amount at which he was assessed

The expression 'the amount for the time being payable in respect of rates,' means the amount which at the material time (*i e*, at the time when the rent is raised) the landlord is compelled to pay in respect of rates. Thus if he has agreed with the tenant

S 5

to pay the rates and has not entered into a compounding agreement he can be compelled to pay the tenant's rates in full, and can, of course, take credit for the full amount of the increase. ' But if he has entered into an agreement with the overseers under the Poor Rate Assessment and Collection Act, 1869, to pay the rates on the premises, whether they are occupied or not, on being allowed a commission of 25 per cent on the rates, then he cannot (except by reason of his own default) be compelled to pay more than 75 per cent of the rates as aforesaid, and this is the amount for the time being payable by him.   (Per Viscount Cave in *Nicholson v. Jackson*, 37 T. L. R. at p. 889.   In that case it was held by the House of Lords that a landlord who had compounded for rates could increase the rent, not by the amount of any increase in the actual rates, but merely by the amount of the increase in the net sum payable by him after deducting the commission.   In this connection may also be noted sect. 16 (1) of the 1920 Act which amends sect. 3 of the Poor Rate Assessment and Collection Act, 1869 (32 & 33 Vict. c. 41).(*d*)   That Act, by sect. 3 provides that where the owner of a hereditament is willing to enter into a written agreement with the overseers to become liable for the poor rates for a term of not less than one year from the date of the agreement, and to pay such poor rates whether the hereditament is occupied or not, then the overseers may, subject to the control of the vestry, agree to receive the rates from the owner and to allow him a commission not exceeding 25 per cent thereon.   This provision is, however, limited to hereditaments, the rateable value of which does not exceed in the Metropolis, 20*l*, in Liverpool 13*l*, Manchester, 10*l*, and elsewhere, 8*l*.   Now the 1920 Act, by sect. 16 (1), provides that for these limits of value are to be substituted limits of values 25 per cent in excess of such limits except in the case of the Metropolis.   Such limits of value are also to be substituted in sect. 4 of the Act, whereby vestries are empowered to order that the owner should be rated instead of the occupier.

In calculating an increase which will be permitted on account of an increase of rates it will be first necessary to consider the

(*d*) As regards Scotland, sect. 1 of the House Letting and Rating (Scotland) Act 1911, is to be substituted; see sect. 18 (1) (*a*) of the Act.

date when the new rate will be allowed, and the period for which it is allowed. Thus a new rate may be allowed on May 17th for a six months period, e.g., April 1st to September 30th. One must next consider what was the rate in the corresponding half-yearly period, which included the 3rd August, 1914, assuming that rates were payable for the house during the latter period. That would be the rate for April 1st to September 30th, 1914.

The next question is as to how one is to arrive at the weekly monthly, or other sum which is to be added to the original rent as an increase. As the rates are levied for a half-yearly period, the proper divisor will be twenty-six in the case of a weekly tenancy (had the rates been for a yearly period, the proper divisor would have been fifty-two). If it is a monthly tenancy, the proper divisor would be six or twelve according as the rates are for half or for the whole of the year. Assuming then that there is a weekly tenancy, and that the rates are payable half-yearly, the proper divisor will be twenty-six. Assuming that the new rate exceeds the rate for the 1914 period by 26*l*, the proper increase on account of rates will be 1*l* per week.

The next question will be—from and until what date can the increase of 1*l* per week be legally recovered by the landlord? The new rate it will be observed in the above illustration, was allowed on May 17th. Presumably the landlord will give notice of increase on that date, May 17th, therefore he will have to wait a week, till May 25th (see sect. 3 (2)), before he can recover any increase. The question arises, can he recover anything for the period April 1st—May 25th? This question has been answered in the negative in the case of *Cardiff Corporation* v *Isaacs, Same* v *Croste* 37 T. L. R. 649. He is only entitled to an increase of 1*l* per week, assuming the facts to be as stated in the illustration, from May 25th. As regards the period during which the landlord will be entitled to the increase, reference should be made to the definition of rates as given in sect. 12 (1) (d) of the Act, which is as follows:— 'The expression rates includes water rents and charges, and *any increase in rates payable by a landlord shall be deemed to be payable by him until the rate is next demanded.*' Therefore this increase of 1*l* will be legally recoverable by the

5 (2)

landlord *until the next rate is made.* Supposing, taking the
above illustration again, the next rate is made on some date subsequent to September 30th (the last date of the half-yearly period),
say on October 21st. In such a case the landlord will be entitled
to the increase until at any rate the 21st October. See *Cardiff
Corp. v. Isaacs, &c. supra.* If on the 21st October the landlord
gives a further notice of increase, if the rates have been increased
he will be entitled to a further increase as from October 28th.
As regards the week October 21st—October 28th it is submitted
that the landlord will be entitled to the same rent as he was previously charging.

The Act, however, it is to be noted, makes no provision for a
case where the rates have been *decreased.* In such a case a
question would arise whether the landlord is entitled to the previous rent or whether he must make a corresponding allowance on
account of the decrease of the rates. It would seem that the
tenant is entitled to such a deduction. The Act speaks in
sect. 2 (1) of the amount by which the increased rent may
exceed the standard rent. The Act has fixed a standard rent,
but has mitigated the burden which the landlord would otherwise
have to bear owing to an increase of rates in cases where the
landlord pays the rates by allowing him to add the amount of
that increase to the tenant's rent. It is submitted, considering
the whole policy of the Act and especially the opening words
of sect. 2 (1) (c) that the landlord is not to make a profit out
of the decrease in the amount of rates and that he must accordingly
make a deduction in the rent charged in favour of the tenant
where there is actually a decrease in the rates.

It is submitted that the periods to be contrasted are firstly, the
period in respect of which the rent is to be increased owing to an
increase of rates and secondly, the corresponding period which
included the 3rd August, 1914 or alternatively, the date on which
the rates first became payable thereafter. The case of *Sutton
v. Hollerton,* however, might seem to be at first sight an authority
to the contrary.

In that case the defendant was tenant of a house let to him by the plaintiffs before the war, the rates being paid by the plaintiffs. The rating period was from June 25th—June 24th. For the year 1915—1916 the rates showed an increase of 12s. 2d. over the corresponding period in 1914—1915. For the year 1916—1917, the increase was 2s. 9d. for the year 1917—1918, 6s. 9d.; i.e., a total increase of 1l. 1s. 8d. for the three years. The Court of Appeal held that the landlord was only entitled to increase the weekly rent by the amount arrived at by dividing the sum of 6s. 9d. by fifty-two. The report is not as clear as may be but apparently the judgment of the Court proceeded on the ground that this sum of 6s. 9d. represented the increase not over the corresponding period 1916—1917 but over the period 1914—1915, and the Court held that the landlord could not allow an increase of rates to run on from year to year, and then afterwards require the tenant to pay the *whole* increase on the current year as it would be very oppressive to require the tenant to pay a large sum in respect of past claims. If however the facts of the case were that the rates for the period 1917—1918 were actually 1l. 1s. 8d. in excess over the corresponding period in 1914—1915, the rates having gradually risen during all these years, it is impossible to see how the judgment can be supported since the two periods which are brought into comparison are (1 the period in respect of which the increase is to be calculated, and (2 the corresponding period in 1914 which included the 3rd August 1914. The comparison is not between the period in respect of which the increase is to be calculated and the next preceding period, which would be in this case 1916—1917. In other words, it is submitted that the judgment is an authority for the proposition that a landlord cannot allow arrears of increases which he would have been entitled to demand from the tenant to accumulate, and afterwards throw the whole burden of those arrears on the tenant but on the other hand, it is submitted that the judgment is not, and should not, be an authority for the proposition that if a landlord fails to increase the rent on account of increases of rates when he would have been entitled to do so he cannot afterwards raise the rent of his premises to the maximum allowed by the Act which he would have been entitled to do had he taken advantage of each opportunity as it occurred of raising the rent owing to an increase of rates.

> The standard rent can further be exceeded by an additional amount of 15 per cent. of the net rent (sect. 2 1, c (g.

In the case of a dwelling-house, however, to which any of the previous Rent Acts also applied (h), i.e. in the case of 1915 and 1919 houses, an additional increase of 5 per cent. only of the net rent was allowed during a period of one year from the passing of the Act viz., 2nd July, 1920—2nd July, 1921. Subsequently to that date, however, the landlord would be entitled to the full increase of 15 per cent.

The "net rent" is arrived at as follows:—Where the landlord at the material date, by reference to which the standard rent is to be calculated paid the rates chargeable on, or which but for the provisions of any Act would be chargeable on the occupier, then the net rent is the standard rent, less the amount of such rates. In any other case the net rent is the standard rent (Sect. 12 1 (c).

Thus if the material date with reference to which the standard rent is to be calculated is the 3rd August 1914, and if the landlord paid the rates at that date which amounted to, say, 15l. then if the rent at that date were 75l., the standard rent would be 75l., but the net rent would be 75l. – 15l. = 60l.

By sect. 14 (1) of the Amendment Act, 1923, the County Court is given the power on the application of either the landlord or the tenant to determine summarily any question as regards the net rent of the premises.

By sect. 2 2 of the Act of 1920 and by sect. 5 (1) of the Amendment Act, 1923 provision is made in certain cases for

---

g In the case of business premises 35 per cent. was allowed Sect. 13 (1) 1 .

As regards suspension of increase under this head see infra p. 72

h See supra p. 3

i See infra p. 13

the suspension of any increase of rent which the tenant may be liable to pay under para (c) as well as para (d) As to these matters, see *infra*, p 72, and compare a similar provision in sect 3 (3) of the Notices of Increase Act, 1923

(d On account of repairs (Sect 2 (1) (d))

In further addition to any of the above amounts the standard rent may be exceeded—

(i) Where the landlord is responsible for the whole of the repairs by an amount equivalent to 25 per cent of the *net* rent (*h*

(ii) Where the landlord is responsible for part and not the whole of the repairs, by such lesser amount (*i e*, less than 25 per cent of the net rent) as may be agreed, or as may on the application (*l*) of the landlord or the tenant, be determined by the County Court, and the County Court alone (*m*) to be fair and reasonable, having regard to such liability Such decision of the County Court will be final and conclusive (*n*)

By the expression 'repairs' is meant 'any repairs required for the purpose of keeping premises in good and tenantable repair, and any premises in such a state shall be deemed to be in a reasonable state of repair and the landlord shall be deemed to be responsible for any repairs for which the tenant is under no express liability (Sect 2 (5) of the Act of 1920 and sect 18 (5) of the Amendment Act, 1923)

In *Brown* v *Holland*, a landlord was held entitled to the full increase of 25 per cent without any deduction for certain repairs done by the tenant inasmuch as these repairs were merely for the tenant's greater comfort and convenience, but not in discharge of any legal liability

It will be observed that while the increases (a and (b) might vary increases (c) and (d) must necessarily be fixed increases

(*k*) See *supra* p 70
(*l*) For form of summons see Appendix of Forms Form 1 which will have to be varied to meet the circumstances of the case
(*m*) See X *Rays Ltd* v *Armitage* (1922) W N 27
(*n*) See sect 2 (6)

and it might be as well to point out once again that all these increases are cumulative

But as regards the increases (c) and (d), provision is made by the Act of 1920 for a suspension of such increases in certain cases. By sect. 2 (2) it is provided that at any time or times after the expiration of three months from the date of an increase permitted under sect. 2 (1) (d) of the Act, the tenant or the sanitary authority (o) may apply (p) to the County Court, which alone is given jurisdiction in such a case (q), for an order suspending such increases, on the ground that the house is not in all respects reasonably fit for habitation

If the County Court is satisfied by the production (r) of a certificate of the sanitary authority (or as regards Scotland the local authority under the Public Health (Scotland) Act 1897), or otherwise, that —

1. the house is not in all respects reasonably fit for human habitation or is otherwise not in a reasonable state of repair, *and*

2. the condition of the house is not due to the tenant's neglect or default, or breach of express agreement,

then the Court shall order that the increase be suspended until the Court is satisfied, on the report of the sanitary authority or otherwise, that the necessary repairs (other than the repairs, if any for which the tenant is liable) have been executed. On the making of such an order which will be final and conclusive (s), the increase shall cease to have effect until the Court is so satisfied

Sect. 5 (1) of the Amendment Act contains a similar provision though in order to take advantage of it an application to the Court is not essential

(o) By Rule 6 the sanitary authority must give notice of the summons to the tenant.

(p) For forms of summons and order, see Appendix (Forms 7 and 8).

(q) See X Rays Ltd. v. Armitage

(r) Whether the Court can go behind the certificate qu. (See Smith v. Primrose (1921) W. N. 291, Britton v. Anderson) It would seem not but see sect. 5 (1) of the Amendment Act

(s) There is no right of appeal, whether the application is by the tenant or the sanitary authority. Glasgow Corporation v. Muir(?)

The tenant, however, must perform two conditions before he will be entitled to rely on sect 5 (1) of the Amendment Act Firstly he must obtain from the sanitary authority or apparently the committee (t) appointed by the sanitary authority for the purpose of the Acts, a certificate (u that the house is not in a reasonable state of repair This certificate must state what works, if any, require to be executed in order to put the house into a reasonable state of repair (Sect 18 (1) of the Amendment Act) Secondly, the tenant must serve a copy of this certificate upon the landlord

Where the tenant has performed these two conditions it will be a good defence to a claim by his landlord against him for any increase of rent permitted under paras (c) or (d) of sect 2 (1) of the Act of 1920 which is in respect of a rental period subsequent to the date of the service of the copy of the certificate on the landlord, that the house was not in a reasonable state of repair during that period Not only can the tenant avail himself of the benefits of sect 5 (1) of the Amendment Act where the claim is one for recovery of these increases of rent but even where the claim is one for possession or ejectment on the ground of non-payment of rent, in so far as the rent unpaid includes such increase

The production of the certificate will be sufficient evidence that the house was and continues to be in the condition therein mentioned, unless the contrary is proved (sect 5 (1) of the Amendment Act), and an instrument purporting to be a certificate or report of a sanitary authority and to be signed by an officer of the authority, will without further proof be taken to be a certificate of the authority unless the contrary is proved (Sect 18 (3) ib)

The tenant, however, will not be able to rely on the above defence if the landlord can show that the condition of the house is due to the tenant's neglect, or default or breach of express agreement (Sect 5 (1) proviso)

(t) Sect 18 (4) of the Amendment Act, 1923
(u) A fee of one shilling is payable on application, which may be deducted from any subsequent payment of rent if a certificate is issued (Sect 18 (1) of the Amendment Act)

Where a sanitary authority has issued a certificate that the house is not in a reasonable state of repair, the landlord may execute the necessary repairs to the house, and if the sanitary authority is satisfied that the dwelling-house is, after the execution of the repairs in a reasonable state of repair, the authority must on the application of the landlord, and on the payment of a fee of one shilling, issue a report (z) to that effect   (Sect 7 (2))

On an application by the tenant to a sanitary authority for a certificate or report, whether under the Act of 1920 or the Act of 1923, a fee of one shilling is payable, but if as the result of such application such certificate is issued, the tenant is entitled to deduct the fee from any subsequent payment of rent   (Sect 2 (4) of the Act of 1920, sect 18 (1) of the Act of 1923)

For a case in which the Court made an order suspending the increase see *Lynch* v *Kenans*, 55 I L T p 59

Reference should also be made for the definition of 'repairs' to sect 2 (5) of the Act of 1920, and sect 18 (5) of the Act of 1923

(c   In the case of dwelling-houses let by a railway company to persons in the employment of the company (Sect 2 (1) (c))

In the above case the standard rent may further be exceeded by such additional amount, if any, as is required in order to give effect to the agreement dated 1st March, 1920, relating to the rates of pay and conditions of employment of certain persons in the employment of railway companies, or any agreement, whether made before or after the passing of the Act (2nd July, 1920) extending or modifying that agreement   (Sect 2 (1) (c))

The agreement referred to provides that employees who are housed by the railway companies shall pay rent, so that they may be placed on an equality with the other employees for whom no housing is provided

(z) As regards the proof of the report cf sect 18 (3) of the Amendment Act

(f) Where *part* of a dwelling-house (which may itself be part
of a house or rooms in a house) to which the Act applies
is lawfully sub-let, and the part sub-let is also a dwelling-
house within the Act (e g , does not consist of furnished
or business premises), in addition to any of the increases
(a) to (e) mentioned above, an amount not exceeding
10 per cent of the net rent (*y*) of the dwelling-
house comprised in the *sub-tenancy* shall be deemed to
be a permitted increase in the case of that dwelling-house,
and an amount equivalent to half of the above amount
shall be deemed to be a permitted increase in the case of
the dwelling-house comprised in the *tenancy* (Sect 7
(1) of the Amendment Act)

It will be observed that this additional increase is permitted only
where *part* of the dwelling-house is sub-let The immediate landlord of the sub-tenant is entitled to an additional increase of 10
per cent. of the net rent of the dwelling-house contained in the
sub-tenancy, and the landlord of the immediate landlord of the
sub-tenant is entitled to an additional increase of half that amount

In order to be entitled to these increases it is not necessary to
serve a notice of increase

Where part of a dwelling-house is so sub-let, the tenant of the
whole must, if so requested in writing by his landlord, supply him
within fourteen days with a written statement of any sub-letting,
giving particulars of the occupancy and the rent charged If the
tenant fails to do so, or supply a statement false in any material
particular, he will be summarily liable to a fine not exceeding
2*l* (Sect 7 (2) of the Amendment Act)

Sect 4 —*Limitation on Rent of Furnished Houses*

Where the dwelling-house is otherwise within the Act, but is
let at a rent which *includes* (*z*) payments in respect of furniture,
the maximum rent is not to exceed by more than 25 per cent the
' normal profit viz the profit which might reasonably have

(*y*) *Supra* p 70
(*z*) As to the meaning of the term includes see *supra* p 31

been expected from a similar letting on the 3rd August 1914 (Sect 9) The same principle is to be applied where part of a dwelling-house or even presumably rooms (a) are let at a rent which includes payment in respect of furniture

It is immaterial whether the premises have been let before or since the passing of the Act (2nd July 1920) and presumably it will make no difference whether the rent has been increased or not since the 25th March 1920 inasmuch as sect 1 of the Act speaks of rent and mortgage interest being increased beyond the standard rent and the standard rate of interest but no mention is made of rent being increased beyond 25 per cent of the normal profit

Another moot point is whether a landlord and tenant can contract themselves out of the provisions of sect 9 It will be observed that the words "notwithstanding any agreement to the contrary" are omitted in the above section

Where the County Court judge has been satisfied on the application (b) of the tenant (c) that the rent charged is yielding and will yield to the landlord (c) a profit more than 25 per cent in excess of the "normal profit" the Court *may* order that the rent so far as it exceeds such sum as would yield such normal profit and 25 per cent shall be irrecoverable The tenant however, will be entitled to recover sums paid in excess only in respect of any period after the passing of the Act (Sect 9 (1) of the Act of 1920)

The Act further affords a penal sanction in that by sect 10 a fine not exceeding 100*l* may be imposed on the landlord (d) if the Court is of opinion having regard to all the circumstances of the case and in particular to the margin of profit allowed by sec 9, that the rent is extortionate

_____

(a) Sects 12 (2) 12 (8)

(b) For forms of summons and order see Appendix of Forms (Forms 11 and 12 see also Rule 1)

(c) By sect 10 (2) of the Amendment Act 1923 tenant is to be substituted for lessee and landlord is to be substituted for lessor wherever these terms are used in sects 9 and 10 of the principal Act

(d) Cf sect 10 (2) of the Amendment Act 1923

Sect. 5.—Restrictions on Levy of Distress for Rent.

No distress for the rent of any dwelling-house to which the Act applies can be levied except with the leave (e) of the County Court. The Court has, with respect to any application for such leave, the same powers of adjournment, stay, suspension, postponement or otherwise as are conferred by sect. 5 (2) of the Act with regard to applications for recovery of possession or ejectment. (Sect. 6.)

The above provision (sect. 6) does not affect a distress levied under sect. 160 of the County Courts Act, 1888. That section provides, in substance, that the provisions of 8 Anne, c. 14, s. 1 (whereby goods and chattels lying or being in or upon premises are not to be taken in execution until all arrears of rent (not exceeding one year's rent) are paid to the landlord of the premises) are not to apply to goods taken in execution under the warrant of the Court; but that in such a case the landlord of the premises on which the goods are taken may, within five clear days from the date of the seizure of the goods, or before their removal, claim any rent in arrear in the manner indicated; whereupon the bailiff or officer making the levy will distrain, in addition, for the rent and the costs of such distress.

In the case of an application for leave to distrain under sect. 6, the Court is given a very wide discretion, and must take into consideration any matters that might legitimately be urged by the tenant; as, for instance, that there is a reasonable and *bonâ fide* dispute as to the rent to be paid, and leave to distrain ought not to be given in such cases (f).

(e) See Rule 1 (c). For forms of summons and order for leave to distrain, Forms 5 and 6 under the Consolidated County Courts (Emergency Powers) Rules, 1915, are to be adopted.

(f) *Townsend* v. *Charlton.*

CHAPTER V

THE NOTICES OF INCREASE ACT, 1923

This Act which was passed on the 7th June 1923 was intended to meet the difficult situation created by a series of decisions culminating in *Kerr* v *Bryde* to the effect that a landlord was not entitled by reason of sect. 3 (1) of the Act of 1920 to an increase of rent unless the tenancy had first been determined, the service of a valid notice of increase alone being insufficient

Apart from its retrospective operation the effect of the Notices of Increase Act is to make a valid notice of increase, served in conformity with sect. 3 (2) of the Act of 1920 (*a*) do double service by operating as a notice to terminate the tenancy in such cases where the tenancy can be determined only by such notice Even if the notice of increase was not originally valid by reason of some defects in it, it may nevertheless have this fictitious effect if the Court by virtue of the power conferred on it by sect. 6 (1) of the Amendment Act 1923 amends the notice of increase and directs that the notice is to be deemed to have effect as a valid notice for by sect. 20 of the Amendment Act, the principal Act the Notices of Increase Act and the Amendment Act are to be construed as one

The Notices of Increase Act has also a retrospective effect so that when an otherwise valid notice of increase has been given prior to the passing of the Act, but no notice to quit, the increase of rent which was invalid according to the Act of 1920 is expressly validated

It will be observed that the only element of invalidity which

(*a*) The Notices of Increase Act therefore applies only in the case of notices of increase served subsequently to 2nd July 1920 (date of the passing of the Act of 1920)

the notice of increase is allowed is that of being unaccompanied or preceded (b) by a valid notice to terminate the tenancy where such latter notice was necessary

The notice of increase may have one of two artificial effects mentioned in sect 1 (1) of the Notices of Increase Act Firstly, it may have effect as if it were a notice to terminate the existing tenancy on the day immediately preceding the day as from which the increase is to take effect The following example may be given as an illustration —T is a weekly tenant paying a rent of 15s per week The landlord serves on the 31st March a notice of his intention to increase the rent, on account of an increase of rates, to 17s 6d per week such increased rent first being payable after a period of one clear week (c) from the date of the service of the notice of increase, say the 8th April. which also happens to be a recurring day of the tenancy Then if the landlord has not served any notice to quit terminating the tenancy the Act provides that the notice of increase is to have effect as if it were also a notice to terminate the tenancy on the date preceding the day as from which the increase is to take effect, which would in this case be the 7th April

But the Act also provides for cases where the notice of increase. even if it is regarded as a notice to terminate the tenancy cannot be a good notice to terminate the tenancy by reason of the fact that the date as from which the increase is stated in the notice of increase to take effect, would be a date falling short of the date on which the tenancy can be properly determined, assuming that the notice of increase was also a notice to terminate the tenancy. Thus the increase may be stated to take effect too soon to allow a sufficient interval of time to elapse in order to satisfy the requirements of a proper notice to quit In such cases sect 1 (1) of the Notices of Increase Act provides that the notice of increase shall have effect as if it were also a notice to terminate the existing tenancy on the earliest day. after the day as from which the increase is to take effect on which if the notice of increase had been a notice to terminate the tenancy, it would have been effective for that purpose

Take again the above illustration. If T was a monthly instead of a weekly tenant and the landlord had served on him on the 31st March the notice of increase given in the illustration the notice of increase would have effect as if it were a proper notice to terminate the tenancy, the date of the termination of such tenancy being the 31st of March

Whether the increase would be effective from the 1st April in the above illustration may however, be open to some doubt because in the notice of increase the increased rent would be stated to become due at a date prior to the fictitious date of the termination of the tenancy. According to the previous law, such a notice of increase would be bad inasmuch as it does not state the correct date as from which the increased rent would begin to run, and dates are matters of substance for the purposes of a valid notice of increase (d)

If, however the notice of increase in the above illustration had been served prior to the passing of the Notices of Increase Act (7th June 1923), it would further have effect, by sect 1 (1) of that Act, as if such earliest date had been specified in the notice as the date as from which the increase was to take effect, and in such a case the increase would be effective

The Act, however, in this connection provides only for the case of a notice of increase served prior to the date of the passing of the Act It would seem, therefore that the notice of increase in the above illustration in so far as it was merely a notice of increase would be a bad notice if it was served subsequently to the 7th June 1923 and in such a case it is submitted, a further valid notice of increase would be necessary in order that the increase might be legally recoverable from the tenant

Sect 1 (1) of the Notices of Increase Act provides also for cases where notices of increase in conformity with sect 3 (2) of the Act of 1920 were served before the passing of the Act (7th June 1923) without a notice to terminate the tenancy where such latter notice was necessary and validates these increases if they come within the provisions of sect 1 (1)

It is to these increases of rent, made before the passing of the Notices of Increase Act, but rendered valid by that Act, that the term "validated increase of rent," it is submitted, is to be applied (Sect 1 (2) of the Notices of Increase Act, 1923)

It is not all arrears of validated increases, however, which a landlord is entitled to recover Sect 1 (1), provisos (a) and (b, together with which should be read sect 2 paras (a) and (b) deal with this question, and their effect is as follows —

The landlord will be unable to recover from the tenant —

(a,—(i) Any unpaid validated increase of rent in respect of any period prior to the 1st December, 1922

(ii) Any unpaid validated increase of rent even in respect of a period subsequent to the 1st December 1922 if such validated increase has been the subject of a judgment of a Court of competent jurisdiction given before the 15th February 1922 It is immaterial whether any sum has or has not been paid under such judgment

(b)—(i) Any sums which have been paid by the tenant but subsequently recovered (e) by him from the landlord whether by means of deductions from rent or otherwise, where they have been so recovered by the tenant prior to the 1st December, 1922, or even subsequently to the 1st December, 1922 if in the latter case such sums represent validated increases of rent in respect of a period prior to the 1st December, 1922

(ii) Any sums which have been paid by the tenant but subsequently recovered from the landlord (whether by means of deduction from rent or otherwise), even though such sums have been so recovered by the tenant subsequently to the 1st December, 1922 and even though such sums represent validated increases of rent

_____

(e) Cf sect 14 (1) of the Act of 1920

in respect of a period subsequent to the 1st December, 1922,

> if,

such sums have been the subject of a judgment of a Court of competent jurisdiction given before the 15th February, 1923 whether or no any sum has been paid under such judgment

(c)—(i) Any rent due before the 1st December, 1922 which has not been paid by reason of the tenant deducting therefrom the amount of any 'validated increase' of rent paid to the landlord previous to such deduction,

> or it is submitted,

(ii) Any rent due since the 1st December 1922, which has not been paid by reason of the tenant deducting therefrom the amount of any validated increase of rent paid to the landlord previous to such deduction,

> if,

such validated increase is in respect of a period prior to the 1st December 1922,

> or

(iii) Any rent due even since the 1st December, 1922 which has not been paid by reason of the tenant deducting therefrom the amount of any validated increase of rent paid even in respect of a period since the 1st December, 1922,

> if,

such rent has been the subject of a judgment of a Court of competent jurisdiction given before the 15th February, 1923 whether or no any sum has been paid under such judgment

On the other hand, a tenant cannot recover from the landlord any validated increase of rent paid by or recovered from the tenant prior to the 1st December 1922 and sect 14 (1) of the Act of 1920 is stated expressly in sect 1 (1 proviso (a) of the Notices of Increase Act, not to apply to such cases

Furthermore it is submitted that a tenant will not be able to recover any validated increase, even though such increase was paid by or recovered from the tenant subsequently to the 1st December 1922 whether such rent has or has not been the subject of a judgment given before the 15th February 1922

A landlord will not be debarred from recovering a validated increase by reason only of the fact that such increase has formed the subject of a judgment delivered subsequently to the 15th February, 1923, under which judgment the tenant has recovered the increase from the landlord   Otherwise sect 1 (1) (b) of the Notices of Increase Act would be quite an unnecessary provision   In support of the above contention reference should also be made to sect 2 (b) of Notices of Increase Act, which speaks of "any sum which during the said period (from 15th December, 1922 to 7th July 1923, has been recovered by the tenant from the landlord by deductions from rent or *otherwise*, &c   as being the amount due under the Act on account of any arrears of rent Now sect 14 (1) of the Act of 1920 gave the tenant the right to recover sums which were irrecoverable by the landlord   without prejudice to any other method of recovery,' by deduction from the rent   The words 'or otherwise' in sect 2 (b) of the Notices of Increase Act are the equivalent of the words ' without prejudice to any other method of recovery' in sect 14 (1) of the Act of 1920, and according to the latter Act the tenant of course had the right to recover such irrecoverable sums by judgment or by an order of a Court of competent jurisdiction

It is further submitted that the rights and obligations of landlords and tenants in respect of the recovery of any sums under the Notices of Increase Act would respectively rest, on death in their personal representatives   (See definition of "landlord" and "tenant" in sect 12 (1) (1) of the Act of 1920 and note sect 4 of the Notices of Increase Act)

The Notices of Increase Act in sect 2 (1) provides that the validated increases of rent (f) and other sums (g) which the landlord has the right of recovering (h) from the tenant by virtue of

(f) Sect 2 (1) (a)   (g) Sect 2 (1) (b)
(h) As to what validated increases of rent are irrecoverable by the landlord see *ante* pp 81 82

the provisions of that Act shall be recovered in a special manner (*i*), viz., they shall be payable by instalments with, and as part of, the periodical payments of rent.   Each of such instalments shall be 15 per cent. of the standard rent (*k*) for the week, month, or other period for which the rent is payable, fractions of a penny being disregarded.   Such instalments are to be paid until the whole of the amount of arrears is paid off.

The tenant, however, may at any time pay to the landlord the full amount of arrears, and if he has already paid part of the arrears, he may pay the balance in one lump sum if he chooses. (Sect. 2 (1), proviso (i))

If the tenant by whom such instalments are payable at any time gives up possession of the premises, whether voluntarily or on any order or judgment of a Court, the whole balance of the sum which is payable by instalments will immediately become due, and the whole of such balance can be recovered by the landlord if unpaid. (Sect. 2 (1), proviso ii)

Before the landlord will be entitled to recover the arrears which he is entitled to recover by virtue of the Notices of Increase Act he must serve a notice (*l*) on the tenant. (Sect. 2 (2))

This notice must specify (i) the amount claimed, and (ii) the amount of the instalments claimed to be payable. (Sect. 2 (2)) The notice must further be in the form (*m*) contained in the Schedule to the Notices of Increase Act, or in a form substantially to the same effect. (Sect. 2 (3))

The landlord must further furnish the tenant with a written statement, which must accompany (*n*) the notice.   The statement must show how the amount claimed is arrived at, and how the amount of the instalments has been calculated. (Sect. 2 (3))

(*i*) This method of recovery, of course, does not apply to any increase of rent in respect of a period subsequent to the 7th June, 1923, to which the provisions of the Notices of Increase Act apply.

(*k*) Cf. *supra* pp. 11—14.

(*l*) As to the criminal liability of the landlord for a false or misleading statement in the notice see *infra* p. 159.

(*m*) *Infra*, App.

(*n*) See Form in Schedule, *infra*, App.

The first instalment will not be payable by the tenant until the expiration of one clear week from the date (o) of the notice (Sect. 2 (2).)

Any question as to (1) the amount of arrears due from a tenant or (11) the amount of any instalment, shall be determined by the County Court and the County Court alone, and the decision of the County Court shall be final and conclusive (p), and there will be no appeal from such decision. An application to determine any of the above questions may be made at the instance of either the landlord or the tenant. Sect. 2 (4). The application must apparently be made under the existing rules.

Where a tenant becomes liable by virtue of the Notices of Increase Act to pay either (1) any arrears of rent representing validated increases of rent in respect of a period prior to the 7th June, 1923 or (11) any sum by way of rent representing increases of rent made effective solely by the service of a notice of increase (q) in respect of a period subsequent to the 7th June 1923 the tenant may avail himself of the benefits of sect. 3 of the Notices of Increase Act. That section provides in sub-sect. (1), that in the above cases, the tenant or the sanitary authority may apply to the County Court for an order suspending such liability, on the ground that the house (r e. the premises in respect of which the claim is made) is not in all respects reasonably fit for human habitation or that it is otherwise not in a reasonable state of repair (s). Such applications are to be made and dealt with in the same manner as similar applications made under sect. 2 (2) of the principal Act of 1920 (t).

Where the liability in respect of the payment of instalments is so suspended the instalments which would have become payable during the period of suspension shall for the purpose of calcu-

o. Not due to of service of the notice. Contrast sect. 3 (2) of the Act of 1920.

p. Cf. sect. 2 (6) of the Act of 1920, sect. 11 (1) of the Amendment Act. The High Court will have no jurisdiction to determine these questions. (Cf. various titles, limitation.

q. See sect. 3 (1) of the Notices of Increase Act.

s. Cf. sect. 2 (3) of the Act of 1920 for the definition of repairs.

t. Sect. 3 (1) of the Notices of Increase Act. Cf. supra, p. 72.

lating the aggregate of instalments paid, be deemed to have been paid Sect 3 (2). In other words the liability of the tenant for the arrears in respect of such period will be completely extinguished. The importance to the landlord of keeping the premises in at least that amount of repair which is required by the Act is great inasmuch as the decision of the County Court suspending the payment of the instalments will be conclusive and final *u* and that, too whether the application is made by the sanitary authority or the tenant *Glasgow Corporation* v *Michel*. The tenant however it is submitted, will not be able to avail himself of sect 3 of the Notices of Increase Act if the Court is satisfied that the condition of the house is due to the tenant's neglect or default or breach of express agreement *x*

Where a tenant has obtained from the sanitary authority a certificate that the house is not in a reasonable state of repair— which certificate must according to sect 3 (4) specify what works if any require to be executed in order to put the house into a reasonable state of repair—and has further served a copy of the certificate upon the landlord it will be a good defence to any claim against the tenant for the payment of any sum which he may be liable to pay by virtue of the Notices of Increase Act, either (i) by way of rent (*y*), or (ii) on account of arrears (*z*) in respect of any rental period subsequent to the date of the service of the certificate, that the house was not in a reasonable state of repair during such subsequent rental period, provided that the condition of the house is not due to the tenant's neglect or default, or breach of express agreement (*a*). The above defence will be open to the tenant not only where the claim put forward by the landlord takes the form of a money claim but even where the claim is one for

---

(*u*) This is the combined effect of sect 3 (1) of the Notices of Increase Act and sect 2 (2) (6) of the Rent Act of 1920

(*x*) See sect 2 (2) of the Act of 1920

(*y*) In respect of a period subsequent to the passing of the Notices of Increase Act 7th June 1923)

(*z*) I e arrears of validated increases of rent which can only be in respect of some period prior to the date of the passing of the Notices of Increase Act (7th June 1923)

(*a*) Sect 3 (3) proviso

recovery of possession or ejectment on the ground of non-payment of rent, so far as the rent unpaid includes any such sum (b) (Sect 3 (3))

In any such proceedings the production of the certificate of the sanitary authority will be sufficient evidence not only that the house was, but also that it continues to be in the condition mentioned in the certificate unless the contrary is proved (c (Sect 3 (3)) An instrument purporting to be a certificate of the sanitary authority and to be signed by an officer of the authority, will without further proof be taken to be a certificate of the authority unless the contrary is proved (Sect 3 (5))

A sanitary authority may appoint a committee for the purposes of the Notices of Increase Act, and may delegate with or without restrictions, to such committee or to an existing committee of the authority, all or any of the powers of the authority under the Notices of Increase Act (Sect 3 (6. (d)

(b) I e which the tenant is liable to pay by the Notices of Increase Act, either by way of rent or on account of arrears

(c) The Court can therefore go behind the certificate Contrast the cases decided under the Act of 1920 (Cf *Smith* v *Primrose* and *Britton* v *Anderson*)

(d) Cf sect 18 (4) of the Amendment Act 1923

CHAPTER VI

RESTRICTIONS ON PREMIUMS

If the dwelling-house is within the Act the payment in addition to the rent of any fine (a) premium or other like sum as a condition of the grant renewal or continuance of a tenancy or a sub-tenancy of the dwelling-house is forbidden and is also made an offence summarily punishable (b). (Sect. 8 (1) of the Act of 1920.) The same provision would apply in a case where part of a dwelling-house (c) or where even rooms (d) only were let.

The scope of the above provision is wider than that of the corresponding provision (sect. 1 (2)) of the Act of 1915 in that sub-tenancies are included and the taking of any pecuniary consideration is prohibited. Then it is submitted that the lessor will not be able to evade the Act by demanding as a condition of the grant renewal or continuance an excessive payment on account of fixtures or furniture. (*Turner v Ives*, 10 L. J. C. C. R. 3.) At any rate statutory confirmation is given to this view by sect. 9 (1) of the Amendment Act which provides that where the purchase of any furniture or other articles is required as a condition of the grant, renewal or continuance of a tenancy or a sub-tenancy the price demanded shall, at the request of the person on whom the demand is made, be stated in writing and if the price exceeds the reasonable price of the articles the excess shall be treated as if it were a fine or premium and sect. 8 of the Act of 1920 (including penal provisions) shall apply. It may be argued however if the view is taken that the lessor was

---

(a) *I.q.* a fine payable in the case of the renewal of a lease, or for a licence to assign or sub-let

(b) *Infra,* p. 156

(c) Sect. 12 (2)

(d) Sect. 12 (8)

not prevented under the Act of 1920 from demanding an excessive price that the provisions of sect 9 (1) of the Amendment Act are not retrospective

Where such payment or such consideration has been made or given under an agreement made subsequent to the 25th March 1920, the amount of such payment or the value of such consideration is recoverable by the person who made or gave it (Sect 8 (1))

In the case however of *houses to which none of the Rent Acts prior to 1920 applied* where an agreement for a tenancy (or presumably for a sub-tenancy) (e) has been *made between the 25th March*, 1920, *and the 2nd July*, 1920 and such agreement includes a provision for the payment of any fine, premium or other like sum or the giving of any pecuniary consideration then the agreement for the tenancy or sub-tenancy is voidable at the option of either party, but the payment of the fine premium or other sum or the giving of the consideration can in no event be demanded and if paid or made the amount paid in the one case and the value of the consideration in the other can be recovered (Sect 8 (1), proviso)

By sect 2 (2) of the Amendment Act 1923 a landlord is entitled to the payment of any agreed sum as part of the consideration for a lease or tenancy agreement executed or made subsequently to the 31st July 1923, where the term thereby created (i) is for a period not less than two years, and (ii) ends at some date after the 24th June 1926

Where however any tenancy or sub-tenancy is granted renewed or continued for a term of fourteen years or upwards the provisions of sect 8 of the Act of 1920 will not apply (Sect 8 (3)) In the Act of 1915 there was no exception made in the case of long terms and accordingly, in *Rees v Marquis of Bute, Davies v Same* the Court held that the landlord could not take a premium, even though the term to be created was one of ninety-nine years In consequence the Courts (Emergency Powers) Act 1917 s 4 (1) provided an exception in the case of leases

(e) Sect 12 (g)

for twenty-one years and upwards and this limit has now been reduced to fourteen years by sect. 8 (3) of the present Act as has been mentioned above.

An interesting question arises as to the position of the parties in a case where an agreement has been entered into for a lease of under fourteen years a premium being payable as a consideration of the grant of the lease. If the tenant has taken possession of the premises he would undoubtedly be able to recover the premium if paid or to resist its payment as the case may be nor would the landlord in such a case be entitled to recover possession except in the cases mentioned by sect. 5 (1) of the Act. because the tenant would immediately come within the protection of the Act. What would be the position however where the tenant has not taken possession and refuses to pay the premium and where the landlord consequently refuses to allow him to enter into possession? Now in *Rees v. Marquis of Bute, supra* where the circumstances were very similar the Court refused specific performance and ordered the contracts to be rescinded on the landlord repaying all the sums of money which had been received by him by way of purchase-money for the leases. But that was a decision under the Act of 1915 and the Court especially took into consideration the fact that by making an order for specific performance it would be imposing a great hardship on the landlord and would at the same time be conferring an undue benefit on the lessees inasmuch as the latter would be obtaining leases for ninety-nine years at a nominal rent and without having to pay anything for the benefit thereby obtained. On the other hand it will be observed that sect. 8 (1) of the Act of 1920 expressly provides that in certain cases if the agreement is to be voidable at the option of either party, and according to the maxim of construction *expressum facit tacitum cessare* the natural conclusion would be that with the exception of the cases expressly provided for by the Act, such agreements or leases for terms not exceeding fourteen years where premiums are paid or are payable are not voidable but on the contrary will be specifically enforced by the Courts such parts of the agreements regarding the payment of premiums being considered as void and wholly negligible

It is only *in consideration of the grant renewal or continuance* of a tenancy that a premium is prohibited under sect 8 Accordingly where a tenant assigned the unexpired residue of his lease for a money consideration the Court held that the assignment did not come within the provisions of sect 8 and was not a grant and that accordingly the payment was not prohibited (*Mason Herring and Brooks v Harris*) (*g*)

In this connection however, should be noted the provisions of sect 15 (2) of the Act whereby a person retaining possession of premises solely by virtue of the provisions of the Act (*i e* under no agreement with his landlord and against his will) is forbidden to ask or receive any sum or the giving of any other consideration *as a condition of his giving up possession* from anyone except his landlord such consideration if paid or given being recoverable Thus if the tenant in *Mason's Case* had been merely a statutory tenant, and did not hold the premises by virtue of a lease or agreement the payment of the consideration it is submitted, would have been contrary to the provisions of the Act, and, if paid could have been recovered, for a statutory tenant is not to make a profit out of his position (*h*)

It is further submitted that a sub-tenant retaining possession by virtue of sect 15 (3), where the interest of the tenant has been determined, is to be considered a tenant ' retaining possession by virtue of the Act ' as well within the meaning of sect 15 (2)

An excessive charge for furniture and other articles may amount to a sum as a condition of giving up possession for the purpose of the above provision (Sect 15 (2)) By sect 9 (2) of the Amendment Act 1923 where a tenant retaining possession by virtue of the Act of 1920 requires that furniture or other articles shall be purchased as a condition of giving up

(*g*) Approved in *Remmington v Larchin* had there been the grant of a sub tenancy however sect 8 would have applied

(*h*) See *Barton v Fincham*, (1921) 2 K B at p 295

possession the price demanded shall at the request of the person
on whom the demand is made be stated in writing and if the
price exceeds the reasonable price of the articles the excess shall
be treated as a sum asked to be paid as a condition of giving
up possession and sect. 15 (2) of the Act of 1920 (including
penal provisions) shall apply accordingly.

It is only the person granting the tenancy or a renewal or
continuance thereof who is prohibited by sect. 8 of the Act of
1920 from charging a premium and there is nothing to prevent
a third person from receiving one. Thus in *Remmington v.*
Larchen a tenant was desirous of surrendering his lease to his
landlord and came to an arrangement with a third person
whereby in consideration of a payment of 150l. he would vacate
the premises and procure the landlord to grant him a head lease
for three years. The arrangement was carried out and the money
paid. It was held that the new tenant could not recover the
money under sect. 8 (1) as the person aimed at was the person
who required the payment of the premium *in addition to the*
rent viz. the landlord. The Court considered the section as
being of a penal nature and accordingly construed it strictly.
In this case again had the tenant in question been a statutory
tenant merely, it is submitted that the taking of the consideration from the incoming tenant would have been illegal as being
a payment made *as a condition of giving up possession* within
the meaning of sect. 15 (2) of the Act the phraseology of which
section being somewhat different from that of sect. 8 (1).

It would appear that a fine or premium or other pecuniary
consideration is recoverable even where the amount is spread
over the whole term and added to the rent even though the total
rent is less than the maximum amount permitted by the Act (*r*)

(*r*) See *Reeve v. Bate* (1916) 2 Ch. at p. 71.

CHAPTER VII

RESTRICTIONS ON RIGHT TO POSSESSION (*a*)

The security of tenure afforded to the occupier of premises within the Act is in addition to any security hitherto enjoyed by him under the normal law regulating the relationship between landlord and tenant. Thus if premises are held under a lease or an agreement the landlord must first show that he has a right to recover possession irrespective of the Rent Act (*b*) before he can avail himself of the provisions of sect. 5 (1). The tenant moreover is not deprived of any right to relief against forfeiture of which he can avail himself. However while this section imposes restrictions on the former rights of landlords, at the same time it does not confer any new rights on tenants (*c*). The Act is not an enabling Act and does not create any new right of action.

The protection afforded by the section is not confined to tenants who are in occupation of premises by virtue of a lease or an agreement but extends also to statutory tenants. A statutory tenant, however, is not entitled to the benefit of such provisions is sect. 212 of the Common Law Procedure Act or sect. 14 of the Conveyancing Act, 1881 (*d*) though the discretion vested in the Court by sect. 5 would appear to be an ample substitute.

Before the provisions of sect. 5 can apply it will be first necessary to determine whether both the house (*e*) and the tenancy (*f*

(*a*) Sect. 5 (1) of the Act as amended by sect. 4 of the Amendment Act, 1923
(*b*) *Goodwin v. Rhodes* (1921), 2 K. B. at p. 185, *Hilcock v. Booth* (1920), K. B. 861
(*c*) *Ellis v. Rhodes* 37 T. L. R. p. 310
(*d*) *Davis v. Tuchs*
(*e*) *Supra* pp. 21 sq. 41 sq.
(*f*) *Supra* pp. 56

are such as to fall within the Act, and whether the occupier (g)
is a tenant within the Act. It is to be observed that sect. 5
will not apply in the case of dwelling-houses *bonâ fide* let at a
rent which includes payments in respect of board, attendance or
use of furniture (h).

Before entering in detail into the circumstances in which an
order for possession or ejectment will be made two important
principles should be mentioned. Firstly, that in every case a
discretion is given to the Court, and it will not necessarily
follow that an order for possession will be made as a matter of
course merely because the landlord can bring himself within any
of the provisions of sect. 5. The discretion, however, must be
exercised in a judicial manner, regard being paid on the one
hand to the general scheme and purpose of the Act and on the
other to the special conditions which each case presents. Where
the Court has exercised its discretion on reasonable grounds an
Appeal Court, it seems, would not disturb an order that has been
made although it might differ in the way it would itself have
exercised its discretion. (*Grandison v. Mackay.*)

The second principle to be observed is that in making an order
under sect. 5, the proper time for the Court to consider is the
time when the Court is asked to make an order. Thus, if since
the date of the writ circumstances have changed, the Court should
consider the circumstances of the case as they are at the date when
the order is asked for and not as they may have been at the date
of the writ, much less at the date of the notice to quit (i).

Reference may also be made to *Hipps v. Hughes*, where an
order for possession was made on appeal on the strength of fresh
affidavits.

It should be further observed that even if the Act is not pleaded
as a defence at the trial of an action for possession or ejectment
the judge is bound to see that judgment for possession is not
given except in accordance with the Act where the evidence

(g) *Supra* pp. 36 sq.
(h) Sect. 12 (2) and see *supra* pp. 29 sq.
(i) *Hermann v. Toms.* See also *Nash v. Hardy, Kempson v. Mallson*

discloses that the case falls within the Rent Restrictions Acts (Rule 18 *Salter v Lash*)

Sect 1 —Cases in which an order or judgment for recovery of possession or ejectment may be made or given

To deal however with the various cases in which the landlord may recover possession the Act provides (k), *subject in all cases to a discretion to be exercised by the Court* as to whether it is reasonable to make or give the order or judgment (*and notwithstanding any agreement to give up possession* (l)), that no order or judgment for recovery of possession or ejectment shall be made or given except in the following cases (m) —

1 —(1) Where some rent lawfully due from the tenant has not been paid or,

(a) Some other obligation of the tenancy (whether under the contract of tenancy or under the Act) so far as the same is consistent with the provisions of the Act, has been broken or not performed (Sect 5 (1) (a))

Rent is not "lawfully due" within the meaning of the above provision where a question has arisen in reference to the amount of rent payable under the Act and has not been determined in the manner provided by the Act (*Dun Laoghaire U D C v Moran*, (1921) 2 I R at p 411) It is further submitted that rent is not ' lawfully due where there is any *bona fide* dispute as regards the validity of the notice to quit or the notice to increase, or as to the amount payable, even though the tenant s contention might ultimately prove to be unfounded Where an action is brought in the High Court, and any dispute arises as to a matter

(k) Sect 5 (1)

(l) These words are not in the Act itself, but it has been held that this is the effect of the section (*Barton v Fincham*) See *infra* p 101

(m) Sect 5 (1) It is is well to remember that even though the landlord recovers possession by force, and without the intervention of the Court the late occupier may nevertheless be entitled to regain possession of the premises (*Remon v City of London Real Property Co*) which by sect. 2 (6), of the Act is to be determined by the County Court alone, the proper procedure it seems would be to adjourn the action until the determination of such question, or to give judgment on any other unconnected issues (n).

It should also be observed that failure to pay any increases of rent which the landlord is entitled to recover under the Notices of Increase Act, 1923, may constitute a ground for ordering possession under sect. 5 (1) (a) of the principal Act. (Cf. sect. 3 (3), of the Notices of Increase Act.)

Whether a tenant in arrears with his rent can remedy the defect by subsequent payment, and thereby be entitled to claim the protection of the Act is a moot point. In *Bevans* v. *Carman* it was held that a tenant failed to bring himself within the protection of sect. 1 (3) of the Act of 1915 merely by tendering rent after action brought. Again in *Kelly* v. *White* and *Ivan Gatrell* v. *Roberts*, the Divisional Court held that the judge had no power to make an order for possession "with execution stay" so long as the tenant pays the rent at the agreed rate, inasmuch as this had the effect of creating a tenancy of infinite duration, and further held that the protection of the Act was not extended to tenants who did not pay their rent. Now these were decisions under the previous Acts, and it is important to note that the phraseology of sect. 5 (1) of the Act of 1920 is very different (o), that the Court is given a discretion in every case, and that by sect. 5 (2) it is expressly given power to adjourn the case, to stay or suspend execution on any order or judgment made or given for recovery of possession or ejectment and to postpone the date of possession. Moreover the above cases have not been followed in later cases decided under the present Act. Thus in *Crutcher* v. *Gotham* the Court refused to make an order for possession, although the rent was in arrear, and in *Reeks* v. *Shelley* a similar case the Court made an order for possession with costs, the order to be discharged if within three weeks the tenant paid the amount claimed. It is submitted therefore, that the cases of *Bevans* v.

(n) X Rays Ltd. v. Lmdau.
(o) See Brandts v. Hornsey.

Corman and *Kelly* v *White* are no longer authoritative (p), that the Court is entitled to take into consideration that the arrears of rent have been subsequently paid and that an order in the form of the order made in *Kelly* v *White* will be quite valid suspending execution, on the terms therein mentioned provided it is limited to apply only while the Act is in force, and no fresh grounds arise on which the landlord may be entitled to recover possession

Where the tenant in arrear with his rent has already lawfully sub-let the premises a difficult question arises as to whether the sub-tenant will nevertheless be entitled to remain in possession Sect 15 (3 of the Act which appears expressly to meet such a case provides that where an order for possession has been made against the tenant the sub-tenant shall be deemed to become the tenant of the landlord on the same terms as he would have held from the tenant if the tenancy continued However in *Hylton* v *Heal*, Rowlatt J was of opinion that the definition of ' tenant' in the Act as including a sub-tenant except where the context otherwise requires) did not apply in such a case and that a tenant could not at the last moment of his tenancy prevent the landlord from recovering possession by sub-letting to another person from whom no rent was yet due It is nevertheless submitted that where the premises have already been lawfully sub-let, the sub-tenant is entitled to protection of the Act by virtue of sect 15 (3`

As regards the breach of any other obligation of the tenancy the provisions of sect 15 (1` and (3, of the Act as to the conditions on which a statutory tenancy will be deemed to be held should be borne in mind as well as the provisions of sect 16 (2, of the Act whereby the tenant is to provide the landlord with all reasonable facilities for the execution of repairs

A condition of course which is contrary to any of the provisions of the Act is not to be regarded as a condition at all Thus

(p, See also the Irish case of *Charles* v *Muldoon* where the Court held that it had no discretion since the rent had not been paid as it accrued due

there will be no breach of a condition if the tenant refuses to give up possession on the determination of the tenancy (q)

In *Gildea v. Conway*, the tenant of a public-house covenanted, *inter alia* to keep up the licence and to do no act that would imperil it. He subsequently acquired other premises which he used as a public-house and thereupon virtually closed the first house and starved its trade. The Court held that this was a breach of the spirit of the tenancy and made an order for possession (r) Similarly it would be a breach of an obligation to be implied in the tenancy if the tenant should behave in such a way as to deter prospective tenants or purchasers from taking the premises in question (*Chapman v. Hughes*)

Where a tenant sub-let premises in breach of a covenant contained in his lease thereby incurring a forfeiture of the lease the Court nevertheless refused to make an order for possession taking into consideration *inter alia*, the fact that the breach was committed innocently the tenant having only entered into the lease under the mistaken belief induced by the landlord's agents that the landlord had expressly consented to underletting (s)

Where possession is claimed under the circumstances mentioned in clause (a) of sect 5 (1) as also in clauses (b) or (c) the Court is not concerned with the question of alternative accommodation the only point for its consideration being whether it is reasonable or not to make the order (t)

Although it is not an implied obligation of a tenancy that a house shall be kept open and unoccupied it nevertheless is an implied obligation on the tenant to use a reasonable degree of diligence in preserving it from harm and this would carry an obligation to do such firing and airing as is necessary to preserve the house from damp (u)

(q) See *Artizans Labourers and General Dwellings Co v. Whiteley* (1919) 2 K. B. at p. 304

(r) See also *Waller and Son Ltd v. Thomas* 1921, 1 K. B. 541 and see now sect 5 (1) (b)

(s) *Lindo v. McFarlane*

(t) *Waller v. Thomas* ib. at p. 553

Roberts v. Wilson 1922 Sc L. T. Sh Ct Rep) at p 24

11.—(1) Where the tenant or *any person residing with him*, or lodging with him or being his sub-tenant—

> (a) has been guilty of conduct which is a nuisance or annoyance to adjoining occupiers; or
>
> (b) has been convicted of using the premises or allowing the premises to be used for an immoral or illegal purpose; or

(11) Where the condition of the house has in the opinion of the Court deteriorated owing to (α) acts of waste by, or (β) the neglect or default of the tenant or any such person.

Where, however, such person is a lodger or sub-tenant, the Court must be satisfied that the tenant has not before the making or giving of the order or judgment taken such steps as he ought reasonably to have taken for the removal of the lodger or sub-tenant. (Sect. 5 (1) (b) as amended by sect. 4 of the Amendment Act, 1923.)

It will be observed that the tenant will be held responsible for the acts of anyone else who is residing or lodging with him or who is his sub-tenant.

The Amendment Act slightly alters the corresponding provision in the Act of 1920 by making the tenant liable for the acts not only of himself and anyone residing with him, but also of anyone lodging with him or being his sub-tenant. In the two latter cases, however, the tenant will secure immunity if the Court is satisfied that he has taken reasonable steps for the removal of the lodger or sub-tenant before the making or the giving of the order or judgment. The burden of proving that such reasonable steps for their removal have been taken will apparently rest on the tenant.

In *Paterson v. Calham* conduct by a tenant which prevented his landlord from letting adjoining premises was considered as *ejusdem generis* with nuisance or annoyance to adjoining occupiers and is being a ground for making an order for possession.[1]

[1] See also *Chapman v. Hughes*

7 2

Again where a tenant on several occasions allowed the water-closet and the sink to become choked as a consequence of which the water overflowed and soaked through the ceiling of a shop occupied by another tenant immediately below the Court held that the tenant had thereby depreciated the value of the property and had committed waste and had been guilty of conduct which was a nuisance and annoyance to an adjoining occupier (y)

The words "used for an immoral or illegal purpose" refer to a case where the house is put to an improper use for the purpose of carrying out an unlawful purpose and not to a case where there are merely isolated instances of illegality in carrying out a purpose which is lawful in itself (z)

Where a case falls under sect 5 (1) (b) the landlord apparently will be entitled to recover possession even though the tenant may have sub-let the premises (a)

III. Where the tenant has given notice to quit *and* in consequence the landlord has contracted to sell or let the dwelling-house or has taken any other steps as a result of which he would, in the opinion of the Court be seriously prejudiced if he could not obtain possession (Sect . (1 (c))

As has been mentioned above the fact that the tenant has given notice to quit will not of itself preclude him from retaining possession (b) (*Hunt* v *Bliss*) But if by doing so he has thereby seriously prejudiced his landlord an order for possession may be made

Where a tenant gave notice to quit for valuable consideration and agreed to vacate the premises but subsequently refused to do so the Court nevertheless held that the landlord was not entitled to possession unless he brought himself within the other provision of clause (c) and showed that he would be seriously prejudiced

(y) *Ferguson* v *Butler* (1918), 2 Sc L T R 228
(z) *Walley* v *Thomas*
(a) *Hulton* v *Heal* (1921) 2 K B at pp 446 448
(b) As regards the landlord's remedy see *Flannagan* v *Shaw*

if he failed to obtain possession (c) The Court arrived at this conclusion on the ground that its jurisdiction to make an order for possession was confined to the cases mentioned in sect. 5 (1), and that no agreement between the parties could give the Court jurisdiction where it had none. At the same time, however, it would appear that there is nothing to prevent the Court from making such an order, where the parties are agreed, and the Court is satisfied that the tenant is willing to give up possession of the premises.

The notice to quit must be given voluntarily (d), though it need not be in any particular form. Thus, where tenants were presumed to have entered into an agreement to give up possession of the premises, which were to be put up for auction in the event of their not being the purchasers, the Court was inclined to the view that this was not a proper notice to quit, inasmuch as it was not a voluntary act on the part of the tenants (e). On the other hand, a letter written by a tenant in answer to the landlord and informing him that he did not intend to hold over was considered a sufficient notice to quit (f).

The word "tenant" in sect. 5 (1) (e) does not include a sub-tenant. Thus, where a tenant had given notice to quit, but, with the consent of the landlord, had sub-let the premises for the remainder of the unexpired residue of his term, the landlord was held entitled to recover possession from the sub-tenant, notwithstanding that the sub-tenant himself had not given any notice to quit (g).

IV. Where the dwelling-house is reasonably required (at the time of the hearing) (h) by the landlord (i) for occupa-

(c) Barton v. Fincham. See also Green-Price v. Webb, Hunt v. Bliss, Smith v. Barclay, Citizens Labourers &c. v. Whitaker.
(d) Barrett v. Marshall 54 T. L. R. at p. 215.
    Ibid. at p. 215.
(f) Gilbert v. Jordan.
(g) Hylton v. Heal.
(h) See Verde v. Hardy.
(i) For a case where the under-tenant of the tenant subsequently purchased the premises and so became the landlord of his immediate lessor (the tenant),

tion as a residence for (a) himself or (b) any son or daughter of his over eighteen years of age or (c) any person bona fide residing with him, or (d) some person engaged in his whole-time employment or in the whole-time employment of some tenant from him or with whom conditional on housing accommodation being provided a contract for such employment has been entered into,

and

the landlord _k_, proves to the satisfaction of the Court that alternative accommodation is available (at the time of the making of the order or giving of the judgment _(l)_, which is—

(i) reasonably suitable to the—

(a) means of the tenant,

(b) needs of the tenant and his family as regards (α) extent (β) character (γ) proximity to place of work and

(ii) consists of—

(a) a dwelling-house to which the Act applies (i.e. a controlled house or part of a house or rooms in a house), or

(b) premises to be let as a separate dwelling on terms which will afford to the tenant security of tenure reasonably equivalent to the security afforded by the Act in the case of a dwelling-house to which the Act applies

(Sect. 5 (1) (d) as amended by sect. 4 of the Amendment Act.)

Exceptions.—The existence of alternative accommodation however shall not be required as a condition of an order or judgment

see _Roe_ v. _Buele_ The term landlord moreover is not confined to the owner of a dwelling-house but it will also include a tenant who has sub-let to a sub-tenant (_Jonoy_ v. _Tan_ (1922) S C 76 (1922) Sc L T R 1)

(k) The onus is on the landlord (_Kempson_ v. _Markham_ _Neale_ v. _Hardy_)

(l) _Ib_

on any of the above grounds mentioned in (IV) in the following cases —

A Where the tenant was in the employment of the landlord
or a former landlord, and the dwelling-house was let
to him in consequence of that employment, and he has
ceased to be in that employment (Para (i))

B Where the Court is satisfied by a certificate of the proper
agricultural committee (m), or of the Minister of Agriculture and Fisheries (n) pending the formation of such
committee that the dwelling-house is required by the
landlord for the occupation of a person engaged in work
necessary for the proper working of an agricultural
holding, or with whom, conditional on housing accommodation being provided, a contract for employment on
such work has been entered into (Para (ii), as
amended by the Amendment Act, 1923)

C Where the landlord gave up the occupation of the dwelling-
house in consequence of his service in any of H.M.'s
forces (Para (iii))

D Where the landlord or the husband or wife of the landlord
became the landlord before the 30th June 1922
     and
the dwelling-house is reasonably required by him for
occupation as a residence for (a) himself or (b) any
son or daughter of his over eighteen years of age
(Para (iv) as amended by sect 4 of the Amendment
Act, 1923)

E Where the landlord or the husband or wife of the landlord
became the landlord after the 30th June 1922
     and
the dwelling-house is reasonably required by him for

(m) As regards Scotland, the body of persons constituted with respect to any
area by the Board of Agriculture for Scotland under sect 11 (2) of the Corn
Production Act 1917 (sect 18 (1) (a))
(n) As regards Scotland, the Board of Agriculture for Scotland

occupation as a residence for (a) himself (b) any son
or daughter of his over eighteen years of age

and

the Court is satisfied that greater hardship would be
caused by refusing to grant an order or judgment for
possession than by granting it. (Para (v) of sect.
5 (1) is amended by sect. 4 of the Amendment Act.)

As regards the persons who will be entitled to claim the benefit
of sect. 5 (1) (d) it should be noted that the term "landlord"
will include any person from time to time deriving title from
the landlord. A *bonâ fide* purchaser therefore, will not be
debarred from obtaining possession even though his vendor might
not have been able to bring himself within the provisions of
sect. 5 (1) (d) o)

Apparently, however no privity need exist between the plaintiff and the defendant. Thus in *Neale v Hardy* the landlord
had let part of a house to A. and had subsequently given him
due notice to quit. During the currency of the notice the landlord let to B the whole of the house including the portion let to
A. B entered into possession of the unoccupied portion of the
premises, and on the expiration of the notice to quit given by the
landlord brought an action against A. to recover possession of
the remaining portion of the premises which A. refused to quit
The Court made an order for possession

The landlord will have to prove that the premises are reasonably required (at the date of the hearing (p)) and that he is
acting reasonably in requiring them (q). Evidence that there
was alternative accommodation previous to the date of the hearing, if there is no evidence that there is such alternative accommodation available at the date of the hearing itself, or on the
other hand evidence that there will be such accommodation at

(o) *Macdonald's Trustees v Hayes Grandison v Mackay, Paul's Trustees
Blanch Duncan v Fitzpatrick*. As regards an instance where a tenant
and his sub-tenant were the parties to the action see *Logan v Law* (1922),
Sct. L. T. R. 1 (1922) S. C. 76.

(p) *Kempson v Markham*

(q) Per Bankes L. J. in *Accommodation & Steel Association Ltd v Clarke*

some future date (r), will be insufficient. In the latter event the proper course to be adopted, if the Court is of opinion that there will be alternative accommodation available at a future date, is to adjourn the case until such date (s).

It is only when the occupation required by the landlord is for residential purposes that sect. 5 (1) (d) will apply. A landlord, for instance, cannot avail himself of its provisions if he wishes to occupy the premises for business purposes (t).

If the landlord requires the premises for occupation by some person (u) in his employment such person must be in his whole-time (x) employment. The Acts previous to 1920 have been altered in this respect by the addition of the word "whole-time," in order to meet the case of Hall v. Gibbs, where it was held that the employment need not be exclusive. Further the employment must be actually existing at the time, and must not be prospective (y), unless it is conditional on housing accommodation being provided. Possibly it will suffice if the person is in the landlord's employ at the time when the ejectment order is to be made (z).

Formerly, it was held that the fact that there was a contract of employment even in existence would not be sufficient, and that the employee had actually to be working for his employer at the material date (Spencer v. Fox). The law has now been altered to this extent, viz., that it is not necessary for the employee to be actually working for his employer in cases where a contract for employment has been entered into conditional on housing accommodation being provided.

Where a landlord has obtained an order or judgment under sect. 5 on the ground that he *requires the dwelling-house for his own occupation*, and it subsequently appears that such order was

(r) Lees v. Duley
(s) See sect. 5 (2)
(t) Laird v. Graves (1921), 55 I. L. T. 55
(u) See S. S. for War v. Pratt
(x) A soldier is in the whole time employment of the Crown (S. S. for War v. Pratt)
(u) R. v. Rogers, Johnston v. Curran
(z) R. v. Rogers, per Atkin, L. J., Spencer v. Fox

obtained by misrepresentation or the concealment of material facts the Court (a) may order the landlord to compensate the tenant for damage or loss sustained by him as the result of such order or judgment (Sect 5 (6))

Furthermore by sect 5 (7) is amended by sect 4 of the Amendment Act in any case where after the 31st July, 1923, a landlord has obtained an order or judgment for possession or ejectment on any of the grounds specified (above) in the amended para (d) of sect 5 (1) and it is subsequently made to appear to the Court that the order or judgment was obtained by misrepresentation or concealment of material facts the Court is given th discretionary powers of making an order for payment of compensation by the landlord to the former tenant and *in addition* of directing that the dwelling-house shall not be excluded from the Act by reason of the landlord having come into possession thereof under the order or judgment In such a case th house will become controlled again as from the date mentioned in the direction

Alternative Accommodation

The onus of proving that alternative accommodation is available *at the date of the hearing* rests on the landlord (b). and apparently the tenant is not obliged to seek such accommodation himself Under the previous Acts however it was held (c) that th tenant was equally bound to show that no alternative accommodation existed but these cases can no longer be considered authoritative

The existence of alternative accommodation is made a condition of the making of any order for possession (d) In this respect the phraseology of the Acts prior to 1920 was different

(a) The application must be made to the Court in which the order or judgment complained of was made (Rule 4 (e)) (For forms of summons and order see Forms 15 and 16)

(b) Neville v Hardy G N R Co (h) v Best

(c) Bazalgette v Hampson Kirian v Dunn

(d) Except in the cases mentioned in paras 4—8 For other cases in which alternative accommodation is required see sect 5 (1) (e) and (f) *infra* pp 115-117 the question of alternative accommodation being only made a circumstance to be considered by the Court in exercising its discretion. Thus under the earlier Acts, the Court held that if the circumstances warranted, an order for possession might be made although no evidence of the existence of any alternative accommodation was offered (e). Such a decision could not, of course, be given under the present Acts.

The alternative accommodation required by the Act of 1920 was to be ' reasonably equivalent as regards rent, and suitability in all respects.' The Amendment Act of 1923 attempts to define the meaning of 'alternative accommodation.' It is necessary, therefore, to examine the previous decisions with regard to alternative accommodation in the light of the new statutory definition.

According to the Amendment Act the alternative accommodation must be reasonably suitable *inter alia*, to the needs of the tenant and his family as regards extent, character, and proximity to place of business. In *Chicerton v Ede* and in the Scotch case of *Fraser v Midgeley*, it was held that the accommodation offered must also be sufficient for those persons who usually reside with the tenant. Family is an elastic term, yet it is not so wide as the phrase ' persons who usually reside with the tenant.' It is therefore doubtful whether such decisions as in *Fraser v Midgeley*, which decided that a lodger who lived rent free was to be taken into consideration and *Chicerton v Ede (f)* which decided that the accommodation must be also sufficient for the tenant's lodgers where the tenant was in the habit of taking in lodgers, would be followed now.

Under the Acts previous to 1920 the phraseology of which again differs materially from that of the later Acts, it was held in *Wilcock v Booth*, that although in considering the question of alternative accommodation the Court might consider the position of the house offered as for example its accessibility to the tenant's place of business (g) yet it was only dwelling-house accommodation that was to be considered and that if the premises were occupied by the tenant partly as a dwelling and partly for business purposes all that the Court was concerned with was the question whether alternative *dwelling-house* accommodation only was available. It is doubtful whether this decision would now be followed in view of the phraseology of the Act of 1920 and the Amendment Act 1923, and also in view of the provisions of sect. 12 (2) (ii) of the Act of 1920 whereby a house may be a dwelling-house within the Act although it is at the same time used for business purposes (h). In the Irish case of *Irene v. Nelson*, moreover, it was expressly decided that the offer of a house without a shop would not suffice where the premises sought to be so recovered consisted of a dwelling-house with a shop attached thereto. Further in the Scotch case of *Cameron v. Wilson* the Court considered that it was necessary to take into consideration the professional needs of a dentist against whom an order was craved.

For instances where the Courts have held under the Act that the alternative accommodation was not suitable in all respects reference may be made to *Flint v. Earl* where a public-house in London was not considered to be as conducive to health as a cottage in the country; *Neale v. Hardy*, where two dark rooms in a basement and situated in an interior neighbourhood were not considered a sufficient substitute for two bright and airy upper floors of a house in Knightsbridge.

Even where the tenant is in possession of more than one dwelling-house it was held under the principal Act that the Court might nevertheless refuse to make an order for possession unless alternative accommodation is offered and this would be so under the Amendment Act as well. Much will depend however on the circumstances of each case and the particular needs of the tenant. Thus in *Crutchley v. White*, the Court considered it reasonable for the tenant to require more than one

g. See also *Pozelquith v. Hempson*. The Amendment Act now expressly states that this factor is to be taken into consideration.

h. See the Act of 1919, s. 1 (1) (c).

house, inasmuch as he was separated from his wife and the other house was needed for occupation by her. In *Flint v. East*, the Court considered a cottage in the country necessary for the health of the manager of a London public-house and refused to make an order for possession of the country cottage, although there was ample dwelling accommodation in the London public-house. However, in *Cruse v. Terrell* (i) Darling, J., made an order for possession of a cottage in the country although there was no adequate alternative accommodation inasmuch as the cottage in question was used by the tenants merely as a pleasure resort and on very rare occasions, the learned judge observing that it was not the intention of Parliament specially to favour those who make use of cottages not for continuous occupation but for week-ends and for pleasure and that is was more just that those who wanted the cottage to live in continuously should have the prior claim. It must not be thought, however, because a dwelling-house is not dwelt in continuously that therefore a landlord may obtain possession without showing the existence of alternative accommodation if he intends it for some person specified in sect. 5 (1) (d). In the case of *Cruse v. Terrell*, the tenant had already a dwelling-house elsewhere, and different considerations may apply in a case where the tenant has but one dwelling-house which for some reason or another he may happen to un-infrequently (k).

In the following cases, as has been mentioned above, the existence of alternative accommodation will not be required as a condition for the making of an order for possession under sect. 5 (1) (d) :—

Exception A (para. (i)).—A landlord will not be able to avail himself of the benefit conferred by this paragraph unless he can show—

    1. that the tenant was in the employment of the landlord or of a former landlord (l)

(i) Cf. also *Robertson v. Wilson.*
(k) Reference may also be made to the following decisions with regard to the question of alternative accommodation viz.—*McGilchrist v. Wallace, Tomms v. Graham & c. v. R. Coates v. Best, Cameron v. Wilson.*
(l) As to the position of a servant of the Crown see *Whyte v. Pratt.*

2 that the dwelling-house was let to him in consequence of that employment

3 that he has ceased to be in that employment

4 that there has been no fresh letting subsequent to the termination of the employment

In *Bond v Pettle* an agricultural labourer was required to occupy certain premises in consequence of his employment no tenancy *in,* apparently being created thereby although the value of such accommodation (3s per week) was deducted from his wages   On the termination of his employment he was permitted to occupy the cottage at 3s per week but subsequently he was given notice to quit as the landlord required the premises for occupation by another employee   It was held by the Divisional Court that the landlord could not obtain possession without providing alternative accommodation on the grounds that his case did not fall within para (1) inasmuch as there was no tenancy at all until after the employment ceased

On the other hand in *Lever v Caton* the Court decided that no alternative accommodation need be offered in the following circumstances   Caton was a tenant in consequence of his employment to Lever Bros   On the termination of his employment he was allowed to continue in possession because there was at that time no means under the then existing Act for evicting him   He was therefore merely a "statutory tenant"   The Act of 1920 was subsequently passed and the landlords served a notice to quit and on its expiration took proceedings to recover possession   The Court held that there was no necessity to prove the existence of any alternative accommodation as the case came within the provisions of para (1) inasmuch as Caton on the termination of his employment was merely a statutory tenant

Bond v Pettle is therefore distinguishable from *Lever Bros v Caton* inasmuch as in the former case there was (1) no tenancy in consequence of employment and (11) there was a fresh letting after the termination of the employment

It is therefore submitted that if there is any fresh letting after the termination of the employment and for this purpose a statutory tenancy will not amount to a fresh letting the landlord will not be able to rely on para (i). As Lush, J. said in *Lever Bros. v. Caton* 'The question is whether there was a new letting after the termination of the employment. Here, on the cessation of the employment, the tenant became a statutory tenant. . . . I do not think it possible to infer that the parties entered into a new agreement in substitution for the agreement under which the premises were let to him in consequence of his employment.'

Reference may also be made to the Irish case of *G. N. R. Co. (I.) v. Best*. In this case the Court found as a fact that some sort of agreement was entered into at the termination of the employment and that the fresh agreement was not made in consideration of the tenant's employment. The Court held that the case did not fall within para. (i) (*n*).

According to the definition of the term tenant in sect. 12 (1) (g), the term may include the widow of a tenant dying intestate, but where the tenant dying intestate and leaving a widow has been in the employment of the landlord within the meaning of para. (i) it could not be said that alternative accommodation must be offered in such a case by the landlord before he will be entitled to possession (*o*).

Exception B (para. (ii)).—The existence of alternative accommodation will not be a necessary condition for the making of an order for possession under sect. 5 (1) (d), where the dwelling-house is proved (in the manner required by para. (ii) (*p*)) to be required for the occupation of a person engaged on work necessary for the proper working of an agricultural holding, or with whom conditional on housing accommodation being provided, a contract for employment on such work has been entered into.

Where a certificate as provided by para. (ii) is produced, the Court has no power to go behind it (*q*).

(*n*) See 55 I. L. T. R. at p. 59, per Pim, J. in *G. N. R. Co. (I.) v. Best*.
(*o*) *Dalton v. Heal*, (1921) 2 K. B. at p. 447.
(*p*) *Supra*, p. 103.
(*q*) *Smith v. Primrose*, (1921) W. N. 291.

An instrument purporting to be a certificate of the county agricultural committee and to be signed by an officer of the committee will without further proof be taken to be a certificate of the committee unless the contrary is proved. (Sect. 18 (3) of the Amendment Act, 1923.) On the application for a certificate under this provision a fee is payable, the amount of which is to be determined by regulations made by the Minister of Agriculture and Fisheries. (Sect. 18 (2) of the Amendment Act.)

Exception C (para. (iii).)—Alternative accommodation will not be required where the landlord gave up the occupation of the dwelling-house in consequence of his service in any of H.M.'s forces during the war. It is doubtful, however, whether the privilege given by this para. (iii) to the ex-Service man would be extended to his widow (r). Whether a person served in H.M.'s forces will depend on whether he was subject to military law (s).

Exception D (para. (iv).)—This Exception as well as Exception E is for the benefit of purchasers of houses. The corresponding paragraph (t) in the Act of 1920 is considerably altered by this Exception and the next. It is not only in cases where the landlord became the landlord, but also where the husband or wife of a landlord became the landlord prior to the 30th June, 1923, that this paragraph will apply.

The landlord will further have to prove that the dwelling-house is reasonably required by him for occupation as a residence for himself or for any son or daughter of his over eighteen years of age.

The landlord therefore cannot avail himself of this provision should he need the house for occupation as a residence for any other relative, not even for his wife, nor would a stepson or stepdaughter or an adopted child be described as a son or daughter of his.

A purchaser is to be regarded as the landlord as from the date

(r) See *Squire v. How.*
(s) *Tudor v. Ardenne.*
(t) *Chambers' App.*

on which a binding agreement has been entered into (*Barrett v. Marshall*)

For the purposes of this provision moreover a sub-tenant who has purchased the head interest in the whole of the premises subsequently to becoming the sub-tenant is entitled to be regarded as a person who has become the landlord (*Rock v. Burke*)

Exception L — To come within this Exception three conditions must be satisfied —

 (i) The landlord or the husband or wife of the landlord must have become the landlord on or after the 30th June 1922

 (ii) The dwelling-house must be reasonably required for occupation as a residence for the landlord or for any son or daughter of the landlord over eighteen years of age (Cf. Exception D)

 (iii) The Court must be satisfied that greater hardship would be caused by refusing to grant an order or judgment for possession than by granting it

As regards the question of greater hardship reference may be made to the following cases decided under the previous Act —

McQuillan v. Clinton — Where it was the custom of the owner of premises to grant a fresh lease to the person who happened to be in occupation of the premises at the expiration of the head lease, the Court made an order for possession in favour of the head lessee

Great Northern Ry. Co. (Ir.) v. Best — Where a railway company required a house for the purpose of accommodating employees and were greatly inconvenienced by being out of possession the Court nevertheless refused to make an order because it was satisfied that the tenant would have nowhere else to go

Barrett v. Marshall — Where the purchaser had bought a house intending it for her own occupation and the tenants had agreed to give up possession on the termination of the tenancy and had attended the sale of the premises in question and read the conditions of sale in which was a statement that the tenants had agreed to give up possession the Court made an order for possession

Dowling v Butler - In this case the plaintiff had taken a lease of the premises in question from the date of the expiry of the defendant's lease The plaintiff was at the time living with his family (consisting of his wife and four children) in a house which was unsuitable for his requirements The premises in question however had been occupied by the defendant's family for over twenty-five years and were at that time occupied by the defendant his two sisters and two paying guests The defendant moreover had searched for accommodation elsewhere but without success The Court refused to make an order for possession

Menzies v Rankins -- In this case the pursuer (plaintiff) had originally built a small cottage as a house for an under-gardener Subsequently during the war he let it to tenants on the express understanding that they would give up possession when he again wanted the house for occupation by a servant The pursuer at the time of action brought required the house for his chauffeur Failure to obtain possession inflicted a double hardship both on the pursuer and on his servant on the former because he could not get from his servant the full service he was entitled to and on the latter because he was obliged to walk or cycle nine miles daily The pursuer offered the tenant other accommodation, which had however some disadvantages viz that the house offered was smaller that it necessitated going outside for water and wc and that it was not situated so conveniently for the purpose of the defender's business The Court however made an order for possession

Christie v Bridgeshan - The pursuer who was fifty-eight years of age and in failing health desired possession of her own house in order to obviate the necessity of working which she was medically advised she should no longer do She hoped to increase her slender means by taking in lodgers in her own house The tenant of the house was a widow with two young daughters, and was herself the owner of some property in a working-class neighbourhood The Court, although feeling that the tenant would suffer hardship by an order for possession nevertheless considered that greater hardship would be inflicted on the landlord by refusing to make such order Possession granted

V Where the dwelling-house is reasonably required (i) for the purpose of the execution of the statutory duties or powers of a local authority or statutory undertaking or (ii) for any purpose which in the opinion of the Court, is in the public interest and the Court is satisfied as aforesaid as respects alternative accommodation (Sect 5 (1) (e) as amended by sect 4 of the Amendment Act, 1923)

This provision differs from the corresponding provision in the Act of 1920 in that it is not necessary that the local authority or the statutory undertaking should be the landlord of the premises of which possession is required Furthermore, another ground for ordering possession provided, of course there is alternative accommodation is mentioned in the amended paragraph i e , if the house is required for any purpose which is in the public interest as for example the widening of a road or the clearing of an insanitary area Reference may be made to a very similar provision no longer in force contained in sect 13 (1) (e) of the Act of 1920 According to that section however the premises had to be *bonâ fide* required for the purpose of a scheme of reconstruction or improvement which appeared to the Court to be desirable in the public interest ' In *Mitchell v Townend*, decided under that sub-section, it was held that it was not sufficient if the scheme was a private scheme even though it might in effect benefit a number of persons and accordingly the intended conversion in that case of the premises of which possession was required into a training school for girls who could then be employed in a company's factories was held not to satisfy the requirements of the section This case might serve perhaps as a guide in construing the above provision in sect 5 (1) (e), as amended by the Act of 1923

Lastly it should be noted that alternative accommodation similar to that required by para (d) [a] must be provided in any case

By sect 12 (1) (i) of the Act the expression "statutory undertaking" and "statutory duties or powers" include any undertaking duties or powers established imposed or exercised under any order having the force of an Act of Parliament

> XI Where (i) the landlord became the landlord after service in any of H M's forces during the war, and (ii) requires the house for his personal occupation and (iii) offers the tenant accommodation on reasonable terms in the same dwelling-house such accommodation being considered by the Court as reasonably sufficient in the circumstances (Sect 5 (1) (f))

Before a landlord will be entitled to rely on the above provision he will have to show that he was a member of H M's forces during the war and that as such he was subject to military law [b] The privilege given to the ex-Service man however will not be extended to his widow Thus in *Squire v Hore* the Court refused to make an order for possession under sect 5 (1) (c) in favour of the widow of a deceased soldier, notwithstanding the fact that the deceased had, on his return from service given notice to the tenant that he required the premises for his own occupation

The accommodation required in this case is somewhat different from that required by paragraphs (d) and (e) of the same subsection (g) in that (i) it may be offered in the same dwelling-house and (ii) it need only be reasonably sufficient in the circumstances of the case

In considering however whether the accommodation is reasonably sufficient it is not only the tenant who is to be considered but also all those persons who usually and properly reside with

---

(a) What has been said as regards alternative accommodation (supra pp 106-109) will equally apply

(b) *Index v Indemus Law* 1 Debtor

(g) *Supra* pp 104-116

him including lodgers where he is in the habit of taking them in (z). The Court will also have to take into consideration such matters as those of character, health, social amenities and so forth The fact that the offer of the landlord would necessitate the joint use of the kitchen, bath and lavatories or the removal of the tenant's furniture for storage might well be a good ground for refusing an order for possession (a).

Apparently there is nothing to prevent an ex-Service man from bringing himself within this provision by buying property for that express purpose so long as he intends to occupy it himself Thus, in *Kentish v Sneath*, a father conveyed premises which he desired to occupy to his son who was an ex-soldier in order to enable him to recover possession The Court granted the latter possession considering that the benefit was not intended for the father alone but for the son as well

VII. Where the dwelling-house is required for occupation as a residence by a former tenant thereof who gave up occupation in consequence of his service in any of H M 's forces during the war (Sect. 5 (1) (g).)

This provision, though it may appear at first sight to do so, does not confer any *rights* on the tenant (b), which he had not before, so that if the landlord does not wish to take any action in the matter the ex-tenant is entirely without remedy

It is not necessary, however, for the party claiming possession to prove that he was himself the former tenant and sub-let the house on joining the forces (c) The landlord himself may eject a tenant from the house in order to put a former tenant into occupation provided he can persuade the Court to make the order Of course any existing tenancy will, in any case have to be duly determined before the landlord can avail himself of the provisions of sect. 5 (1) (g)

(z) *Churston v. Fox* (1921) 2 K B at pp 39, 40
(a) *Ibid*
(b) *Goodwin v Rhodes*
(c) *Messenger v Hatton*

VIII Where the tenant has subsequently to the 31st July,
      1923 and without the consent of the landlord—

      (i) assigned the whole of the dwelling-house or

      (ii) sub-let the whole of the dwelling-house or

      (iii) sub-let part of the dwelling-house the re-
      mainder being already sub-let

      Sect 5 (1) (h   see sect 4 of the Amendment Act)

This is entirely a new provision affording yet another ground
on which the landlord will be entitled to possession provided
of course he is entitled to possession under the law ordinarily
in force

IX Where the dwelling-house consists of or includes premises
    licensed for the sale of intoxicating (d) liquor
    and the tenant has —

    (i) committed an offence as holder of the licence or

    (ii) not conducted the business to the satisfaction of
    the licensing justices or the police authority or

    (iii) carried the business on in a manner detrimental
    to the public interest or

    (iv) the renewal of the licence has for any reason
    been refused

    (Sect 5 (1) (i) see sect 4 of the Amendment Act)

This provision also is new   The wording of the paragraph impliedly gives statutory confirmation to the view (e) that premises
may constitute a dwelling-house within the Act although they
may consist partly of premises licensed for the sale of intoxicating liquor

Reference may also be made to the following cases on posses-
sion decided under the Acts passed previously to 1920 viz —
_Storm v Fanbrass Green-Price v Webb Hunt v Bliss
Pope v Pritchard Stephens v Latham Hipps Ltd v_

(d) As regards Scotland   excisable   liquor sect 19 (a) of the Amendment Act 1923
(e) Sup c p 21

Hughes Paul and others Paul's Trustees v Blanch (f); Lamb v Graham.

Sect 2 – Powers of the Court in making or giving an order or judgment for possession or ejectment under sect 5

In actions for recovery of possession and ejectment the Court is given a very wide discretion (g, as regards the order to be made in the circumstances. At the trial of the action at the time of the making or giving of any order or judgment for recovery of possession or ejectment the Court has a full discretion which however must be exercised judicially (1, to adjourn the application (2, to stay or suspend execution on any such order or judgment or (3, postpone the date of possession for such period or periods as it thinks fit, and subject to such conditions (if any as regards payment by the tenant of arrears of rent rent, or mesne profits and otherwise. And if such conditions are complied with the Court may discharge or rescind any such order or judgment. Applications (h, may also be made to the Court subsequently to the making or giving of the order or judgment, and the Court has the same power to deal with the application in the manner indicated above (i,

Similar powers are also given to the Court in cases where apparently an *unconditional* order or judgment has been already made or given but not executed (h. An application may be subsequently made to the Court to stay or suspend execution or for any of the purposes mentioned above.

In the case of an unexecuted order or judgment which was made or given before the passing of the Act of 1920, where the Court was of opinion that such order or judgment would not have

---

(f) Cf also Grandison v Maclay Macdonald's Trustees v Hut...
(g) Sect 5 (2)
(h) For forms of summons and order see Appendix, Forms 9 and 10
(i) See also Rickes v Shelley Benabo v Horsley Crucibles v Gatliff
(k) The Court has this power even where the order or judgment was given prior to the Act of 1920 but it is not likely that any need for the exercise of this power will arise now

been made or given if the Act was in force at that time the Court had a discretion on application by the tenant to rescind or vary such order or judgment in such manner as the Court might think fit for the purpose of giving effect to the Act (m) This provision however did not give the judge a rigid power which he had to exercise if he was satisfied the order would not be met but merely a discretion to re-open the matter if he thought fit (n) Moreover the order contemplated by this section was an order made by the judge in invitum, and did not contemplate a consent order (o)

Sect 3 — Position of Sub-tenants

Protection is further afforded to sub-tenants by sect 5 5 whereby an order or judgment against a tenant for the recovery of possession of any dwelling-house within the Act or ejectment therefrom under sect 5 will not affect the right of any sub-tenant whether of the whole or part of the premises in question to retain possession thereof or be in any way operative against any such sub-tenant But in order to avail himself of this provision it will be necessary for the sub-tenant to show 1 that the premises or any part of them have been lawfully sub-let and 2 that they were so sub-let before proceedings were commenced for their recovery (p)

This sub-section (q) means that where there is a sub-tenant lawfully and de facto in possession the landlord who desires to recover possession cannot avail himself as against the sub-tenant of any order or judgment which he may have recovered against the tenant but must commence separate proceedings against the sub-tenant in which the latter may urge whatever matters he

l) The Court has this power now but no need for its exercise is likely to arise at the present time

(m) Sect 5 (3)

(n) Taylor v Lawes

(o) Hillesley v White, see also Comyns v Frost

(p) Sect. 5 (5), Chapman v Hughes, Ward v Larkins

(q) Sect 5 (5)

may think fit, including matters personal as between himself and the landlord affecting the reasonableness of the landlord's demand, which is one of the elements to be taken into account in the proceedings (r).

Even where the premises are not within the Act by reason for instance of the rent payable by the original tenant being beyond the limits of the Act or being less than two-thirds of the rateable value (s), under-tenants will nevertheless be entitled to the protection of the Act whether they are under-tenants of the whole or only a portion of the premises if the rent payable by such under-tenants are within the limits of the Act (t). Where an order for possession is made against the original tenant in such a case, the order must be limited to such parts of the premises (if any) as are occupied by the original tenant (u).

Further by sect. 15 (3) where the interest of a tenant of a dwelling-house within the Act is determined either as the result of an order or judgment for possession or ejectment or for any other reason any sub-tenant to whom the premises or any part thereof have been *lawfully* sub-let shall *subject to the provisions of the Act*, be deemed to become the tenant of the landlord on the same terms as he would have held from the tenant if the tenancy had continued. This sub-section merely means that where the interest of the original tenant has been lawfully determined (e.g. by surrender (x) but not by notice to quit (y)) then any sub-tenant assuming that he is entitled to retain possession under the provisions of the Act shall notwithstanding that the title under which he derived his interest has come to an end continue to be tenant, the terms on which he retains possession being the same as those on which he would have held from the tenant if the tenancy had continued (z). If under

(r) Per Rowlatt J. in *Hylton v. Heal*, (1921) 2 K. B. at p. 449.

(s) Sect. 12 (7).

(t) *Cottell v. Baker*, *Murphy v. Porter and Blane*, *Hall v. Lanyon*.

(u) *Cottell v. Baker* see however *Murphy v. Porter and Blane*.

(v) *Barton v. Fincham* (1921) 2 K. B. at p. 297.

(y) *Hylton v. Heal*.

(z) Per Rowlatt J., in *Hylton v. Heal* (1921) 2 K. B. at p. 441.

the Act the sub-tenant has a right to continue to be a sub-tenant, or his other rights then these rights are preserved to him by sect. 15 (3), but if he has no such rights as, for example, if he has no right to continue in possession of the premises under sect. 5 (1) (c) then sect. 15 (3) does not assist him (a).

As has been observed, under-tenants will not be entitled to the protection of the Act where the premises have not been lawfully sub-let to him, though in such a case there will be nothing to prevent them from obtaining relief under the Conveyancing Act, 1892 (b).

Even where a sub-tenant performs all the obligations existing between him and his own lessor (the tenant) he will neverthe-less have no rights afforded him by the Act if the tenant in letting the premises to him commits a breach of one of the obligations of his own tenancy, e.g. by sub-letting without consent. The word "tenancy" in sect. 5 (1) (a) is not confined merely to the "statutory tenancy" created by the Act but extends to the original contractual tenancy as well (c).

A tenant, unless he is a tenant at sufferance or at will, has a right to sub-let unless there is an agreement to the contrary and even where there is such an agreement an under-letting of part of the premises only will not amount to a breach of covenant not to under-let (d) unless the covenant is so worded as to include such an under-letting.

In this connection might also be noted how far a statutory tenant has power to sub-let. It is submitted that this question will depend on whether the right of sub-letting was expressly excluded or not under the original contract of tenancy since by sect. 15 (1) the statutory tenant is entitled to the benefit of all the terms and conditions of the original contract of tenancy. This view has been upheld by the Divisional Court in *Keeves v. Dean* and *Nunn v. Pellegrini*.

a. Per Rowlatt J. in *Hutton v. Hcal* (1921) 2 K. B. at p. 340.
b. *Dat v. Jacques*, see also *Head v. Whaley* (1918) 1 K. B. 1S.
c. *Chapman v. Hughes*.
d. *Wilson v. Rosenthal*, see also *Jay v. Coll v. ct.*

Where a tenant lawfully sub-lets premises he will not be liable to his immediate landlord for rent or for use and occupation during such time as his sub-tenant remains in statutory (e) possession of the premises after the expiration of the tenant's lease or agreement provided the tenant has given due notice to his sub-tenant to vacate the premises on or before the expiration of his own lease or tenancy agreement (f). Inasmuch as the sub-tenant in such a case has acquired a statutory tenancy the tenant must be regarded as having done all that he was required to by giving due notice. It would be otherwise if the tenant left the sub-tenant in possession willingly or as having assented to the continuation of the sub-tenancy by not taking any steps to determine such sub-tenancy (g).

Sect. 4 - Warrants for Possession

By sect. 143 of the County Courts Act 1888 a warrant for possession whenever issued is to bear date on the day succeeding the last day for delivery of possession allowed by the judgment and to continue in force for three months from that date and no longer and by the Small Tenements Recovery Act 1838 s. 1 a warrant for possession must be executed within thirty clear days from its date. The Act by sect. 5 (1) provides that notwithstanding the above provisions every warrant for delivery of possession of or to enter and give possession of any dwelling-house within the Act shall remain in force for three months from the day next after the last day named in the judgment or order for delivery of possession or, in the case of a warrant under the Small Tenements Recovery Act 1838 from the date of the issue of the warrant and in either case for such further period or periods (if any) as the Court shall from time to time, whether before or after the expiration of such three months direct

(e) 1. by virtue of the provisions of sect. 15 (3) of the Act
(f) Reynolds v. Bannerman
(g) Ibid (1922) 1 K. B. at p 723

Sect. 5.   Acceptance of Rent after service of Notice to Quit

Questions of difficulty have arisen with regard to the effect of an acceptance of rent by the landlord after the expiration of a notice to quit.   Now sect. 16 (3) of the Act expressly provides that where a landlord of any dwelling-house within the Act has served a notice to quit on a tenant, the acceptance of rent by the landlord for a period not exceeding three months from the expiration of the notice to quit shall not be deemed to prejudice any right to possession of such premises, and if any order for possession is made any payment of rent so accepted shall be treated as mesne profits (*h*).   In *Town Properties Development Co., Ltd. v. Winter,* Avory, J., following *Davies v. Bristow* in preference to *Hartell v. Blackler* (*i*), decreed possession in a case where the landlord had received two quarters' rent after the expiration of the notice to quit   It is to be observed, however, that the attention of the Court, as far as can be gathered from the report, was not called to sect. 16 (3) of the Act   The same question arose in the subsequent case of *Shuter v. Hersh*   The County Court judge had come to the very natural conclusion that the effect of sect. 16 (3) was to invalidate a notice to quit where there had been an acceptance of more than three months' rent after the expiry of the notice   The Divisional Court, however, overruled the learned County Court judge   Bankes, L. J., expressly accepted the view of Shearman, J., in *Davies v. Bristow* which is as follows :—" As long as a landlord is prevented from getting recovery of possession of premises after the expiration of the notice to quit   (i.e., owing to the provisions of the Rent Act) ' it is correct to say that the former tenant by holding over, no longer becomes a trespasser, but is in lawful statutory occupation of the premises, unless there is proved in fact any other lawful agreement subject to the provisions of the Act which the landlord and tenant choose to make."

The result is that acceptance of rent for a period even exceed-

(*h*) There was no similar provision in the earlier Acts
(*i*) See also *Hunt v. Bliss; Evans v. Enever*

ing three months will not in itself create a fresh tenancy and prevent the occupation of the tenant from being any other than statutory. It will be necessary to prove that a fresh agreement has been entered into between the landlord and the tenant.

A further question arises as to whether a landlord of premises within the Act will by the subsequent acceptance of rent waive his right to recover possession by way of forfeiture for breaches of covenant or otherwise. Sect. 16 (3) only deals with the cases where a notice to quit has been given. It is submitted that it is a question of fact in each case as to whether the landlord has waived the breach, and it would appear that the subsequent acceptance of rent would amount to conclusive evidence of waiver. As Lush J. said in *Davies v. Bristow*[1]: "Where a breach of covenant available for forfeiture has been committed by the tenant it is correct enough to say that the landlord can waive the forfeiture, for by the breach of covenant the term is not avoided; it is only rendered voidable at the landlord's option. He can elect whether to affirm or disaffirm the tenancy, and if he by some act evinces an unequivocal intention to affirm it, as by the acceptance of rent with notice of the breach, he cannot afterwards insist on the forfeiture; and no statement made by him at the time of doing that act that he does it without prejudice to his right to re-enter will affect the conclusion that the forfeiture is waived. Now when one looks at *Hartell v. Blackler* one sees that the authorities which were cited to the Court, viz., *Croft v. Lumley* and *Davenport v. Reg.* were cases of forfeiture; they were not cases in which the term had been brought to an end by a notice to quit; and, in my opinion, the principle which is applicable to the former class of cases is not applicable to the latter. When once the notice to quit has expired the position of the parties is precisely the same as it would be if the original lease had provided for the determination of the term at the date mentioned in the notice. There is in that case no room for election by the landlord. The landlord and tenant may of course agree that a new tenancy shall be created on the old terms and that is what in effect they do when they agree that the notice to quit shall be waived. But the agreement to continue the tenancy must be proved. It must be shown that the parties were *ad idem* as to the terms.

In the light of these authorities it would appear that sect 16 3 is a useless and purposeless provision and has no effect whatever.[1]

[1] Cf. also *Sherman* v. *Cooley*

CHAPTER VIII

MORTGAGES

Sect. 1.—*Application of the Act* (a)

In no case is a mortgage created after the 2nd July, 1920, affected by the Act (b). But in considering the application of the Act with regard to mortgages created before that date it would be best to keep distinct (1) the class of premises, and (2) the kinds of mortgages to which the Act applies. Not only the mortgaged property but the mortgage itself must fall within the provisions of the Act.

A. *Premises to which the Act applies.*

It will be necessary in the first instance that the mortgaged property should come within the description of a " dwelling-house " (c) as defined by the Act, and for this purpose it should be remembered that a house may be a dwelling-house even though it is also used as a shop or office or for business, trade or professional purposes (d).

Further, the standard rent or rateable value of the dwelling-house must have been at the material date within the limits prescribed by sect. 12 (2) (a) (b) and (c), though, if the dwelling-house once falls within the provisions of the Act, it will always remain within the Act whether it continues or not to be one to which the Act applies (e).

(a) The reader is recommended to read Chapter III before reading this section.

(b) Sect. 12 (4) (c).

(c) As to what is a dwelling-house, see *supra* pp. 21—23.

(d) Sect. 12 (2) (n), *supra*, p. 21.

(e) Sect. 12 (6), *supra*, p. 24.

Similarly, if the Act once applies to a mortgage it will continue to apply to the mortgage whether or not the mortgaged property still remains within the Act. If, however, the mortgaged property *f* becomes decontrolled under the Act of 1923 it seems that the Act will cease to apply to the mortgage as well.

The house, moreover, must not have been in course of erection on or erected after the 2nd April, 1919, nor must it have been in course of being *bonâ fide* reconstructed by way of conversion or so reconstructed after the above-mentioned date within the meaning of sect. 12 (9) *g*.

In cases where the rent payable in respect of any tenancy is less than two-thirds of the rateable value the Act will not apply to any mortgage by the landlord from whom the tenancy is held of his interest in the dwelling-house (*h*) but such a mortgage will apparently come within the Act on the termination of the tenancy or on the creation of a new tenancy where the rent is more than two-thirds of the rateable value.

As regards a mortgage of a dwelling-house which is otherwise within the Act except for the fact that the rent includes payments in respect of board attendance or use of furniture (*i*) it is submitted that the Act will not be wholly excluded in such a case but only so long as such a tenancy is in existence, provided the other conditions of the Act are satisfied.

The Act further will not apply to a mortgage of a house where the house is let together with land other than the site of the house or other premises if the rateable value of such other land or premises would, if let separately, be more than one quarter of the rateable value of the house *k*. In this case also the mortgage will presumably be excluded from the operation of the Act only so long as the tenancy continues, provided of course the premises are otherwise within the Act.

(f) Cf. *supra* p. 41.
(g) *Supra* pp. 25, 26.
(h) Sect. 12 (7). *supra* pp. 34, 36.
(i) Sect. 12 (2). *supra* pp. 29—31.
(k) Sect. 12 (2). *m. supra* p. 27, and see *In re Heyn*.

Where the mortgaged property consists of one or more dwelling-houses to which the Act applies *and other land*, then if the rateable value of such dwelling-houses is *less* than one-tenth of the rateable value of the whole of the land comprised in the mortgage the Act will not apply to such a mortgage (*l*). This provision must be kept distinct from sect 12 (2) (iii) inasmuch as the latter merely provides a criterion to be applied in determining whether a dwelling-house is within the Act or not. If a dwelling-house is excluded by virtue of sect 12 (2) (iii) from the provisions of the Act, it is to be treated for all purposes as outside the scope of the Act. On the other hand sect 12 (4) (a) deals with cases in which the mortgaged property consists of one or more dwelling-houses *within the Act*, and other land (which will apparently include buildings *outside the Act*

Where, however the mortgaged property consists of one or more dwelling-houses to which the Act applies and other land (or presumably buildings to which the Act does not apply) and the rateable value of the dwelling-houses is *more* than one-tenth of the rateable value of the whole of the land comprised in the mortgage the mortgagee may apportion the principal money between such dwelling-houses and such other land by giving one calendar month's notice in writing to the mortgagor such notice to state the particulars of such apportionment and at the expiry of the notice the Act will not apply to the mortgage so far as it relates to such other land. The mortgage will then operate for all purposes including the mortgagor's right of redemption, as if it were a separate mortgage for the respective portions of the principal money secured by the dwelling-houses and such other land respectively, to which such portions were apportioned (*m*)

The mortgagor however before the expiration of the calendar month's notice will be entitled to dispute the amounts so apportioned and in default of agreement the matter must be determined by a single arbitrator appointed by the President of the

(*l*) Sect 12 (4)   (*l*) sect 2 (1) (i) of the Act of 1915 and sect 4 of the Act of 1919
(*m*) Sect 12 (5)

Surveyors Institution or in Scotland by the Chairman of the Scottish Committee of the Surveyors Institution (o)

It is immaterial whether there is more than one dwelling-house comprised in the mortgage provided they are each within the provisions of the Act. The Act moreover will equally apply where any interest in such premises has been mortgaged.

But where the mortgaged property consists partly of premises within the Act and partly of premises outside the provisions of the Act then, as has been mentioned above p, the Act will not apply at all if the rateable value of the premises within the Act is less than one-tenth of the rateable value of such other premises outside the provisions of the Act. If however the rateable value of the property within the Act is more than one-tenth of the rateable value of the other premises then the landlord will have the right to apportion the principal money by virtue of sect. 12 (5) and in the manner indicated therein (q). This provision thus obviates a difficulty which arose under the earlier Acts in *Re Dunn's Application* in which case it was held that where the mortgaged property consisted partly of premises within and partly of premises outside the Act and the case was not excluded by sect. 2 (4) (i) of the Act of 1915 which was a provision similar to that of sect. 12 (4) (i) of the present Act the mortgagee was precluded from realizing his security even in respect to the property to which the Act did not apply.

The Act moreover will not be excluded merely because the mortgaged house or houses cannot be said to have been let at the material times or at all. It has been held in *Woodfield v. Bond* that the words let as a separate dwelling in sect. 12 (2) only qualify the words part of a house (r) and accordingly the Court decided in that case that the Act would apply although

(p) Sect. 12 (5)
(o) Sect. 18 (1) (i)
(p) Supra p. 129, sect. 12 (1) (a)
(q) Supra p. 129
(r) Supra p. 24. A contrary view has been taken in Ireland. (See
[illegible]

the mortgaged property was at all times occupied by the mortgagor and could not be said to have been let.

Furthermore it must be remembered that once the Act applies to a mortgage of a dwelling-house within the Act it will continue to do so whether or no the dwelling-house continues to be one to which the Act applies s though this provision will not it seems apply in the case of houses decontrolled by the Act of 1923.

For the purposes of the Act the expression "mortgagor" and "mortgagee" will include any person deriving title under the original mortgagor or mortgagee t. In *Martin v Watson and Egan* a mortgagor's interest had vested in A. A demised the premises to B whose title was not a good one since it was void against the mortgagee. The Court nevertheless held that B was a person deriving title under the mortgagor.

B — *Mortgages to which the Act applies*

Although the mortgaged property may be within the Act the Act nevertheless may not apply to the mortgage in question. The Act does not state definitely the class of securities to which it applies. Sect 12 (1) (h) does not attempt to define "mortgage" but merely states that the expression includes a land charge under the Land Transfer Acts 1875 and 1897 u while sect 12 (4) (h) expressly excludes from the provisions of the Act equitable charges by deposit of title deeds or otherwise. The matter however has received the judicial interpretation of the Courts and it is to the decided cases that one must turn for enlightenment.

In *Jones v Woodward* which was decided under the previous Act of 1915 Sargant J held that by "mortgage" was meant

(s) Sect 12 (b), *supra* pp 24 128

(t) Sect 12 (1) (t) As regards Scotland "mortgagor" and "mortgagee" mean respectively the debtor and the creditor in a heritable security and "mortgaged property" means the heritable subject or subjects included in a heritable security (Sect 18 (1) (a))

(u) As regards Scotland, "mortgage" and "encumbrance" mean the heritable security including a security constituted by absolute disposition qualified by back bond or letter (Sect 18 (1) (a))

9 (2)

an instrument which conveyed the property out and out but gave a right to redeem. The Act of 1915 also contained a similar provision, excepting from its operation an equitable charge by deposit of title deeds or otherwise, and in the same case it was held that the words "or otherwise" were not *ejusdem generis* but would also bring within the exception equitable charges effected by any other means whatever. Accordingly the learned judge held that the charge which was one given by a builder on certain dwelling-houses to secure all moneys due or to become due, and which contained a provision that the borrower would give the lender formal charges within a stipulated time, was an equitable charge within the meaning of sect. 2 (4) (b) of the Act of 1915 and was therefore excluded from the operation of that Act.

The meaning of these words was further considered by the Court of Appeal in *London City and Westminster Bank v. Tompkins*. In that case Pickford L. J. was of the same opinion as Sargant J. that the expression mortgage should not be construed in an extensive sense, and in favour of this view may be urged the fact that the Acts expressly define (y) "mortgage" as including a land charge under the Land Transfer Acts 1875 and 1877 z. Bankes L. J. however who took a contrary view considered that the word "mortgage" would include equitable mortgages as well but he held that all equitable charges were excluded from the Act by virtue of the exception. Scrutton L. J. was also of the same opinion and considered that the exception was wide enough to include an equitable security in the wide sense a security not intended to be of a permanent character, and therefore made in an informal way which needs equitable assistance to enforce it in most cases and in most respects (a).

It would seem therefore that the Act will apply to a mort-

(x) Sect 2 (4) (b)
(y) Sect 2 (1) (c) of the Act of 1915 and sect 12 (1) (h) of the Act of 1920
z See *Jones v. Woodward* 1917; W N at p 61
a 1918 1 K B at p 530

gage whether of legal or equitable (b) estate where there is a conveyance of property subject to a proviso of redemption. As regards other equitable mortgages using the word mortgage in a wide sense equitable charges created by deposit of deeds are expressly excluded by the Act and so it is submitted would other equitable mortgages if they are of an informal character and are intended only as a security for a temporary purpose even though the lender may be given the power to realise his security without the intervention of the Court as undoubtedly the intention of the Acts was to protect what may be called the permanent mortgagors of small property and not to interfere with temporary securities (c). Thus in *Tomkins Case supra* where title deeds were deposited with a bank as a security for an overdraft and a deed executed charging the defendant's interest in the property the Court held that the charge did not come within the Act although there was a clause in the deed whereby the borrower declared that he held the charged property as trustee for the lender and two further clauses one of which authorised the lender to remove the borrower as trustee and to appoint new trustees with a declaration vesting the borrower's estate in the new trustees (thus enabling the lender to get the legal estate in himself without the intervention of the Court (d), and another clause whereby under sect 8 of the Conveyancing Act, 1882 the borrower appointed the lender his irrevocable attorney to execute a conveyance of his legal estate on a sale by the lender as mortgagee

Sect 2 - Restrictions on Increasing Mortgage Interest

It is only where the rate of mortgage interest has been increased since the 25th March 1920 (e) that such increase is effected (f), and in such a case any excess beyond the limits per-

---

(b) *I q* a second mortgage *ibid* at p 522

(c) *Ibid* at p 522

(d) *London and County Banking Co v Goddard* (1897) 1 Ch 642

(e) See however *Hollands v Cooper*

(f) Sect 1

mitted by sect. 1 of the Act will be irrecoverable from the mortgagor (g), notwithstanding any agreement to the contrary, and
if already paid, can be recovered from the mortgagee (h), subject now, however, to the provisions of sect. 8 (2) of the Act of
1923 (i). In considering whether the interest has been increased
since the 25th March 1920, the same observations will apply
as have already been made in the case of increase of rent (k).

By virtue of sect. 19 (3) of the Act and of sect. 38 of the
Interpretation Act, 1889, increases of interest, in the case of
1915 houses since the 3rd August 1914, and in the case of
1919 houses since the 25th December 1918, will also be
affected (l). But if there is an increase prior to the 25th March
1920, and such increase is either valid or not affected by the
provisions of the Acts passed prior to 1920, then it is submitted such increase will not be affected by the Act of 1920.
Holland v. *Cooper* however is a case distinctly to the contrary,
but it is submitted that it is a decision which cannot be supported. It certainly conflicts with the judgment of Atkin L. J.
in *Sinclair* v. *Powell* (m). In that case (*Hollands* v. *Cooper*)
houses to which the 1915 Act applied had been mortgaged prior
to the 4th August 1914. By an agreement dated the 29th
September 1914 the rate of interest which was formerly 4½ per
cent. was raised to 6 per cent. The interest was thus raised
since the 3rd August 1914 (though not since the 25th March
1920). The increase however was valid by virtue of sect.
1 (3) (c) of the Act of 1915 inasmuch as it had been increased
in consequence of a notice to repay given prior to the 4th August.
1914 and therefore was not affected by that Act. Interest
at the rate of 6 per cent. was paid until the passing of the Act
of 1920 when the mortgagor contended that the amount of

(g) Sect. 1
(h) Sect. 14 (1)
(i) *Intra* p. 148
(k) *Supra* pp. 1—6 and see *Goldsmith* v. *Orr* *Radley* v. *Gale* *Dickson*
v. *H.* .
(l) *Supra* pp. 6—53
(m) (1922) 1 K. B. at p. 405 See also p. 402

interest was beyond the limits permitted by the Act. The Court adopted his contention and held that the Act of 1915 was repealed by the Act of 1920; that the standard rate of interest was $4\frac{1}{2}$ per cent, and all that the mortgagee was entitled to was an increase above the standard rate of $\frac{1}{2}$ per cent for a year from the 2nd July, 1920 (n), and subsequently an increase of 1 per cent. Astbury J. in arriving at the above decision considered that the Act did not provide that all increases validly made before the 25th March, 1920, should continue valid.

It would seem that the effect of this decision is really to maintain that where the rent or interest has been lawfully increased prior to the 25th March, 1920, then although such rent or interest which accrued due before the 25th March, 1920, is not affected by the Act, the rent or interest which accrued due subsequently to that date will be irrecoverable if it is above the limits permitted by the Act. Now it is submitted, to use the words of Lush J. in *Sinclair v. Powell* (o), that all that the Act does is to prevent subsequent increases after a specified date; it does not affect already existing and lawful agreements, whether for the payment of increased rent or increased mortgage interest, and therefore that where rent or interest has been lawfully increased prior to the 25th March, 1920, the same rent or interest will be legally recoverable even subsequent to the above date, although such rent or interest may be above the limits permitted by the Act (p).

As in the case of increase of rent, so in the case of increase of mortgage interest, the Act does not override any agreements made by the mortgagor and mortgagee, provided such agreements are not contrary to the provisions of the Act itself. Thus if a mortgage provides that interest below the maximum payable under the Act is payable, and contains a proviso for redemption on a certain date, the interest can in no event be increased by virtue of the Act solely so long as the interest is paid and the other

---

(n) Sect. 4 (b) of the Act of 1920.

(o) But see *Woodhead v. Debnam.*

(p) See also *Goldwith v. Orr; Barnes v. Orr.*

covenants observed at any rate until after that date   Sect 3 (1)
of the Act expressly provides that nothing in the Act shall be
taken to authorise any increase in the rate of interest on a mortgage *except in respect of a period during which but for the
Act of 1920 q the security could be enforced*   It is unfortunate
that increase of mortgage interest has not been treated with such
fulness in the Act as increase of rent and in the absence of any
judicial decisions on the subject the matter becomes merely one
of conjecture   One can therefore only suggest the problems
that may arise and attempt to discover their solutions

For instance can the mortgage interest be increased apart from
the mortgagor's assent?   It is submitted on the analogy of *Cork
Improved Dwellings Co v Barry(r)* that such an increase can
be imposed *in invitum*, provided there is no agreement in
existence which of course the mortgagee is not entitled to
override

It is further submitted that some sort of notice intending to
increase the interest must be served before the higher rate of
interest can be claimed   There is no provision in the Act
similar to that dealing with increase of rent (s whereby the rent
cannot be increased until the tenancy is determined and a notice
of increase is given in the manner prescribed by the Act

It would appear moreover that such increase would be only
effective is from the date on which the mortgagee would be
entitled to enforce his security or call in his mortgage   For
instance he might serve a notice of his intention to increase the
rate is from the date provided in the agreement for the redemption of the mortgage   But what if he allows that date to pass
by before serving a notice?   Will the increase be immediately
effective?   Any answer to such a question must be given with
the greatest diffidence but perhaps an analogy showing how this
sect 3 1 has been interpreted in the case of increase of rent
may be of assistance   This section provides that no increase of

q One might also add   and the previous Rent Acts
r *Supra* pp 51, 52
s Sect 3 (1) and (2)

rent will be recoverable except for a period during which, but for the Act, the landlord would be entitled to obtain possession, and it has been held that the words "entitled to obtain possession" mean that the landlord has done everything that is necessary in order "to complete his title to submit to the Court" that his right to obtain possession is complete. The landlord, for instance, will not have to wait till the expiration of the time within which it would be competent for him to obtain an order for possession, i.e., until after he could have issued and served the writ and all the other proceedings could have taken place, which were necessary to entitle him to an order for possession (l). So in the case of mortgage interest it may be argued that such increase will be effective as from the time when the mortgagee has the right to recover the money he has lent, or, in the alternative, to enforce his security. Where therefore, the date of redemption has passed, and there is no provision that the mortgagee must give the mortgagor a notice of his intention to call in the mortgage after a stipulated time if the money is not repaid, it is submitted, on a strict view, that the increase will become recoverable immediately on the giving of a notice increasing the mortgage interest.

The amount by which the rate of interest payable in respect of a mortgage to which the Act applies can be increased is not to exceed by more than 1 per cent. the standard rate of such mortgage (u), but in no event is the rate to be increased so as to exceed $6\frac{1}{2}$ per cent. per annum (x). In the case, however, of '1915' and '1919' houses an increase of only $\frac{1}{2}$ per cent. above the standard rate was permitted during the period 2nd July, 1920, to 2nd July, 1921 (y), but subsequently the full increase of 1 per cent. could be demanded.

'Standard rate of interest' is defined as meaning, in the case of (1) a *mortgage* in force on the 3rd August, 1914, the rate of

---

(l) See *Kerr* v *Bryde*, per Lord Sumner, also *Hall* v *Hasler*, (1921) 3 K. B. at p 651

(u) Sect 4

(x) Sect 4 (a)

(y) Sect 4 (b)

interest payable at that date, and (ii) in the case of a *mortgage* created since that date, the original rate of interest (z).

In the case of a mortgage created after the 3rd August, 1914, where more than one rate has been charged, it is submitted that the first or original rate will be the standard rate. Thus if a mortgage provides that interest at the rate of 5 per cent. shall be payable, but that at a certain date the interest is either to be increased or decreased, the standard rate in such a case will be 5 per cent. the original rate of interest. And further, it is submitted that, in arriving at the standard rate, no deduction is to be made for income tax in cases where the mortgagee is to receive interest free of income tax (a). It is quite possible for the standard rate to exceed the maximum of $6\frac{1}{2}$ per cent. permitted by sect. 4 (a) of the Act of 1920. Thus if property within the Act was mortgaged at the rate of 4 per cent. in 1914, and the mortgage was paid off, and subsequently the owner happened to mortgage the property again at 7 per cent., then assuming that the property was not within the provisions of the earlier Acts and the mortgage was created prior to the passing of the present Act, the mortgagee would nevertheless be entitled to interest at the rate of 7 per cent. which would be the standard rate, though of course by virtue of the Acts the rate could not be further increased. $6\frac{1}{2}$ per cent. being the maximum allowed by the Act.

An illustration will serve to explain the manner in which the increase is to be calculated. Assume the mortgaged house to be one to which the Acts passed previously to 1920 applied. and assume the interest on the mortgage of the house in question to have been 6 per cent. in August, 1914. The rate of interest may be increased as follows:—For a period of one year from the 2nd July, 1920, to 2nd July, 1921, interest at the rate of $6\frac{1}{2}$ per cent. may be charged. Subsequently to that date the mortgagee would have been entitled to the full increase of 1 per cent. bringing the rate up to 7 per cent., but for the provision

(z) Sect. 12 (1) (b)
(a) See *supra* p. 12 on standard rent and the cases cited

of sect. 1 (a) of the Act whereby in no case can more than 6½ per cent be charged and therefore rate cannot be increased beyond 6½ per cent. In the case of 1919 houses where, by virtue of the Act of 1919, the interest has been already increased by ½ per cent no further increase will be allowed during the period of a year from the 2nd July, 1920.

A brief survey of the provisions of the earlier Acts with regard to increases in mortgage interest may prove useful. Under the Act of 1915 in the case of 1915 houses with certain exceptions, increases since the commencement of the war and beyond the standard rate of interest (b) (which was defined (c) in that Act in identical terms with the definition in sect 12 (1) (b) of the present Act) were forbidden. In no case did the Act apply, however, to increases subsequent to the 4th August, 1914 where such increase was in compliance with or in consequence of a notice in writing demanding either repayment or an increased rate given prior to the 4th August, 1914 (d) nor did the Act affect any mortgage interest which accrued due before the 25th November 1915 (e)

In the case of 1919 houses under the Act of 1919 (f), that Act only applied to increases since the 25th December 1918 (g) but did not affect mortgage interest which had accrued due before the 4th March, 1919, and in the case of these houses an increase of ½ per cent above the standard rate of interest was allowed

Sect 3 - Restrictions on calling in Mortgages

In the case of mortgages to which the Act applies sect 7 enacts that it shall not be lawful for the mortgagee which term will of course include anyone deriving title under him (h) to call in his mortgage or take any steps for exercising any right of

(b) The Act of 1915 s 1 (1)
(c) Ibid sect 2 (1) (b)
(d) Ibid. sect 1 (1) (x)
(e) Ibid sect 1 (1) (i)
(f) 9 Geo V c 7
(g) Ibid sect 4 (i)
(h) Sect 12 (1) (f)

foreclosure or sale, or for otherwise enforcing his security or for
recovering the principal money thereby secured (*i*) so long as—

   (*a*) interest at the rate permitted under the Act is paid and
       is not more than twenty-one days in arrear; and

   (*b*) the covenants by the mortgagor (other than the covenant
       for the repayment of the principal money secured) are
       performed and observed; and

   (*c*) the mortgagor keeps the property in a proper state of
       repair and pays all interest and instalments of principal
       recoverable under any prior encumbrance.

The provisions of Rule 12 of the Increase of Rent Rules should
be noted, whereby, on an application for an order authorising a
mortgagee to call in and enforce a mortgage, the Court may,
after considering all the circumstances of the case and the position of all the parties, make or refuse to make the order subject to such conditions as the Court may think fit.

The Act, it is to be observed, does not take away any right,
but merely suspends the particular form of remedy which might
otherwise have been made to enforce the mortgagee's rights (*k*).

The meaning of the words "take any steps for . . . enforcing
his security" was considered in *Welby* v. *Parker*. In that case
a mortgagee, before the Act of 1915 came into force, had issued
a writ to enforce his security by foreclosure and sale, and subsequently to the passing of that Act applied by summons in
chambers for an order *nisi*. The summons was adjourned to
Eve J., who refused to make an order. On appeal the Court
of Appeal, affirming the judgment, held that the application
by summons and the giving of the notice of appeal were "steps
for enforcing a security." In *Martin* v. *Watson and Egan* the
interest of the mortgagee of certain premises vested in the plaintiff. The interest of the original mortgagor vested in one Mary
Watson, who demised the premises to the defendant Egan, such
demise being void against the mortgagee. The plaintiff took
proceedings in ejectment, and it was held that this was a "step

---

(*i*) For forms of summons and order, see Appendix, Forms 2 and 4.
(*k*) *Welby* v. *Parker*.

for enforcing the security. Again in *In re Whiteside Park and another* v *Whiteside*, the Court held that the application for an order for administration of the estate of a deceased person by the assignees of a mortgage debt of the deceased was a step and the Court accordingly refused the application.

While the mortgagee's right to recover his principal or enforce his security is suspended protection is at the same time given to him by requiring the mortgagor to fulfil the conditions mentioned in paras (a) (b) (c) of sect 7 so that the mortgagee's right might not be otherwise prejudiced and the general position left in *statu quo* (l)

One of the conditions to be fulfilled by the mortgagor before he will be entitled to the protection given by sect 7 is the punctual payment of interest at the rate permitted by the Act (m) The mortgagor himself must pay the interest. The retention of rent as a payment of interest by a mortgagee in possession will not amount to payment of interest within the meaning of sect 7 (a) (n). It is submitted that the words rate permitted under the Act do not mean merely the rate permitted by sect 1 of the Act it will also include a rate which exceeds $6\frac{1}{2}$ per cent but which is not illegal under the Act by reason for instance of its being the standard rate or its having been increased prior to the 25th March 1920 (o)

Property will not have been deemed to have been kept in repair by the mortgagor merely because the mortgagee in possession might have applied the surplus rents for the purpose of keeping it in repair or merely because the mortgagees were in possession and the mortgagor could not have entered without being guilty of trespass (p)

The meaning of the phrase keep in a proper state of repair was considered in *Woodifield* v *Bond*, and it was there pointed out that the standard of repair to be reasonably required or

(l) *Woodifield* v *Bond* (1922) 2 Ch at p 50
(m) Sect 7 (a)
(n) *Walters* v *White*
(o) See however *Holland* v *Cooper*
(p) *Walters* v *White*

which is proper — for the protection of a mortgagee is obviously more elastic than that appropriate in the case of a landlord (q) The Court accordingly held that "the proper state of repair in which a mortgagor has to keep his property in order to obtain the benefit of sect. 7 must be measured by the general condition of the property at the date of the mortgage, and must not be extended beyond the preservation of the property in a state corresponding with its condition at that date (r). The property must be kept in such a state as not to be substantially deteriorated, and so that it should remain as good a security for the mortgage money as it was (s); nor does the word "repair" involve a rebuilding of the whole or any integral part of the structure of the security." In this connection it should be observed that in the Act "repairs" are contrasted with "improvements and structural alterations" (t)

Exceptions. The provisions of sect. 7 will not apply in the following cases—

1. To a mortgage where the principal money secured thereby is repayable by means of periodical instalments extending over a term of not less than ten years from the creation of the mortgage (u)

2. To any power of sale exerciseable by a mortgagee who was on the 25th day of March 1920 a mortgagee in possession (x)

These words have only been inserted *ex abundanti cautela* and do not mean that where a mortgagee is in possession on the 25th March 1920 his remedies are limited by the Act to the exercise of his power of sale (y)

(q) (1922) 2 Ch. at p. 51
(r) *Ib.* at p. 51
(s) *Ib.* See also *Hetherington's Trustees v. Huntress Trustees* (1923), Sc. L. Times, pp. 49 et seq. (neglect to make good damage resulting from minor workings and neglect to provide additional sanitary accommodation)
(t) Sect. 2 (1) (d)
(u) Sect. 7 (1)
(x) *Ibid.*
(y) *Hetherington v. ...*

By virtue of sect 19 (3) of the Act and sect 38 of the Interpretation Act 1889 the 25th November 1915 and the 4th March 1919 are to be substituted for the 25th March 1920 in the case of " 1915 " and ' 1919 ' houses respectively

A mortgagee in possession has been held to mean under the Courts (Emergency Powers) Act 1914 s 1 (1) (b) a mortgagee who has taken possession without the leave of the Court (a), and apparently the same meaning is to be given to the term as used in the Rent Act A mortgagee therefore who has gone into possession with the leave of the Court will not be able to take any further step for enforcing his security without the leave of the Court as otherwise the Act would provide a means for deceiving the Court because it would enable a mortgagee to procure an order merely for leave to go into possession while his real purpose would be to realise his security by a sale (a)

> (3) To cases where the mortgagor consents to the exercise by the mortgagee of the powers conferred by the mortgage (b)

In a Scotch case where the trustees of a debtor's estate consented to the first bondholder's trustees entering into possession of and administering the mortgaged estate it was held that a third bondholder could not object or avail himself of the provision of sect 1 (4) of the Rent Act of 1915 and that apparently will be the same position under sect 7 (4) of the Act of 1920 (c)

> (4) If in the case of a mortgage of a *leasehold* interest the mortgagee satisfies the County Court that (i) his security is seriously diminishing in value or is otherwise in jeopardy and (ii) that for that reason it is reasonable that the mortgage should be called in and enforced, the Court may by order authorise him to call in and enforce the same and thereupon sect 7 shall not apply to such mortgage

---

(a) *In re Provident Association of London Ltd and Golloughy's Contract*
(a) *Ib* at p 243
(b) Sect 7 (1)
(c) *Graham's Trustees v Dous' Trustees* (1917) 2 Sc L T R 174

Any such order, however, may be made subject to a condition that it shall not take effect if the mortgagor within such time as the Court directs pays to the mortgagee such *portion* of the principal sum secured as appears to the Court to correspond to the diminution of the security (*d*).

(*d*) Sect. 7 (11). — As to the Court to which application should be made, see Rule 2.

CHAPTER IX

RECOVERY OF SUMS IRRECOVERABLE BY LANDLORD OR MORTGAGEE

WHERE any sum has whether before or after the passing of the Act of 1920 (2nd July, 1920) been paid on account of any *rent or mortgage interest*, being a sum which is by virtue of that Act or any Act repealed by that Act (a), irrecoverable by the landlord or mortgagee, the sum so paid is recoverable from the landlord or mortgagee who received the payment, or his legal personal representative, by the tenant or mortgagor by whom it was paid (or presumably, his legal personal representative (b)). Any such sum, or *any other sum*, which under that Act is recoverable by a tenant from a landlord or payable or repayable by a landlord to a tenant may without prejudice to any other method of recovery be deducted by the tenant or mortgagor from any rent or interest payable by him to the landlord or mortgagee (c) (or presumably, his legal personal representative (d))

In the case of the original mortgagor and mortgagee and the original landlord and tenant no difficulty arises In such a case the mortgagor and the tenant may recover such sums by action, or, if they prefer they may deduct the amount from interest or rent respectively

Where the original mortgagee or landlord is dead, such sums can be recovered from their legal personal representatives, but it is not quite clear whether they can be deducted from the interest or rent It is submitted however that this method of

(a) See the Second Schedule of the Act
(b) The words in brackets are not in the Act
(c) Sect 14 (1)
(d) Sect 12 (1) (t) The words in brackets are not in the Act

S   10

recovery can also be adopted since 'mortgagee' and 'landlord' are defined by sect. 12 (1) (f) as including any person from time to time deriving title under the original mortgagee and landlord.

No express provision is made for a case where the original mortgagor or tenant is dead but it is also submitted that in such a case their legal personal representatives can adopt either method of recovery as mentioned above by virtue of sect. 12 (1) (f) which defines mortgagor and tenant as including persons deriving title under the original mortgagor and tenant.

The earlier Acts made no provision for the recovery of such sums and in *Sharp Bros.* v. *Knight* it was held that the tenant could not recover sums paid in excess of the rent, legally recoverable by the landlord, if such payments were made under a mistake of law as they usually would be (e). This state of affairs was remedied by sect. 2 of the Courts (Emergency Powers) Act 1917 whereby it was provided, *inter alia*, that where such excess payments of rent or mortgage interest had been made which would have been irrecoverable under the Rent Act of 1915, such sums, within six months after the date of payment, or in the case of payments made before the passing of the Courts (Emergency Powers) Act 1917 within six months of the passing thereof should be recoverable from the landlord or mortgagee or their personal representatives or be deducted from any rent or interest payable within such six months. This provision was replaced by sect. 14 (1) of the Act of 1920.

Together with sect. 14 (1) should be read sect. 19 (3) of the Act of 1920 and also sect. 38 of the Interpretation Act 1889. The combined effect of these sections may be summarised as follows. Payments should be divided into two categories, into payments made before and payments made after the 2nd July 1920 the date when the Act of 1920 came into operation. As regards payments made prior to that Act of 1920 the tenant can be met by any objection which could have been raised at the date of the passing of the Act of 1920. In *Rawlinson* v. *Algar* the tenant claimed to recover excess payments of rent covering a

period of 266 weeks from September, 1915, till October, 1920
As regards the excess payments made prior to the 2nd July,
1920, the Court held that the landlord could plead in defence
sect 5 of the Courts (Emergency Powers) Act 1917

As regards payments made subsequently to the 2nd July 1920
no limit of time was set within which such payments might be
recovered

The object of the Act in this respect was thus twofold
firstly, to enlarge by sect 14 the tenant's right to recover or
set off sums overpaid and secondly, by sect 19 (3) not to revive
rights which were not *in esse* at the time of the passing of the
Act (*f*)

The view however is taken in this book that any rights to
recover irrecoverable sums paid prior to the passing of the
Act of 1920 have long since been extinguished since the Courts
(Emergency Powers) Act 1917 s 5 (1) imposed a time limit
of six months within which such sums might be recovered

The above submission is based on the fact that, by sect 19 (3)
of the Act of 1920, nothing in the repeal of the enactments mentioned in the Second Schedule is to render recoverable any sums
which were irrecoverable on the 2nd July 1920 without prejudice to the operation of sect 38 of the Interpretation Act 1889
This latter Act in sect 38 (2) (c) provides that where an Act
passed after 1st January 1890, repeals any other enactment
unless a contrary intention appears the repeal shall not affect
any right, privilege obligation or liability acquired, accrued or
incurred under any enactment so repealed ' The liability incurred by the landlord or mortgagee under the Acts previous to
the Act of 1920 was a liability to pay these irrecoverable
sums only within six months of the date of their payment by
the tenant or the mortgagor as the case must be

There does not seem to be any case which directly deals with
the point though *Rawlinson* v *Alger* and *Smith* v *Lloyd* may
be cited as strong authorities for the contrary proposition that
such sums paid between the period January 2nd to July 2nd

Rawlinson v *Alger* (1921 W N at p 91

10 2

1920 can be recovered at any time since the passing of the Act of 1920

The law has again been altered by sect. 8 (2) of the Amendment Act, 1923, which restores the six months' limit of time within which the tenant or mortgagor may recover by virtue of sect. 14 (1) of the Act of 1920, sums paid respectively to the landlord or mortgagee. By sect. 8 (2) of the Amendment Act, 1923, it is provided that sums which are recoverable by the tenant or mortgagor under sect. 14 (1) of the Act of 1920 shall be recoverable at any time within six months from the date of payment or in the case of a payment made before the 31st July 1923 at any time within six months from the 31st July 1923 but not afterwards. This provision, however, does not affect in any way the operation of the Notices of Increase Act (Sect. 8 (3) of the Amendment Act.)

It is not only excess payments of rent and mortgage interest that are recoverable under sect. 14. That section also provides that any other sum which is recoverable by a tenant from a landlord, or payable or repayable by a landlord to a tenant, may, without prejudice to any other method of recovery, be deducted from the rent. The only two other cases in the Acts are premiums and excessive rents in the case of furnished lettings.

Fines, premiums and other such sums, therefore, are not only recoverable by action, but their amount may also be deducted from the rent. Further, on the conviction of a person for taking a fine premium or other sum the Court may order the amount paid or the value of the consideration given to be repaid, such order being in lieu of any other method of recovery (g)

Where a statutory tenant has been convicted under sect. 15 (2) of taking a fine premium or other sum or any other consideration from any other person than the landlord the Court may also make a similar order.

In the case of furnished lettings, where the rent is such as to yield the lessor a profit of more than 25 per cent over the 'normal profit' (h), such excess may be recovered by action, or deducted from the rent, and in a case where the offender is

(g) Sect. 8 (2)   (h) Sect. 9

convicted under sect. 10 the Court may order the excess to be paid over to the lessee, such order to be in lieu of any other method of recovery (g)

The expiration of the Act will not render recoverable by the landlord any rent, interest or other sum which, during the continuance of the Act, was irrecoverable, or affect the right of the tenant to recover any sum which, during the continuance of the Act, was recoverable by him (h)

The provisions of sect. 1 (1) (a) and (b) of the Notices of Increase Act, 1923 should further be noticed, whereby sect. 14 (1) of the Act of 1920 providing for the recovery of sums made irrecoverable by the principal Act is not to apply to an increase of rent made valid by the Notices of Increase Act where such increase was paid by or recovered from a tenant prior to the 1st day of December, 1922 (i). A tenant, moreover, has no right to recover any validated increase of rent even where such increase was paid by or recovered from the tenant subsequently to the 1st December, 1922 because such increase becomes valid through the operation of the Notices of Increase Act.

The provisions of proviso (b) of sect. 1 (1) of the Notices of Increase Act should further be noted whereby nothing in that Act shall affect the right to enforce any judgment of a Court of competent jurisdiction given before the 15th February, 1923 or render recoverable any sum paid under such judgment. Thus if judgment has been given prior to the 15th February, 1923, in favour of the tenant to recover any validated increase of rent which was paid by the tenant to the landlord even prior to the 1st December, 1923 such judgment will stand and the tenant will be entitled to recover the validated increase in spite of proviso (a)

As to the method of recovery by the landlord of arrears of validated increases of rent under the Notices of Increase Act, cf. supra, p. 84

(g) Sect. 10
(h) Sect. 19 (2)
(i) This provision seems to have been inserted ex abundanti cautela

CHAPTER X

PROCEDURE

IN consequence of the power conferred by sect. 17 (1) of the Act of 1920 Rules (a) have been made under that Act in place of the Rules made under the previous Acts (b) Rules have also been made with regard to Scotland (c) Rule 15 of the original Rules of 1920 has been slightly amended by a fresh Rule made on the 3rd June, 1921 (d, relating to the fees payable in the case of an order giving leave to distrain Rules have also been made under the Act of 1923 (e) whereby the Rules of 1920 with the exception of Rules 2 3 12 19. 20 (most of which apply to mortgages) are extended to include applications under the Act of 1923 except under sect 11 (2) (Rule I)

The County Court is given by sect 17 (2) of the Act of 1920 jurisdiction to deal with any claim or other proceedings arising out of the Act or any of its provisions, notwithstanding that by reason of the amount of claim or otherwise the case would not but for this provision be within the jurisdiction of a County Court If a person takes proceedings under the Act in the High Court which he could have taken in the County Court he shall not be entitled to recover any costs (f)

This section (17 (2), refers to such applications which under the Act are to be made to the County Court applications, for example with regard to increase of rent under sect 2 (6), appli-

---

a See Appendix

b The previous Rules [England] were S R & O 62. L 2. 29th Jan 1916 S R & O 446 L 22. 26th June 1916 S R & O 623 21st May 1919

c See Statutory Rules and Orders, 1920 Vol 1 p 1094 sq

d S R & O 932, L 12 3rd June 1921

e 1923 No 901, L 16

f Sect 17 (2)

cations under sect. 7 (ii) for calling in a mortgage of a leasehold interest on the ground that it is seriously diminishing in value, or applications for apportionment of rent under sect. 12 (3), and so forth (*g*). It is in respect of such applications only, it is submitted, that it will be immaterial whether by reason of the amount of claim or otherwise, the case would be beyond the jurisdiction of the County Court; the jurisdiction of the County Courts and of the High Court is not otherwise interfered with (*h*).

On the other hand, where a claim arises out of the Act and is such that the County Court would have had jurisdiction irrespectively of the Act, then no costs will be awarded by virtue of sect. 17 (2) if proceedings are taken in the High Court, even though such proceedings are successful (*i*). On the other hand, there appears to be no reason why a successful defendant should be deprived of his costs, where proceedings arising under the Act are brought in the High Court.

For an instance of a "proceeding arising out of the Act," reference should be made to *Wolff* v. *Smith*, where a statutory tenant instituted proceedings in the Chancery Division, claiming an injunction to restrain his landlord from interfering with the quiet enjoyment by him of certain rooms of which he was the tenant. In his judgment, Eve, J., said 'As between the plaintiff and his landlady it was necessary to establish possession, and the plaintiff could only do so by showing that he was a statutory tenant by virtue of the Act. Therefore, this proceeding was one arising out of the Act.'

By sect. 11 (1) of the Amendment Act, 1923, the County Court has the power of *summarily* determining on the application of a landlord or a tenant any questions as to the *amount* of the rent standard rent, or net rent, or as to the increase of rent permitted under the Amendment Act or the principal Act of 1920

(*g*) For forms of such application, see Forms in Appendix.
(*h*) Cf. X Rays Ltd. v. Armitage
(*i*) Wolff v. Smith

Where an action is brought in the High Court and some question arises which, by virtue of the Act, is determinable by the County Court alone (k) the High Court will have no jurisdiction to determine the question, and the matter must be referred to the County Court. The High Court, however, will not be prevented from giving its decision on any other independent issue (l). Thus in X Rays, Ltd. v. Armitage, which was an action under Ord. XIV. r. 8 for possession, rent and mesne profits, a question arose as to whether the increase of rent should be suspended under sect. 2 (2) and Rowlatt, J. held that the High Court had no jurisdiction to entertain the question, and that resort for that purpose must be had to the County Court.

Care must be taken in determining the cases in which the County Court alone is given jurisdiction. The provisions of sect. 2 (6) of the Act for instance are at first sight misleading. That section provides that any question arising under sub-sects. 1, 2, 3 of sect. 2 shall be determined by the County Court alone whose decision shall be final and conclusive. No difficulty arises in the case of the two latter sub-sections under which applications can be made to the County Court for the purpose of suspension of increase (sub-sect. 2) and for the purpose of determining whether there has been a transfer of a burden or liability (Sub-sect. (3)). But as regards sub-sect. (1) the applications to which reference are made are applications under sect. 2. 1. (i) for the purpose of suspending or reducing an increase on the ground that the expenditure was unnecessary, and applications under sect. 2 (d) (ii) for determining what is a fair and reasonable increase in cases where the landlord is responsible for part of the repairs.

It must not be thought that by virtue of sect. 2 (6) the County Court alone is given power to determine what is the proper increase payable or what is the standard rent (m). The High Court has the same power of determining this question subject, of course, to the above-mentioned limitations.

(k) Id., under sect. 2 (6).
(l) X Rays, Ltd. v. Armitage.
(m) Connolly v. Whelan, 54 I. L. T. R. at p. 20; X Rays, Ltd. v. Armitage.

Other instances in which applications must be made to the County Court are applications under sect. 7 (11) for calling in a mortgage of a leasehold in which case apparently there will be an appeal against the decision of the County Court judge; applications under sect. 9 (1) in the case of excessive charges for furnished lettings; applications under sect. 12 (1) (g) for the purpose of determining who should be entitled to become the tenant, in default of agreement in cases where the tenant dying intestate leaves no widow or is a woman; under sect. 12 (3) for the purpose of apportioning the rent, in which case the decision of the County Court as regards the amount will be conclusive and final; under sect. 2 (4) of the Notices of Increase Act 1923, as to the amount of arrears due from a tenant or the amount of any instalment payable by him; applications under sects. 2 (4), 3 (1) of the Notices of Increase Act; and applications under Rule 3 of the 1923 Rules, sects. 7 (3), 11 (1) of the Act of 1923

Reference should also be made to sect. 11 (2) of the Amendment Act 1923 whereby the Lord Chancellor may by rules and directions made and given under sect. 17 of the principal Act of 1920 provide for any questions arising under or in connection with the Act of 1920 or Part I of the Amendment Act of 1923 being referred by consent for final determination by the judge or registrar of a County Court sitting as an arbitrator or by an arbitrator appointed by such judge

Where parties desire to have any questions settled by arbitration pursuant to sect. 11 (2) of the Act of 1923, they must sign and deliver to the County Court of the district in which the premises in question are situate a written request in accordance with Form 17. (Rule 4 (1) of the 1923 Rules.)

It is to be noted that the Arbitration Act 1889 will not apply to an arbitration under sect. 11 (2) of the Act of 1923. (Rule 4 (3) of the 1923 Rules.)

The only fee (n) payable on such an arbitration is 1l. 10s., the whole of which is to be paid to the arbitrator where he is a person other than the judge or registrar. (Rule 4 (4).)

(n) The fee should be sent to the Court with the application. (Rule 4 (4).)

Each party will have to bear and pay his own costs in the arbitration and one half of the above fee of 1*l*. 10*s*. '(*o*).

Rule 16 (*p*) provides for the costs of such applications, and such applications only. The corresponding rule under the earlier rules came under the consideration of the Court in the case of *Bensusan* v. *Bustard*. It was held that where an action was brought in the County Court to recover possession of premises under the Rent Act of 1915 costs follow the event under sect. 113 of the County Courts Act, 1888, unless the Court otherwise orders, and that the above section of the County Courts Act was in no way affected by the Rule. The position is the same under the present Act. As was said (*q*) by Lawrence, J., in the above case: "There is no power by rules to repeal sect. 113 of the County Courts Act, 1888. The rule applies to applications under the Act (*i.e.*, the Rent Act), and there are many applications under the Act with reference to questions of rent and mortgages and a variety of things which are well covered by the words 'any application under the Act and these Rules.'" The Rules deal, *inter alia*, with particular forms of applications for relief under the Rent Act. They provide for the form in which they are to be made and the like matters, and it is in regard to these *independent* applications in the County Court, which are not dealt with by the County Court Rules, that these particular Rules were made. Such Rules had to be made because these applications were outside and beyond the prior jurisdiction of the County Court (*r*).

With regard to applications under the Act of 1923, the costs of such applications are in the absolute discretion of the Court, and the Court must in every case fix the amount of such costs. (Rule 2 (2) of the 1923 Rules.) It is immaterial whether such an application could or could not have been made under the principal Act.

The provisions of Rule 18 should also be noted, whereby in

(*o*) See Form 17 in Appendix
(*p*) See Appendix.
(*q*) 89 L. J K. B. at p 1118
(*r*) *Ibid*. at p. 1119.

actions for recovery of rent or mortgage interest or for recovery of possession or ejectment, affected by the Act, the Court must satisfy itself before making an order that such order may properly be made regard being had to the provisions of the Act Even where the Act is not pleaded as a defence, the Court is nevertheless obliged to see that the provisions of the Act are complied with (*Salter v Lash*)

In passing, mention might also be made of the provisions of sect 19 (3) of the Act whereby any proceedings pending in any Court (whether a Court of first instance or not (s)) on the 2nd July 1920, under any enactment repealed by the Act were to be deemed to have been commenced under the Act

Further by sect 3 (2) of the Administration of Justice Act, 1920 it is provided that, notwithstanding anything in any Act, it shall not be lawful for any party in a County Court or other civil Court of inferior jurisdiction to require any action or other matter arising under the Increase of Rent and Mortgage Interest (Restrictions) Act 1920 to be tried by a jury

A point of pleading arose in the Irish case of *O'Hare and others v Ireland* That was a case of ejectment The defence was (1) a plea of possession and (2) a plea of the Rent Act The reply (1) joined issue and (2) denied that the Act applied but at the same time relied on an undertaking by the defendant to give up possession, and also stated that the premises were required by the plaintiffs for the proper working of an agricultural holding The defendant sought to set aside the second part of the reply, and in the alternative asked for leave to deliver a special rejoinder The Court held that the reply was specially pleaded and that there was no need for a special rejoinder

(s) *Brado v Horsley*

CHAPTER XI

SUMMARY OFFENCES UNDER THE ACTS

1. *False or Misleading Statement or Representation in Notice of Increase*

If a notice of increase (a) contains any statement or representation which is *false or misleading in any material respect*, the landlord (b) shall be liable on summary conviction to a fine not exceeding 10l. unless the *landlord* proves that the statement was made (1) innocently and (2) without intent to deceive (c).

2. *Requiring a Fine, Premium &c.*

1. Any person *requiring* any payment of any fine, premium or other like sum or the giving of any pecuniary consideration in addition to the rent, as a condition of the grant, renewal or continuance (d) of a tenancy or a sub-tenancy of any dwelling-house to which the Act applies, shall be liable on summary conviction to a fine not exceeding 100l. (e).

The Court on convicting the offender may order the amount paid or the value of the consideration given to be repaid to the person by whom the same was made or given, but such order shall be in lieu of any other method of recovery prescribed by the Act (f).

Requiring the giving of any pecuniary consideration is not a

(a) See sect. 3 (2) of the Act of 1920.

(b) For definition of landlord see sect. 12 (1) 1) the definition of landlord in sect. 12 (1) (g) will not apparently apply.

(c) Sect. 3 (2).

(d) *Supra*, p. 91.

(e) Sect. 8 (2) of Act of 1920.

(f) *Ibid.*

distinct offence from requiring the payment of a fine or premium (g) In *Crang v Leman* a rent collector and house agent was convicted under sect 8 (2) for receiving from a fresh tenant the payment of arrears of rent due from the previous tenant as a condition of a grant of the tenancy of premises within the Act

Where the purchase of any furniture or other articles is required as a condition of the grant, renewal or continuance of a tenancy or sub-tenancy and the price exceeds the reasonable price the excess is to be treated as a fine or premium for the purposes of the above provision (Sect 9 (1) of the Amendment Act, 1923)

(b) A *statutory tenant*, retaining possession by virtue of the provisions of the Act of any dwelling-house to which the Act applies who as a condition of giving up possession, asks or receives the payment of any sum or the giving of any other consideration by any person *other than the landlord* (h), shall be liable on summary conviction to a fine not exceeding 100l (i)

The Court by which the offender is convicted may order any such payment or the value of any such consideration to be paid to the person by whom the same was made or given, but such order shall be in lieu of any other method of recovery (h)

Where the statutory tenant requires that furniture or other articles shall be purchased as a condition of giving up possession and the price exceeds the reasonable price, the excess will be treated as a sum asked to be paid as a condition of giving up possession for the purposes of the above provision (Sect 9 (2) of the Amendment Act 1923)

3 Excessive Charges for Furnished Lettings

Any person who, after the passing of the Act (2nd July 1920) *lets* any dwelling-house to which the Act applies or any part thereof (including apparently rooms subject to a separate

(g) *Crang v Leman* Times, 11th Nov 1921
(h) For definition of landlord see sect 12 (1) (f)
(i) Sect 15 (3) of Act of 1920
(k, Ibid supra p 91

letting wholly or partly as a dwelling) (*l*) at a rent which includes payment in respect of the use of furniture, and the rent charged yields to the lessor a profit which, having regard to all the circumstances of the case and *in particular, to the margin of profit allowed under sect. 9* is extortionate shall be liable on summary conviction to a fine not exceeding 100*l.* (*m*)

The Court by which the offender is convicted may order that the rent so far as it exceeds the amount permitted by sect. 9 shall be irrecoverable, and that the amount of any excess shall be repaid to the lessee; but any such order shall be in lieu of any other method of recovery prescribed by the Act (*n*).

4. *Failure to supply Statement as to Standard Rent*

A landlord (*o*) of any dwelling-house to which the Act applies shall on being so *requested in writing by the tenant* of the dwelling house supply him with a *statement in writing* as to what is the standard rent, and if *without reasonable excuse* he—

i. *fails* within fourteen days to do so or

ii. supplies a statement which is *false in any material particular*

he shall be liable on summary conviction to a fine not exceeding 10*l.* *p*

Apparently, in order to obtain a conviction a request in writing must first be proved to have been made by the tenant.

5. *False Entries in Rent Books and similar Documents*

A. If *any person* in any rent book or similar document makes an entry showing or purporting to show any tenant as being in arrear in respect of any sum which by virtue of the Act or any Act repealed thereby is irrecoverable such person shall on summary conviction be liable to a fine not exceeding 10*l.* unless he

(*l*) Sect. 12 (5) of Act of 1920.
(*m*) Sect. 10 of Act of 1920.
(*n*) *Ibid.*
(*o*) For definition of landlord see sect. 12 (1) (*i*) of Act of 1920.
(*p*) Sect. 11 of Act of 1920.

proves that he acted (1) innocently and (2) without intent to deceive (*g*)

B Where any such entry (in any rent book or similar document showing or purporting to show any tenant as being in arrear in respect of any sum which by virtue of the previous Rent Acts is irrecoverable) has, *before the passing of the Act* (2nd July, 1920), been made by or on behalf of the landlord (*r*) then if the landlord on being requested by or on behalf of the tenant so to do refuses or neglects to cause the entry to be deleted *within seven days*, the landlord shall on summary conviction be liable to a fine not exceeding 10*l* unless he proves that he acted (1) innocently and (2) without intent to deceive (*s*)

6 *False or Misleading Statement or Representation in Notice claiming Validated Increases of Rent*

If a notice by the landlord claiming that a sum on account of arrears (*t*) of rent is due to him under the Notices of Increase Act 1923 contains any statement or representation which is false or misleading in any material respect, the landlord shall be liable on summary conviction to a fine not exceeding 10*l*, unless the landlord proves that the statement was made innocently and without intent to deceive (*u*)

7 *Failure to supply Statement or supplying False Statement of Sub-Letting*

Where part of any dwelling-house (*x*) to which the principal Act (of 1920) applies is lawfully sub-let, and the part so sub-let is also a dwelling-house within the Act (e g does not consist of business premises) and the landlord makes a written request to

---

(*q*) Sect 14 (2) (a) of Act of 1920
(*r*) See sect 12 (1) (f) for definition of landlord
(*s*) Sect 14 (2) (b) of Act of 1920
(*t*) See sect 2 (1) of the Notices of Increase Act, 1923
(*u*) Sect 2 (2) of the Notices of Increase Act
(*x*) Which may itself be part of, or rooms in a house Cf *supra* p 23

the tenant for a written statement of any sub-letting. the tenant will be summarily liable to a fine not exceeding 2*l* if the tenant without reasonable excuse—

(i) fails within fourteen days of such request to supply the landlord with such written statement of any sub-letting with particulars of occupancy, or

(ii) supplies a statement which is false in any material particulars (*y*)

(*y*) whether knowledge of the falsity on the part of the land-lord must also be proved?

(*y*) Sect 7 (2) of the Amendment Act 1923

CHAPTER XII

RESTRICTIONS AFTER THE EXPIRY OF THE PRINCIPAL ACT

THE Act of 1920 and Part I of the Amendment Act of 1923 expire (a) on the 24th June 1925 in England and on the 28th May 1925 in Scotland (b)

After these dates Part II of the Act of 1923 comes into operation in England and Scotland, respectively and provides a modified form of control for another five years (c) Part II of the Amendment Act however may be determined at an earlier date if a resolution to that effect is passed by both Houses of Parliament (d)

Part II deals with three matters mainly i e Restrictions on Possession (e) Reduction of Rent (f) and Restrictions on Calling-in of Mortgages (g) It also provides for the creation of reference committees (h) and empowers (i) the Lord Chancellor to make such rules and give such directions as he thinks fit for the purpose of giving full effect to the provisions of Part II

The Minister of Health (in Scotland (k), the Scottish Board of Health) is to provide for the constitution and procedure of these reference committees by regulations made by him (Sect 15 (1) Before any such regulation is made it is to be laid in draft before

(a) Sect 1 of the Amendment Act 1923
(b) Sect 19 (3) ibid
(c) Sect 17 ibid
(d) Ibid
(e) Sect 12, ibid.
(f) Sect 13 ibid
(g) Sect 14 ibid
(h) Sect 12 (5), Sect 15, ibid
(i) Sect 16 ibid
(j) Sect 19 (1)

both Houses of Parliament, and the draft must be approved by resolution of both Houses either with or without modifications or additions. In the former case both Houses must agree to the modifications or additions. The Minister of Health may thereupon make the regulation in the form in which it has been approved, and the regulation on being so made shall be of full force and effect. (Sect. 15 (2).

The purpose of such reference committees is in order to assist the Court in the determination of questions arising under Part II of the Act in relation to the rent, character or condition of dwelling-houses. (Sect. 12 (5).)

In addition reference may be made to a reference committee for determination of any questions in relation to the rent (l) payable by or to be paid by a sitting tenant (m) which may be submitted to them by the tenant and landlord.

Sect. 1.—Restrictions on Right to Possession

Sect. 12 of the Amendment Act, 1923, deals with the restrictions on the right to possession of a house to which the principal Act applies after the expiry of the latter Act (n).

The Act employs the phrase 'sitting tenant' and defines it as a person who on the 24th June 1923 (o) is tenant of a dwelling-house (p) to which the principal Act then applies (sect. 12 (1) (q), and then may be a sitting tenant of part of a dwelling-house. Sect. 12 (1). From these two sub-sections the inference seems obvious that the sitting tenant need not necessarily be in actual possession.

Where proceedings are taken against the 'sitting tenant' for recovery of possession or ejectment at any time after the 24th

---

(l) Cf. sect. 12 (2)

(m) For definition see sect. 2 (1)

(n) As amended by Parts I and III of the Amendment Act, 1923.

(o) As regards Scotland 28th May 1923. (See sect. 19 (3).)

(p) Which may include part of or rooms in a house. See sect. 12 (2) and sect. 12 (8) of the Act of 1920.)

(q) I.e. which is still a controlled house. (See secs. 2 and 3 of the Amendment Act, 1923; see also supra pp. 41–46.)

June 1923 it it appears to the Court (1) that the proceedings are harsh and oppressive or (II) that exceptional hardship would be caused to the sitting tenant by the making or giving of an order or judgment for possession or ejectment the Court may—

(a) refuse to make or give the order or judgment

(b) adjourn the application

(c) stay or suspend execution of any such order or judgment

(d) (I) postpone the date of possession for such period or periods and subject to such conditions as it thinks proper

(II) discharge or rescind any order or judgment on the compliance with such conditions (Sect 12 (1) (j))

The Court may further for the purpose of the exercise of its jurisdiction under sect 12—

(e) direct that the tenancy of the sitting tenant shall be treated as a subsisting tenancy notwithstanding any determination of the tenancy by notice to quit or similar notice or otherwise, and the Court may set aside and annul any such notice accordingly (sect 12 (2))

(f) determine what increase of rent, if any, is fair and reasonable regard being had to the character and condition of the dwelling-house and the rents of similar dwelling-houses in the locality (Sect 12 (2) (s))

None of the above powers however is to be exercised by the Court where the Court is satisfied that greater hardship would be caused to the landlord by the exercise of the power than would be caused to the tenant by the refusal to exercise it

As to what may constitute greater hardship reference may be made to the cases on possession under the previous Act, cited above, pp 113—115

Where an order or judgment for possession is made or given against the sitting tenant of the whole of the dwelling-house, the same shall not unless the Court otherwise orders be opera-

(r) Cf sect 5 (2) of the Act of 1920

(s) The County Court can also exercise in any proceedings against the sitting tenant to which sect 12 applies, the power under sect 13 of reducing the rent pending the execution of repairs (sect 13 (2)) cf infra p 164

tive against the sitting tenant of part of such dwelling-house, provided such part was on the 24th June, 1925, lawfully sub-let to the sitting tenant of such part and also constituted a dwelling-house to which the principal Act applies, i.e., a house which on that date is still controlled. (Sect. 12 (1).) The Court, further, has in relation to such part and to the sitting tenant thereof the like powers and jurisdiction as it has in relation to the whole house and to the sitting tenant thereof (t)

Sect. 12, sub-sects (1) (5) do not apply, however, to proceedings under the Small Tenements Recovery Act, 1838 The tenant, however, may apply that proceedings taken under that Act should be discontinued, in which case they will be transferred to the County Court in accordance with the rules that may be made for transfer to the County Court under Part II (Sect. 12 (6) `

Sect 2.—Restrictions with regard to Rent

One of the powers given to the County Court by sect 12 is that of determining what increase of rent (whether payable or to be paid) by the sitting tenant is fair and reasonable, regard being had to the character and the condition of the dwelling-house and the rents of similar dwelling-houses in the locality (Sect 12 (2)) The landlord and the tenant, if they prefer, can submit this question for determination by a reference committee (Sect 15 (2))

If the County Court on the application of the sitting tenant (u) is satisfied by the production of a certificate of the sanitary authority (x), and such further evidence (if any), that the dwelling-house is not in a reasonable state of repair (y) and that its condition is not due to the tenant's neglect or default or

(t) For definition of sitting tenant see supra, p 162
(u) Cf sect 12 (1)
(x) The certificate must state the work which requires to be executed in order to put the dwelling-house into repair (Sect 18 (1)) As to the fee payable and by whom it is to be paid, see ibid As to the proof of the certificate see sect 18 (3)
(y) Cf sect 18 (5) for the definition of "repairs"

breach of express agreement, the Court may order that the rent be reduced until the Court is satisfied on the report of the sanitary authority or otherwise that the necessary repairs (other than those for which the tenant is liable) have been executed Subject to the terms of the order, the rent will be payable at the reduced rate ordered by the Court until the Court is so satisfied (e) (Sect 13 (1))

Sect 3 – Restriction on Calling in of Mortgages

Where a dwelling-house is (1) in the occupation of a sitting tenant (*a e e* still controlled by virtue of Part II) and (2) subject to a mortgage to which the principal Act applied (b) provided it is not a mortgage where the principal is repayable by periodical instalments extending over a term of not less than ten years from the creation of the mortgage (c) the County Court may on application by the landlord make an order, subject to such conditions as regards increase or otherwise and for such time as appears to the Court to be proper (d) restraining the mortgagee from—

(a) calling-in his mortgage,

(b) taking steps for enforcing his security (as to what is such a step cf *supra* pp 110 111)

(c) recovering the principal money

if it is satisfied that such calling-in, enforcement or recovery would cause exceptional hardship

The County Court may, further, on the application of the mortgagee or landlord, rescind or vary any order so made if satisfied that, by reason of any material change in circumstances rescission or variation is necessary (Sect 14 (1))

(e) The powers of the Court under this section may be exercised in any proceedings against the sitting tenant to which sect 12 applies (Cf *supra*, p 163)

(a) For definition see sect 12 (1) *supra* p 162

(b) As to the application of the Act to mortgages, cf *supra* p 127

(c) Sect 14 (3)

(d) Sect 14 (2)

The restrictions that may be imposed under this section will however cease to be operative if at any time after the making of the order

(a) interest is more than twenty-one days in arrear; or

(b) any covenant by the mortgagor (other than that for the repayment of the principal money secured) is broken or not performed; or

(c) the mortgagor fails—

(i) to keep the property in a proper state of repair (as to what will constitute such failure cf. *supra* p. 141); or

(ii) to pay the interest and instalments of principal recoverable under any prior encumbrance; or

(d) the sitting tenant ceases to be tenant of the dwelling-house (Sect. 14 (2)).

These restrictive provisions with regard to mortgages are very necessary in the interests of landlords. It is only fair that while the landlord is saddled with the burden of restrictions he in his turn should have some measure of protection by the imposition of corresponding restrictions on the rights of the mortgagees of his controlled property.

APPENDIX I.

TEXT OF THE RENT RESTRICTIONS ACTS,
1920, 1923

———•———

A

INCREASE OF RENT AND MORTGAGE INTEREST (RESTRICTIONS) ACT, 1920

(10 & 11 Geo. 5 c. 17.)

[2nd July, 1920.]

Be it enacted, &c.

Restrictions on Increase of Rent and Mortgage Interest.

1. Subject to the provisions of this Act, where the rent of any dwelling-house to which this Act applies, or the rate of interest on a mortgage to which this Act applies, has been since the twenty-fifth day of March nineteen hundred and twenty, or is hereafter, increased then if the increased rent or the increased rate of interest exceeds by more than the amount permitted under this Act the standard rent or standard rate of interest the amount of such excess shall, notwithstanding any agreement to the contrary, be irrecoverable from the tenant or the mortgagor as the case may be.

Provided that, where a landlord or mortgagee has increased the rent of any such dwelling-house or the rate of interest on any such mortgage since the said date, but before the passing of this Act he may cancel such increase and repay any amount paid by virtue thereof and in that case the rent or rate shall not be deemed to have been increased since that date.

2.—(1) The amount by which the increased rent of a dwelling-house to which this Act applies may exceed the

Restriction on increasing rent and mortgage interest

Permitted increase in rent

standard rent shall, subject to the provisions of this Act,
be as follows, that is to say:—

(a) Where the landlord has since the fourth day of August
nineteen hundred and fourteen incurred, or hereafter incurs, expenditure on the improvement or
structural alteration of the dwelling-house (not including expenditure on decoration or repairs), an
amount calculated at a rate per annum not exceeding six, or, in the case of such expenditure
incurred after the passing of this Act, eight per
cent. of the amount so expended

Provided that the tenant may apply to the county
court for an order suspending or reducing such
increase on the ground that such expenditure is or
was necessary in whole or in part, and the court
may make an order accordingly.

(b) An amount not exceeding any increase in the amount
for the time being payable by the landlord in
respect of rates over the corresponding amount paid
in respect of the yearly, half-yearly or other period
which included the third day of August nineteen
hundred and fourteen, or in the case of a dwelling-
house for which no rates were payable in respect
of any period which included the said date, the
period which included the date on which the rates
first became payable thereafter

(c) In addition to any such amounts as aforesaid an
amount not exceeding fifteen per centum of the
net rent.

Provided that, except in the case of a dwelling-
house to which this Act applies but the enactments
repealed by this Act did not apply, the amount of
such addition shall not, during a period of one year
after the passing of this Act, exceed five per cent .

(d) In further addition to any such amounts as aforesaid—

(i) where the landlord is responsible for the
whole of the repairs, an amount not exceeding
twenty-five per cent of the net rent, or

(ii) where the landlord is responsible for part and not the whole of the repairs such lesser amount as may be agreed, or as may, on the application of the landlord or the tenant, be determined by the county court to be fair and reasonable having regard to such liability.

(e) In the case of dwelling-houses let by a railway company to persons in the employment of the company such additional amount if any as is required in order to give effect to the agreement dated the first day of March nineteen hundred and twenty relating to the rates of pay and conditions of employment of certain persons in the employment of railway companies or any agreement whether made before or after the passing of this Act extending or modifying that agreement.

(2) At any time or times, not being less than three months after the date of any increase permitted by paragraph (d) of the foregoing subsection the tenant or the sanitary authority may apply to the county court for an order suspending such increase, and also any increase under paragraph (e) of that subsection, on the ground that the house is not in all respects reasonably fit for human habitation, or is otherwise not in a reasonable state of repair.

The court on being satisfied by the production of a certificate of the sanitary authority or otherwise that any such ground as aforesaid is established and on being further satisfied that the condition of the house is not due to the tenant's neglect or default or breach of express agreement, shall order that the increase be suspended until the court is satisfied on the report of the sanitary authority or otherwise that the necessary repairs (other than the repairs if any for which the tenant is liable) have been executed, and on the making of such order the increase shall cease to have effect until the court is so satisfied.

(3) Any transfer to a tenant of any burden or liability previously borne by the landlord shall for the purposes of this Act be treated as an alteration of rent, and where is

the result of such a transfer the terms on which a dwelling-house is held are on the whole less favourable to the tenant than the previous terms the rent shall be deemed to be increased whether or not the sum periodically payable by way of rent is increased, and any increase of rent in respect of any transfer to a landlord of any burden or liability previously borne by the tenant where as the result of such transfer the terms on which any dwelling-house is held are on the whole not less favourable to the tenant than the previous terms shall be deemed not to be an increase of rent for the purposes of this Act Provided that for the purposes of this section the rent shall not be deemed to be increased where the liability for rates is transferred from the landlord to the tenant if a corresponding reduction is made in the rent

(4) On any application to a sanitary authority for a certificate or report under this section a fee of one shilling shall be payable but if the authority as the result of such application issues such a certificate as aforesaid the tenant shall be entitled to deduct the fee from any subsequent payment of rent

(5) For the purposes of this section the expression "repairs" means any repairs required for the purpose of keeping premises in good and tenantable repair and any premises in such a state shall be deemed to be in a reasonable state of repair and the landlord shall be deemed to be responsible for any repairs for which the tenant is under no express liability

(6) Any question arising under subsection (1) (2) or (3) of this section shall be determined on the application either of the landlord or the tenant by the county court and the decision of the court shall be final and conclusive

Limitation of permitted increases in rent

3 (1) Nothing in this Act shall be taken to authorise any increase of rent except in respect of a period during which but for this Act the landlord would be entitled to obtain possession, or any increase in the rate of interest on a mortgage except in respect of a period during which but for this Act the security could be enforced

(2) Notwithstanding any agreement to the contrary, where the rent of any dwelling-house to which this Act applies is increased, no such increase shall be due or recoverable until or in respect of any period prior to the expiry of four clear weeks, or, where such increase is on account of an increase in rates, one clear week, after the landlord has served upon the tenant a valid notice in writing of his intention to increase the rent which notice shall be in the form contained in the First Schedule to this Act, or in a form substantially to the same effect. If a notice served as aforesaid contains any statement or representation which is false or misleading in any material respect the landlord shall be liable on summary conviction to a fine not exceeding ten pounds unless he proves that the statement was made innocently and without intent to deceive. Where a notice of an increase of rent which at the time was valid has been served on any tenant, the increase may be continued without service of any fresh notice on any subsequent tenant.

(3) A notice served before the passing of this Act of an intention to make any increase of rent which is permissible only by virtue of this Act shall not be deemed to be a valid notice for the purpose of this section.

4 The amount by which the increased rate of interest payable in respect of a mortgage to which this Act applies may exceed the standard rate shall be an amount not exceeding one per cent. per annum:

Permitted increase in rate of mortgage interest

Provided that—

    (a) the rate shall not be increased so as to exceed six and a half per cent. per annum; and

    (b) except in the case of a dwelling-house to which this Act applies but the enactments repealed by this Act did not apply, the increase during a period of one year after the passing of this Act shall not exceed one-half per cent. per annum.

Further Restriction and Obligations on Landlords and Mortgagees

5.—(1) No order or judgment for the recovery of possession of any dwelling-house to which this Act applies, or for the ejectment of a tenant therefrom, shall be made or given unless—

    (a) any rent lawfully due from the tenant has not been paid, or any other obligation of the tenancy whether under the contract of tenancy or under this Act, so far as the same is consistent with the provisions of this Act, has been broken or not performed; or

    (b) the tenant or any person residing with him has been guilty of conduct which is a nuisance or annoyance to adjoining occupiers, or has been convicted of using the premises or allowing the premises to be used for an immoral or illegal purpose, or the condition of the dwelling-house has, in the opinion of the court, deteriorated owing to acts of waste by, or the neglect or default of the tenant or any such person; or

    (c) the tenant has given notice to quit, and in consequence of that notice the landlord has contracted to sell or let the dwelling-house or has taken any other steps as a result of which he would, in the opinion of the court, be seriously prejudiced if he could not obtain possession; or

    (d) the dwelling-house is reasonably required by the landlord for occupation as a residence for himself or for any person bonâ fide residing or to reside with him, or for some person in his whole time employment or in the whole time employment of some tenant from him, and (except as otherwise provided by this subsection) the court is satisfied that alternative accommodation, reasonably equivalent as regards rent and suitability in all respects is available; or

    (e) the landlord is a local authority or a statutory undertaking and the dwelling-house is reasonably required for the purpose of the execution of the statutory duties or powers of the authority or undertaking, and the court is satisfied as aforesaid as respects alternative accommodation; or

(f) the landlord became the landlord after service in any of His Majesty's forces during the war and requires the house for his personal occupation and offers the tenant accommodation on reasonable terms in the same dwelling-house, such accommodation being considered by the court as reasonably sufficient in the circumstances; or

(g) the dwelling-house is required for occupation as a residence by a former tenant thereof who gave up occupation in consequence of his service in any of His Majesty's forces during the war;

and in any such case as aforesaid the court considers it reasonable to make such an order or give such judgment.

The existence of alternative accommodation shall not be a condition of an order or judgment on any of the grounds specified in paragraph (d) of this subsection—

(i) where the tenant was in the employment of the landlord or a former landlord and the dwelling-house was let to him in consequence of that employment and he has ceased to be in that employment; or

(ii) where the court is satisfied by a certificate of the county agricultural committee or of the Minister of Agriculture and Fisheries pending the formation of such committee that the dwelling-house is required by the landlord for the occupation of a person engaged on work necessary for the proper working of an agricultural holding; or

(iii) where the landlord gave up the occupation of the dwelling-house in consequence of his service in any of His Majesty's forces during the war; or

(iv) where the landlord became the landlord before the thirtieth day of September nineteen hundred and seventeen, or, in the case of a dwelling-house

8 & 9 Geo 5,
c 7

which section four of the Increase of Rent and Mortgage Interest (Restrictions) Act, 1919, applied, became the landlord before the fifth day of March, nineteen hundred and nineteen or in the case of a dwelling-house to which this Act applies but the enactments repealed by this Act did not apply, became the landlord before the twentieth day of May nineteen hundred and twenty, and in the opinion of the court greater hardship would be caused by refusing an order for possession than by granting it

(2) At the time of the application for or the making of giving of any order or judgment for the recovery of possession of any such dwelling-house, or for the ejectment of a tenant therefrom, or in the case of any such order or judgment which has been made or given, whether before or after the passing of this Act and not executed at any subsequent time, the court may adjourn the application or stay or suspend execution on any such order or judgment or postpone the date of possession, for such period or periods as it thinks fit and subject to such conditions (if any) in regard to payment by the tenant of arrears of rent rent or mesne profits and otherwise as the court thinks fit and if such conditions are complied with the court may if it thinks fit discharge or rescind any such order or judgment

(3) Where any order or judgment has been made or given before the passing of this Act but not executed and, in the opinion of the court the order or judgment would not have been made or given if this Act had been in force at the time when such order or judgment was made or given, the court may, on application by the tenant rescind or vary such order or judgment in such manner as the court may think fit for the purpose of giving effect to this Act

(4) Notwithstanding anything in section one hundred and forty-three of the County Courts Act, 1888 or in section one of the Small Tenements Recovery Act 1838 every warrant for delivery of possession of or to enter and give possession of, any dwelling-house to which this Act applies shall

51 & 52 Vict
c 43
1 & 2 Vict
c 74

remain in force for three months from the day next after the last day named in the judgment or order for delivery of possession or ejectment or in the case of a warrant under the Small Tenements Recovery Act 1838 from the date of the issue of the warrant and in either case for such further period or periods if any as the court shall from time to time, whether before or after the expiration of such three months direct

(5) An order or judgment against a tenant for the recovery of possession of any dwelling-house or ejectment therefrom under this section shall not affect the right of any sub-tenant to whom the premises or any part thereof have been lawfully sublet before proceedings for recovery of possession or ejectment were commenced to retain possession under this section, or be in any way operative against any such sub-tenant

(6) Where a landlord has obtained an order or judgment for possession or ejectment under this section on the ground that he requires a dwelling-house for his own occupation and it is subsequently made to appear to the court that the order was obtained by misrepresentation or the concealment of material facts the court may order the landlord to pay to the former tenant such sum as appears sufficient as compensation for damage or loss sustained by that tenant as the result of the order or judgment

6 No distress for the rent of any dwelling-house to which this Act applies shall be levied except with the leave of the county court and the court shall with respect to any application for such leave, have the same or similar powers with respect to adjournment, stay, suspension, postponement and otherwise as are conferred by the last preceding section of this Act in relation to applications for the recovery of possession

Restriction on levy of distress for rent

Provided that this section shall not apply to distress levied under section one hundred and sixty of the County Courts Act 1888

The provisions of this section shall be in addition to and not in derogation of any of the provisions of the County Emergency Powers Act 1914 or any Act amending or

4 & 5 Geo. 5, c. 78

extending the same except so far as those provisions are
repealed by this Act

Restriction on
calling-in of
mortgages

7. It shall not be lawful for any mortgagee under a mortgage to which this Act applies so long as—

(a) interest at the rate permitted under this Act is paid
and is not more than twenty-one days in arrear,
and

(b) the covenants by the mortgagor (other than the
covenant for the repayment of the principal money
secured) are performed and observed, and

(c) the mortgagor keeps the property in a proper state
of repair and pays all interest and instalments of
principal recoverable under any prior encumbrance,

to call in his mortgage or to take any steps for exercising any
right of foreclosure or sale or for otherwise enforcing his
security or for recovering the principal money thereby
secured

Provided that—

(i) this provision shall not apply to a mortgage where
the principal money secured thereby is repayable
by means of periodical instalments extending
over a term of not less than ten years from the
creation of the mortgage nor shall this provision
affect any power of sale exerciseable by a mortgagee who was on the twenty-fifth day of March
nineteen hundred and twenty a mortgagee in
possession or in cases where the mortgagor consents to the exercise by the mortgagee of the
powers conferred by the mortgage, and

(ii) if in the case of a mortgage of a leasehold interest
the mortgagee satisfies the county court that his
security is seriously diminishing in value or is
otherwise in jeopardy and that for that reason it
is reasonable that the mortgage should be called
in and enforced the court may by order authorise
him to call in and enforce the same and thereupon this section shall not apply to such mortgage but any such order may be made subject to

a condition that it shall not take effect if the mortgagor within such time as the court directs pays to the mortgagee such portion of the principal sum secured as appears to the court to correspond to the diminution of the security

8 —(1) A person shall not, as a condition of the grant renewal, or continuance of a tenancy or sub-tenancy of any dwelling-house to which this Act applies require the payment of any fine premium or other like sum or the giving of any pecuniary consideration in addition to the rent and where any such payment or consideration has been made or given in respect of any such dwelling-house under an agreement made after the twenty-fifth day of March nineteen hundred and twenty the amount or value thereof shall be recoverable by the person by whom it was made or given

Provided that where any agreement has been made since the said date but before the passing of this Act for the tenancy of a house to which this Act applies but the enactments repealed by this Act did not apply and the agreement includes provision for the payment of any fine, premium or other like sum or the giving of any pecuniary consideration in addition to the rent that agreement shall without prejudice to the operation of this section be voidable at the option of either party thereto

(2) A person requiring any payment or the giving of any consideration in contravention of this section shall be liable on summary conviction to a fine not exceeding one hundred pounds and the court by which he is convicted may order the amount paid or the value of the consideration to be repaid to the person by whom the same was made or given but such order shall be in lieu of any other method of recovery prescribed by this Act

(3) This section shall not apply to the grant renewal or continuance for a term of fourteen years or upwards of any tenancy

9 —(1) Where any person lets or has before the passing of this Act let any dwelling-house to which this Act applies

Restriction on premiums

Limitation of rent of houses let furnished

or any part thereof, at a rent which includes payment in respect of the use of furniture, and it is proved to the satisfaction of the county court on the application of the lessee that the rent charged is yielding or will yield to the lessor a profit more than twenty-five per cent. in excess of the normal profit as hereinafter defined, the court may order that the rent, so far as it exceeds such sum as would yield such normal profit and twenty-five per cent. shall be irrecoverable, and that the amount of any payment of rent in excess of such sum which may have been made in respect of any period after the passing of this Act, shall be repaid to the lessee

(2) For the purpose of this section "normal profit" means the profit which might reasonably have been expected from a similar letting in the year ending on the third day of August nineteen hundred and fourteen

Penalty for excessive charges for furnished lettings

10. Where any person after the passing of this Act lets any dwelling-house to which this Act applies or any part thereof at a rent which includes payment in respect of the use of furniture, and the rent charged yields to the lessor a profit which, having regard to all the circumstances of the case and in particular to the margin of profit allowed under the last preceding section of this Act, is extortionate then, without prejudice to any other remedy under this Act the lessor shall be liable on summary conviction to a fine not exceeding one hundred pounds, and the court by which he is convicted may order that the rent so far as it exceeds the amount permitted by the last preceding section of this Act shall be irrecoverable and that the amount of any such excess shall be repaid to the lessee, but any such order shall be in lieu of any other method of recovery prescribed by this Act

Statement to be supplied as to standard rent

11 A landlord of any dwelling-house to which this Act applies shall, on being so requested in writing by the tenant of the dwelling-house, supply him with a statement in writing as to what is the standard rent of the dwelling-house, and if, without reasonable excuse, he fails within fourteen

days to do so, or supplies a statement which is false in any
material particular, he shall be liable on summary conviction
to a fine not exceeding ten pounds

Application and Interpretation of Act

12—(1) For the purposes of this Act, except where the   Application
context otherwise requires—   and Interpretation

(a) The expression 'standard rent' means the rent at
which the dwelling-house was let on the third day
of August nineteen hundred and fourteen, or where
the dwelling-house was not let on that date the
rent at which it was last let before that date or,
in the case of a dwelling-house which was first let
after the said third day of August, the rent at
which it was first let:

Provided that in the case of any dwelling-house
let at a progressive rent payable under a tenancy
agreement or lease the maximum rent payable
under such tenancy agreement or lease shall be the
standard rent, and, where at the date by reference
to which the standard rent is calculated the rent
was less than the rateable value the rateable value
at that date shall be the standard rent

(b) The expression 'standard rate of interest' means in
the case of a mortgage in force on the third day of
August nineteen hundred and fourteen, the rate of
interest payable at that date or in the case of a
mortgage created since that date the original rate
of interest

(c) The expression "net rent' means, where the landlord
at the time by reference to which the standard rent
is calculated paid the rates chargeable on or which
but for the provisions of any Act would be chargeable on the occupier, the standard rent less the
amount of such rates, and in any other case the
standard rent

(d) The expression "rates' includes water rents and
charges, and any increase in rates payable by a

12 (2)

landlord shall be deemed to be payable by him until the rate is next demanded

(e) The expression "rateable value" means the rateable value on the third day of August nineteen hundred and fourteen or in the case of a dwelling-house or a part of dwelling-house first assessed after that date the rateable value at which it was first assessed

(f) The expressions "landlord," "tenant," "mortgagee" and "mortgagor" include any person from time to time deriving title under the original landlord, tenant, mortgagee or mortgagor

(g) The expression "landlord" also includes in relation to any dwelling-house any person other than the tenant who is or would but for this Act be entitled to possession of the dwelling-house and the expressions "tenant" and "tenancy" include sub-tenant and sub-tenancy and the expression "let" includes sub-let and the expression "tenant" includes the widow of a tenant dying intestate who was residing with him at the time of his death or where a tenant dying intestate leaves no widow or is a woman such member of the tenant's family so residing as aforesaid as may be decided in default of agreement by the county court

(h) The expression "mortgage" includes a land charge under the Land Transfer Acts 1875 and 1897

38 & 39 Vict
c. 87

50 & 51 Vict
c. 66

(i) The expressions "statutory undertaking" and "statutory duties or powers" include any undertaking duties or powers established imposed or exercised under any order having the force of an Act of Parliament

2. This Act shall apply to a house or a part of a house let as a separate dwelling where either the annual amount of the standard rent or the rateable value does not exceed—

(a) in the metropolitan police district including therein the City of London one hundred and five pounds

(b) in Scotland ninety pounds; and

(c) elsewhere seventy-eight pounds;

and every such house or part of a house shall be deemed to be a dwelling-house to which this Act applies.

Provided that—

(i) this Act shall not, save as otherwise expressly provided, apply to a dwelling-house bonâ fide let at a rent which includes payments in respect of board, attendance, or use of furniture; and

(ii) the application of this Act to any house or part of a house shall not be excluded by reason only that part of the premises is used as a shop or office or for business, trade, or professional purposes; and

(iii) for the purposes of this Act any land or premises let together with a house shall, if the rateable value of the land or premises let separately would be less than one quarter of the rateable value of the house, be treated as part of the house, but, subject to this provision, this Act shall not apply to a house let together with land other than the site of the house.

3) Where, for the purpose of determining the standard rent or rateable value of any dwelling-house to which this Act applies, it is necessary to apportion the rent at the date in relation to which the standard rent is to be fixed or the rateable value of the property in which that dwelling-house is comprised, the county court may, on application by either party, make such apportionment as seems just, and the decision of the court as to the amount to be apportioned to the dwelling-house shall be final and conclusive.

(4) Subject to the provisions of this Act, this Act shall apply to every mortgage where the mortgaged property consists of or comprises one or more dwelling-houses to which this Act applies or any interest therein, except that it shall not apply—

(i) to any mortgage comprising one or more dwelling-houses to which this Act applies and other land if

the rateable value of such dwelling-houses is less
than one-tenth of the rateable value of the whole
of the land comprised in the mortgage; or

(b) to an equitable charge by deposit of title deeds or
otherwise; or

(c) to any mortgage which is created after the passing
of this Act.

(5) When a mortgage comprises one or more dwelling-
houses to which this Act applies and other land, and the
rateable value of such dwelling-houses is more than one-tenth
of the rateable value of the whole of the land comprised in
the mortgage, the mortgagee may apportion the principal
money secured by the mortgage between such dwelling-
houses and such other land by giving one calendar month's
notice in writing to the mortgagor, such notice to state the
particulars of such apportionment, and at the expiration of
the said calendar month's notice this Act shall not apply
to the mortgage so far as it relates to such other land, and
for all purposes, including the mortgagor's right of redemption, the said mortgage shall operate as if it were a separate
mortgage for the respective portions of the said principal
money secured by the said dwelling-houses and such other
land respectively to which such portions were apportioned:

Provided that the mortgagor shall, before the expiration
of the said calendar month's notice, be entitled to dispute
the amounts so apportioned as aforesaid, and in default of
agreement the matter shall be determined by a single
arbitrator appointed by the President of the Surveyors'
Institution.

(6) Where this Act has become applicable to any
dwelling-house or any mortgage thereon it shall continue
to apply thereto whether or not the dwelling-house continues
to be one to which this Act applies.

(7) Where the rent payable in respect of any tenancy of
any dwelling-house is less than two-thirds of the rateable
value thereof this Act shall not apply to that rent or tenancy
nor to any mortgage by the landlord from whom the tenancy
is held of his interest in the dwelling-house, and this Act

shall apply in respect of such dwelling-house as if no such
tenancy existed or ever had existed

(8) Any rooms in a dwelling-house subject to a separate
letting wholly or partly as a dwelling shall for the purposes
of this Act be treated as a part of a dwelling-house let as
a separate dwelling

(9) This Act shall not apply to a dwelling-house erected
after or in course of erection on the second day of April
nineteen hundred and nineteen or to any dwelling-house
which has been since that date or was at that date being
bona fide reconstructed by way of conversion into two or more
separate and self-contained flats or tenements but for the
purpose of any enactment relating to fixing the gross estimated rental or gross value of any such house to which this
Act would have applied if it had been erected or so reconstructed before the third day of August nineteen hundred
and fourteen and let at that date shall not exceed —

(a) if the house forms part of a housing scheme to which
    section seven of the Housing Town Planning &c   9 & 10 Geo 5
    Act 1919 applies the rent (exclusive of rates)   c 35
    charged by the local authority in respect of that
    house and

(b) in any other case the rent (exclusive of rates) which
    would have been charged by the local authority in
    respect of a similar house forming part of such a
    scheme as aforesaid

(10) Where possession has been taken of any dwelling-
houses by a Government department during the war under
the Defence of the Realm regulations, for the purpose of
housing workmen this Act shall apply to such houses as if
the workmen in occupation thereof at the passing of this
Act were in occupation as tenants of the landlords of such
houses

13 (1) This Act shall apply to any premises used for
business trade or professional purposes or for the public
service as it applies to a dwelling-house and as though
references to dwelling-house house and dwelling

*Application
to business
premises*

included references to any such premises but this Act in
its application to such premises shall have effect subject to
the following modifications—

    (a) The following paragraph shall be substituted for
        paragraph (c) of subsection (1) of section two—

            (c) In addition to any such amounts as afore-
            said an amount not exceeding thirty-five per
            centum of the net rent

    (b) The following paragraph shall be substituted for para-
        graph (d) of subsection (1) of section five—

            (d) the premises are reasonably required by the
            landlord for business trade or professional purposes
            or for the public service and except as otherwise
            provided by this subsection the court is satisfied
            that alternative accommodation reasonably equiva-
            lent as regards rent and suitability in all respects,
            is available

    (c) The following paragraph shall be added after para-
        graph (g) of the same subsection—

            (h) The premises are bonâ fide required for the
            purpose of a scheme of reconstruction or improve-
            ment which appears to the court to be desirable
            in the public interest

    (d) Paragraph (1) of the same subsection shall not apply

    (e) Sections nine and ten shall not apply

    (2) The application of this Act to such premises as afore-
said shall not extend to a letting or tenancy in any market
or fair where the rent or conditions of tenancy are controlled
or regulated by or in pursuance of any statute or charter

    (3) This section shall continue in force until the twenty-
fourth day of June nineteen hundred and twenty-one

General

**Recovery of
sums made
irrecoverable,
&c.**

    11—(1) Where any sum has whether before or after
the passing of this Act been paid on account of any rent or
mortgage interest being a sum which is by virtue of this
Act or any Act repealed by this Act irrecoverable by the
landlord or mortgagee the sum so paid shall be recoverable

from the landlord or mortgagee who received the payment
or his legal personal representative by the tenant or mortgagor by whom it was paid, and any such sum and any other
sum which under this Act is recoverable by a tenant from a
landlord or payable or repayable by a landlord to a tenant
may without prejudice to any other method of recovery
be deducted by the tenant or mortgagor from any rent or
interest payable by him to the landlord or mortgagee

(2) If

    (a) any person in any rent book or similar document
        makes an entry showing or purporting to show
        any tenant as being in arrear in respect of any
        sum which by virtue of any such Act is irre-
        coverable, or

    (b) where any such entry has before the passing of
        this Act been made by or on behalf of any
        landlord the landlord on being requested by or
        on behalf of the tenant so to do refuses or
        neglects to cause the entry to be deleted within
        seven days

that person or landlord shall on summary conviction be
liable to a fine not exceeding ten pounds unless he proves
that he acted innocently and without intent to deceive

15.- (1) A tenant who by virtue of the provisions of this   Conditions of
statutory
tenancy
Act retains possession of any dwelling-house to which this
Act applies shall so long as he retains possession observe
and be entitled to the benefit of all the terms and conditions
of the original contract of tenancy so far as the same are
consistent with the provisions of this Act and shall be
entitled to give up possession of the dwelling-house only on
giving such notice as would have been required under the
original contract of tenancy or if no notice would have
been so required on giving not less than three months
notice

Provided that notwithstanding anything in the contract
of tenancy a landlord who obtains an order or judgment for
the recovery of possession of the dwelling-house or for the

ejectment of a tenant retaining possession as aforesaid shall not be required to give any notice to quit to the tenant

(2) Any tenant retaining possession as aforesaid shall not as a condition of giving up possession ask or receive the payment of any sum or the giving of any other consideration by any person other than the landlord, and any person acting in contravention of this provision shall be liable on summary conviction to a fine not exceeding one hundred pounds, and the court by which he was convicted may order any such payment or the value of any such consideration to be paid to the person by whom the same was made or given, but any such order shall be in lieu of any other method of recovery prescribed by this Act

(3) Where the interest of a tenant of a dwelling-house to which this Act applies is determined either as the result of an order or judgment for possession or ejectment, or for any other reason, any sub-tenant to whom the premises or any part thereof have been lawfully sublet shall, subject to the provisions of this Act, be deemed to become the tenant of the landlord on the same terms as he would have held from the tenant if the tenancy had continued

Minor amendments of law 42 & 43 Vict c 41

16 (1) Section three of the Poor Rate Assessment and Collection Act 1869 shall except so far as it relates to the metropolis have effect as though for the limits of value specified in that section there were substituted limits twenty-five per cent in excess of the limits so specified, and that section and section four of the same Act shall have effect accordingly

(2) It shall be deemed to be a condition of the tenancy of any dwelling-house to which this Act applies that the tenant shall afford to the landlord access thereto and all reasonable facilities for executing therein any repairs which the landlord is entitled to execute

(3) Where the landlord of any dwelling-house to which this Act applies has served a notice to quit on a tenant, the acceptance of rent by the landlord for a period not exceeding three months from the expiration of the notice to quit shall

not be deemed to prejudice any right to possession of such premises and if any order for possession is made, any payment of rent so accepted shall be treated as mesne profits.

17.—(1) The Lord Chancellor may make such rules and give such directions as he thinks fit for the purpose of giving effect to this Act and may by those rules or directions, provide for any proceedings for the purposes of this Act being conducted so far as desirable in private and for the remission of any fees.

Rules as to procedure

(2) A county court shall have jurisdiction to deal with any claim or other proceedings arising out of this Act or any of the provisions thereof notwithstanding that by reason of the amount of claim or otherwise the case would not but for this provision be within the jurisdiction of a county court, and if a person takes proceedings under this Act in the High Court which he could have taken in the county court he shall not be entitled to recover any costs.

18.—(1) This Act shall apply to Scotland subject to the following modifications:—

Application to Scotland and Ireland

> (a) 'Mortgage' and 'encumbrance' mean a heritable security including a security constituted by absolute disposition qualified by back bond or letter: "mortgagor' and 'mortgagee' mean respectively the debtor and the creditor in a heritable security: 'covenant' means obligation: 'mortgaged property' means the heritable subject or subjects included in a heritable security: 'rateable value' means yearly value according to the valuation roll: 'rateable value on the third day of August nineteen hundred and fourteen' means yearly value according to the valuation roll for the year ending fifteenth day of May nineteen hundred and fifteen, 'assessed' means entered in the valuation roll, 'land' means lands and heritages: 'rates' means assessments as defined in the House Letting and Rating (Scotland) Act, 1911: 'Lord Chancellor'

1 & 2 Geo 5, c 53

and "High Court" mean the Court of Session; "rules" means act of sederunt; "county court" means the sheriff court; "sanitary authority" means the local authority under the Public Health

60 & 61 Vict c. 38.

(Scotland) Act, 1897; "mesne profits" means profits, the Board of Agriculture for Scotland shall be substituted for the Minister of Agriculture and Fisheries, the twenty-eighth day of May shall be substituted for the twenty-fourth day of June, the reference to the county agricultural committee shall be construed as a reference to the body of persons constituted with respect to any area by the Board of Agriculture for Scotland under subsection (2) of section eleven of the Corn Production Act, 1917,

7 & 8 Geo. 5, c. 46.

references to levying distress shall be construed as references to doing diligence, the reference to the President of the Surveyors Institution shall be construed as a reference to the Chairman of the Scottish Committee of the Surveyors Institution,

9 & 10 Geo. 5, c. 60

a reference to section five of the Housing, Town Planning &c. (Scotland) Act, 1919 shall be substituted for a reference to section seven of the Housing, Town Planning &c. Act, 1919, and a reference to section one of the House Letting and Rating (Scotland) Act, 1911 shall be substituted for a reference to section three of the Poor Rate

32 & 33 Vict c. 41

Assessment and Collection Act, 1869.

(b) Nothing in paragraph (b) of subsection (1) of the section of this Act relating to permitted increases in rent shall permit any increase in rent in respect of any increase after the year ending Whitsunday nineteen hundred and twenty in the amount of the rates payable by the landlord other than rates for which he is responsible under the House Letting and Rating (Scotland) Act, 1911.

(c) Paragraph (d) of subsection (1) of the section of this Act relating to application and interpretation shall not apply.

(4) Where any dwelling-house to which the Acts repealed by this Act applied is subject to a right of tenancy arising from a yearly contract or from tacit relocation and ending at Whitsunday nineteen hundred and twenty-one the year ending at the said term of Whitsunday shall be deemed to be a period during which but for this Act the landlord would be entitled to obtain possession of such dwelling-house

Application to Ireland

19.—(1) This Act may be cited as the Increase of Rent and Mortgage Interest (Restrictions) Act 1920

(2) Except as otherwise provided this Act shall continue in force until the twenty-fourth day of June nineteen hundred and twenty-three

Provided that the expiration of this Act or any part thereof shall not render recoverable by a landlord any rent interest or other sum which during the continuance thereof was irrecoverable or affect the right of a tenant to recover any sum which during the continuance thereof was under this Act recoverable by him

(3) The enactments mentioned in the Second Schedule to this Act are hereby repealed to the extent specified in the third column of that schedule

Provided that without prejudice to the operation of section thirty-eight of the Interpretation Act, 1889 nothing in this repeal shall render recoverable any sums which at the time of the passing of this Act were irrecoverable or affect the validity of any order of a court or any rules or directions made or given under any enactment repealed by this Act all of which orders rules and directions if in force at the date of the passing of this Act shall have effect as if they were made or given under this Act and any proceedings pending in any court at the date of the passing of this Act under any enactment repealed by this Act shall be deemed to have been commenced under this Act

Short title duration and repeal

52 & 53 V. c. 63

SCHEDULES

FIRST SCHEDULE

FORM OF NOTICE BY LANDLORD

INCREASE OF RENT AND MORTGAGE INTEREST (RESTRICTIONS) ACT 1920

Date

To

Address of premises to which)
this notice refers   -   - |

Take notice that I intend to increase the rent of
l *s* *d* per   at present payable by you
as tenant of the above-named premises by the amount of
l *s* *d* per

The increase is made up as follows -

(a)   *l*   *s*   *d* under paragraph (a) of subsection (1) of section two of the Act being six
eight per cent on *l*   *s*   *d* expended by me since *insert date* on improvements and structural alterations and consisting
of *

(b)   *l*   *s*   *d* under paragraph (b) of subsection (1) of section two of the Act on account
of an increase in the rates payable by me from
l   *s*   *d* per   to *l*   *s*   *d*
per   in respect of the premises

(c)   *l*   *s*   *d* under paragraph (c) of subsection (1) of section two of the Act being
per cent on the net rent of the premises
The net rent is   *l*   *s*   *d*   The
standard rent is   *l*   *s*   *d*

* Here state improvements and alterations effected

(d)   *l*   *s*   *d* under paragraph (d) of subsection (1) of section two of the Act being
    per cent on the net rent of the premises
The net rent is   *l*   s   *d*   The
standard rent is   *l*   s   *d*

The increase under head (b) will date from   being
one clear week from the date of (a) this notice, and the
remaining increases from   being four clear weeks
from the date of (a) this notice

* The increase under head (d) is on account of my respon-
sibility for repairs [or no part, part only, of which are you
under an express liability]

† At any time or times, not being less than three months
after the   day of   19   you are entitled to apply
to the county court for an order suspending the increases
under heads (c) and (d) above if you consider that the premises are not in all respects reasonably fit for human habitation or otherwise not in a reasonable state of repair. You
will be required to satisfy the county court by a report of
the sanitary authority or otherwise that your application is
well founded, and for this purpose you are entitled to apply
to the sanitary authority for a certificate. A fee of one
shilling is chargeable on any application for a certificate,
but if the certificate is granted you can deduct this sum
from your rent. The address of the sanitary authority is

    Signed

    Address

---

a) The words ' service of ' are to be added after ' date of '. See
sect 6 (2) of the Amendment Act 1923

---

* Where the tenant is under an express liability for part of the repairs,
the increase under head (d) is to be settled in default of agreement by the
county court

† This paragraph need not be included if there is no increase under
head (d)

APPENDIX I

SECOND SCHEDULE

ENACTMENTS REPEALED

Session and Chapter	Short Title	Extent of Repeal
5 & 6 Geo 5 c 97	The Increase of Rent and Mortgage Interest (War Restrictions) Act 1915	The whole Act.
7 & 8 Geo 5 c 25	The Courts (Emergency Powers) Act 1917	Ss 4, 5 and 7
9 & 10 Geo 5. c 7	The Increase of Rent and Mortgage Interest (Restrictions) Act 1919	The whole Act
9 & 10 Geo 5, c 90	The Increase of Rent, &c (Amendment) Act 1919	The whole Act.

B

INCREASE OF RENT AND MORTGAGE INTEREST RESTRICTIONS (CONTINUANCE) ACT 1923

[13 & 14 Geo 5 c 7]

[17 March 1923

Be it enacted &c

Continuance of 10 & 11 Geo 5, c 17

1 The Increase of Rent and Mortgage Interest (Restrictions) Act 1920 and any enactment amending that Act shall continue in force until the thirty-first day of July nineteen hundred and twenty-three

Short title and extent

2 This Act may be cited as the Increase of Rent and Mortgage Interest Restrictions (Continuance) Act 1923 and does not extend to Northern Ireland

C

RENT RESTRICTIONS (NOTICES OF INCREASE) ACT 1923

(13 & 14 Geo 5 c 13)

7th June 1923

Be it enacted &c

1.—(1) Where notice of intention to increase rent has whether before or after the passing of this Act been served on a tenant in conformity with subsection (2) of section three of the Increase of Rent and Mortgage Interest (Restrictions) Act 1920 (hereinafter referred to as the principal Act) and a notice to terminate the tenancy was necessary in order to make such increase effective the notice of intention to increase the rent shall have effect and shall be deemed always to have had effect as if it were or had been also a notice to terminate the existing tenancy on the day immediately preceding the day as from which the increase is or was first to take effect or on the earliest day thereafter on which if it had been a notice to terminate the tenancy it would have been effective for that purpose and in the latter case a notice of increase served before the passing of this Act shall be deemed to have had effect as if such earliest date had been specified in the notice as the date as from which the increase was to take effect

Provided that—

> (a) nothing in this Act shall entitle a landlord after the passing of this Act to recover from a tenant in respect of any period before the first day of December nineteen hundred and twenty-two the increase of rent made valid by this Act or any sums which have been recovered from the landlord before that date by means of deductions from rent or otherwise or any rent due before that date which has not been paid by reason of

Effect of notices to increase rent under principal Act 10 & 11 Geo 5 c 17

13

such deductions having been made thereon
but section fourteen subsection (1) of the principal Act shall not apply to an increase of rent
made valid by this Act which was paid by,
or recovered from a tenant prior to the first day
of December nineteen hundred and twenty-two,

(b) nothing in this Act shall affect the right to enforce
any judgment of a court of competent jurisdiction given before the fifteenth day of February,
nineteen hundred and twenty-three, or render
recoverable any sum paid under such a judgment

(2) Any increase of rent made valid by this Act is hereinafter referred to as a validated increase of rent

Payment of
arrears by
instalments

2.—(1) The amount due under this Act on account of any
arrears of rent that is to say

(a) any validated increase of rent in respect of the period
from the first day of December nineteen hundred
and twenty-two to the date of the passing of this
Act both inclusive, and

(b) any sum which during the said period has been recovered by the tenant from the landlord by deductions from rent or otherwise and which would not
have been so recoverable had this Act been then
in force

shall be payable by instalments with and as part of the
periodical payments of rent each instalment being fifteen
per cent of the standard rent for the week, month or other
period for which the rent is payable fractions of a penny
being disregarded and such instalments shall continue payable until the whole of the amount of such arrears is paid off

Provided that—

(i) the tenant may at any time pay to the landlord the
full amount of such arrears subject to the deduction of the aggregate amount of the instalments
(if any) already paid and

(ii) if a tenant by whom any such instalments are payable gives up possession of the premises either

voluntarily or on any order or judgment of a court the balance of the sum payable by instalments shall immediately become due and recoverable

(2) A landlord claiming that a sum on account of arrears of rent is due to him under this Act shall serve on the tenant a notice to that effect and the notice shall specify the amount so claimed and the amount of the instalments claimed to be payable and the first instalment shall not be payable until after the expiration of one clear week from the date of the notice. If such notice contains any statement or representation which is false or misleading in any material respect the landlord shall be liable on summary conviction to a fine not exceeding ten pounds unless he proves that the statement was made innocently and without intent to deceive

(3) The notice shall be in the form contained in the Schedule to this Act or in a form substantially to the same effect and the landlord shall furnish the tenant with details in writing showing how the amount claimed is arrived at and how the amount of the instalments has been calculated

(4) Any question as to the amount of arrears due from a tenant or the amount of any instalment shall be determined on the application either of the landlord or the tenant by the county court and the decision of the court shall be final and conclusive

3.—(1) A tenant who becomes by virtue of this Act liable to pay any sum by way of rent or on account of arrears or the sanitary authority may apply to the county court for an order suspending such liability on the ground that the house is not in all respects reasonably fit for human habitation or that it is otherwise not in a reasonable state of repair and section two of the principal Act shall apply as if the application had been made under subsection (2) of that section

Power to suspend liability if premises unfit for human habitation or in state of disrepair

(2) Where the liability in respect of the payment of instalments is so suspended the instalments which would have become payable during the period of suspension shall for

13 (2)

the purpose of calculating the aggregate amount of instalments paid, be deemed to have been paid

(3) Where a tenant has obtained from the sanitary authority a certificate that the house is not in a reasonable state of repair, and has served a copy of the certificate upon the landlord, it shall be a good defence to any claim against the tenant for the payment of any sum which the tenant is by virtue of this Act liable to pay by way of rent or on account of arrears in respect of any subsequent rental period that the house was not in a reasonable state of repair during that period, and in any proceedings against the tenant for the enforcement of such claim (including proceedings for recovery of possession or ejectment on the ground of non-payment of rent so far as the rent unpaid includes any such sum) the production of the said certificate shall be sufficient evidence that the house was and continues to be in the condition therein mentioned unless the contrary is proved

Provided that the foregoing provision shall not apply in any case where and so far as the condition of the house is due to the tenant's neglect or default or breach of express agreement.

(4) For the purposes of this Act a certificate of a sanitary authority shall specify what works (if any) require to be executed in order to put the house into a reasonable state of repair

(5) An instrument purporting to be a certificate of a sanitary authority and to be signed by an officer of the authority shall without further proof be taken to be a certificate of the authority unless the contrary is proved

(6) A sanitary authority may appoint a committee for the purposes of this Act and may delegate with or without restrictions to such committee or to an existing committee of the authority all or any of the powers of the authority under this Act

Short title and construction

4 This Act may be cited as the Rent Restrictions (Notices of Increase) Act 1923 and shall be construed as one with the principal Act except that this Act shall not extend to Ireland

SCHEDULE

Form of Notice by Landlord

Rent Restrictions (Notices of Increase) Act 1923

Date

To

    Address of premises to which
      this notice refers -   -

    TAKE NOTICE that I claim that the sum of
is due to me from you as tenant of the above premises on
account of arrears of rent under the above-mentioned Act

    The amount due on account of such arrears is payable by
instalments with, and as part of your weekly *monthly or
other periodical rent* until the amount of such arrears is
paid off The first instalment will be payable on the
day of *

    The amount of the instalments claimed by me is
a week *month, or other period as the case may be*

    If you wish to dispute the amount of the sum claimed or
of the instalments you are entitled to apply to the county
court of

    You are entitled to apply to the county court for an order
suspending any sum due from you by way of rent or on
account of arrears under the above-mentioned Act if you
consider that the premises are not in all respects reasonably
fit for human habitation or otherwise not in a reasonable
state of repair You will be required to satisfy the county
court by a report of the sanitary authority or otherwise
that your application is well founded and for this purpose
you are entitled to apply to the sanitary authority for a
certificate A fee of one shilling is chargeable but if the
certificate is granted you can deduct this sum from the sum
due from you as aforesaid The address of the sanitary
authority is

    * The date to be inserted will be the first rent day after the expiration
of one clear week from the date of the notice

If at any time you give up possession of the above premises, either voluntarily or on an order or judgment of the court, the balance of the sum payable by instalments will immediately become due

A statement is sent herewith showing how the amount of the above claim is arrived at, and how the amount of the instalments has been calculated

Signed

Address

D

RENT AND MORTGAGE INTEREST RESTRICTIONS ACT, 1923

(13 & 14 Geo 5 c 32)

An Act to amend and prolong the duration of the Increase of Rent and Mortgage Interest (Restrictions) Act 1920, and any enactment amending that Act and to make provision as to the rent and recovery of possession of premises in certain cases after the expiry of that Act and for purposes in connection therewith

[31st July 1923]

Be it enacted &c

PART I

AMENDMENT AND PROLONGATION OF DURATION OF PRINCIPAL ACT

Prolongation of duration of principal Act

10 & 11 Geo 5, c 17

1 Subject to the provisions of this Act the Increase of Rent and Mortgage Interest (Restrictions) Act, 1920 (hereinafter referred to as the principal Act), shall continue in force until the twenty-fourth day of June nineteen hundred and twenty-five

2.—(1) Where the landlord of a dwelling-house to which the principal Act applies is in possession of the whole of the dwelling-house at the passing of this Act or comes into possession of the whole of the dwelling-house at any time after the passing of this Act then from and after the passing of this Act or from and after the date when the landlord subsequently comes into possession as the case may be the principal Act shall cease to apply to the dwelling-house

Exclusion of dwelling-houses from application of principal Act in certain cases

Provided that where part of a dwelling-house to which the principal Act applies is lawfully sub-let and the part so sub-let is also a dwelling-house to which the principal Act applies the principal Act shall not cease to apply to the part so sub-let by reason of the tenant being in or coming into possession of that part and if the landlord is in or comes into possession of any part not so sub-let the principal Act shall cease to apply to that part notwithstanding that a sub-tenant continues in or retains possession of any other part by virtue of the principal Act

Provided also that where a landlord comes into possession under an order or judgment made or given after the passing of this Act on the ground of non-payment of rent the principal Act shall notwithstanding anything in the foregoing provisions of this sub-section continue to apply to the dwelling-house

(2) Where at any time after the passing of this Act the landlord of a dwelling-house to which the principal Act applies grants to the tenant a valid lease of the dwelling-house for a term ending at some date after the twenty-fourth day of June nineteen hundred and twenty-six being a term of not less than two years or enters into a valid agreement with the tenant for a tenancy for such a term the principal Act shall as from the commencement of the term cease to apply to the dwelling-house and nothing in the principal Act shall be taken as preventing or invalidating the payment of any agreed sum as part of the consideration for such lease or agreement

Provided that where part of the dwelling-house is lawfully sub-let at the commencement of the term and is a

dwelling-house to which the principal Act applies, that part
shall, notwithstanding anything in the foregoing provisions
of this subsection, continue to be a dwelling-house to which
the principal Act applies.

(3) For the purposes of this section the expression "possession" shall be construed as meaning "actual possession,"
and a landlord shall not be deemed to have come into
possession by reason only of a change of tenancy made
with his consent.

3. Where before the passing of this Act the landlord of
a dwelling-house to which the principal Act applies has
granted to the tenant a valid lease of the dwelling-house
for a term ending on some date after the twenty-fourth day
of June nineteen hundred and twenty-three, or has entered
into an agreement with the tenant for a tenancy for such a
term, and the rent thereby reserved is reserved at a rate which
after but not before such last-mentioned date exceeds the
standard rent and the increases permitted under the principal Act or this Act, the landlord may, by three months'
notice in writing expiring not earlier than the twenty-first
day of December nineteen hundred and twenty-three, and
not later than the thirty-first day of March nineteen hundred
and twenty-four, determine the said lease or tenancy, provided that if within one month of the receipt of such notice
the lessee or tenant shall give to the landlord notice in
writing that he elects to abide by the said lease or agreement
and the terms thereof, then the said lease or agreement
shall remain in full force and effect in every respect including the amount of the rent thereby expressed to be
reserved unaffected by the principal Act or this Act.

4. The following section shall be substituted for section
five of the principal Act, namely:—

    "(1) No order or judgment for the recovery of pos-
session of any dwelling-house to which this Act applies,
or for the ejectment of a tenant therefrom shall be made
or given unless—

        (a) any rent lawfully due from the tenant has not been
        paid, or any other obligation of the tenancy

(whether under the contract of tenancy or under this Act) so far as the same is consistent with the provisions of this Act has been broken or not performed; or

(b) the tenant or any person residing or lodging with him or being his sub-tenant has been guilty of conduct which is a nuisance or annoyance to adjoining occupiers, or has been convicted of using the premises or allowing the premises to be used for an immoral or illegal purpose, or the condition of the dwelling-house has, in the opinion of the court, deteriorated owing to acts of waste by, or the neglect or default of, the tenant or any such person, and where such person is a lodger or sub-tenant the court is satisfied that the tenant has not, before the making or giving of the order or judgment, taken such steps as he ought reasonably to have taken for the removal of the lodger or sub-tenant; or

(c) the tenant has given notice to quit, and in consequence of that notice the landlord has contracted to sell or let the dwelling-house or has taken any other steps as a result of which he would, in the opinion of the court, be seriously prejudiced if he could not obtain possession; or

(d) the dwelling-house is reasonably required by the landlord for occupation as a residence for himself or for any son or daughter of his over eighteen years of age, or for any person bonâ fide residing with him, or for some person engaged in his whole-time employment or in the whole-time employment of some tenant from him or with whom, conditional on housing accommodation being provided, a contract for such employment has been entered into, and (except as otherwise provided by this subsection) the court is satisfied that alternative accommodation is available which is reasonably suitable to the means of the tenant and to the needs

of the tenant and his family as regards extent
character, and proximity to place of work and
which consists either of a dwelling-house to which
this Act applies, or of premises to be let as a
separate dwelling on terms which will afford to
the tenant security of tenure reasonably equivalent to the security afforded by this Act in the
case of a dwelling-house to which this Act applies ;
or

" (e) the dwelling-house is reasonably required for the
purpose of the execution of the statutory duties
or powers of a local authority or statutory undertaking, or for any purpose which, in the opinion
of the court, is in the public interest ; and the
court in either case is satisfied as aforesaid as
respects alternative accommodation ; or

" (f) the landlord became the landlord after service in
any of His Majesty's forces during the war and
requires the house for his personal occupation and
offers the tenant accommodation on reasonable
terms in the same dwelling-house such accommodation being considered by the court as reasonably
sufficient in the circumstances ; or

" (g) the dwelling-house is required for occupation as
a residence by a former tenant thereof who gave
up occupation in consequence of his service in any
of His Majesty's forces during the war ; or

" (h) the tenant without the consent of the landlord has
at any time after the thirty-first day of July,
nineteen hundred and twenty-three, assigned or
sub-let the whole of the dwelling-house or sub-
let part of the dwelling-house, the remainder being
already sub-let ; or

" (i) the dwelling-house consists of or includes premises
licensed for the sale of intoxicating liquor, and
the tenant has committed an offence as holder of
the licence or has not conducted the business to
the satisfaction of the licensing justices or the police

authority or has carried it on in a manner detrimental to the public interest or the renewal of the licence has for any reason been refused

and in any such case as aforesaid the court considers it reasonable to make such an order or give such judgment

The existence of alternative accommodation shall not be a condition of an order or judgment on any of the grounds specified in paragraph (d) of this subsection

    (i) where the tenant was in the employment of the landlord or a former landlord and the dwelling-house was let to him in consequence of that employment and he has ceased to be in that employment or

    (ii) where the court is satisfied by a certificate of the county agricultural committee or of the Minister of Agriculture and Fisheries pending the formation of such committee that the dwelling-house is required by the landlord for the occupation of a person engaged on work necessary for the proper working of an agricultural holding or with whom conditional on housing accommodation being provided a contract for employment on such work has been entered into or

    (iii) where the landlord gave up the occupation of the dwelling-house in consequence of his service in any of His Majesty's forces during the war or

    (iv) where the landlord or the husband or wife of the landlord became the landlord before the thirtieth day of June nineteen hundred and twenty-two and the dwelling-house is reasonably required by him for occupation as a residence for himself or for any son or daughter of his over eighteen years of age or

    (v) where the landlord or the husband or wife of the landlord did not become the landlord before the thirtieth day of June nineteen hundred and twenty-two and the dwelling-house is reasonably required by him for occupation as a residence for himself or for any son or daughter of his over eighteen years of age and the court is satisfied that greater hardship would be caused by refusing to grant an order or judgment for possession than by granting it

(2) At the time of the application for or the making or giving of any order or judgment for the recovery of possession of any such dwelling-house or for the ejectment of a tenant therefrom or in the case of any such order or judgment which has been made or given whether before or after the passing of this Act and not executed at any subsequent time the court may adjourn the application or stay or suspend execution on any such order or judgment or postpone the date of possession for such period or periods as it thinks fit and subject to such conditions (if any) in regard to payment by the tenant of arrears of rent rent or mesne profit and otherwise as the court thinks fit and if such conditions are complied with the court may if it thinks fit discharge or rescind any such order or judgment

(3) Where any order or judgment has been made or given before the passing of this Act but not executed and in the opinion of the court the order or judgment would not have been made or given if this Act had been in force at the time when such order or judgment was made or given the court may on application by the tenant rescind or vary such order or judgment in such manner as the court may think fit for the purpose of giving effect to this Act

51 & 52 Vict
c 43
1 & 2 Vict
c 74

(4) Notwithstanding anything in section one hundred and forty-three of the County Courts Act 1888 or in section one of the Small Tenements Recovery Act 1838 every warrant for delivery of possession of or to enter and give possession of any dwelling-house to which this Act applies shall remain in force for three months from the day next after the last day named in the judgment or order for delivery of possession or ejectment or in the case of a warrant under the Small Tenements Recovery Act 1838 from the date of the issue of the warrant and in either case for such further period or periods if any as the court

shall from time to time whether before or after the expiration of such three months, direct

'(5) An order or judgment against a tenant for the recovery of possession of any dwelling-house or ejectment therefrom under this section shall not affect the right of any sub-tenant to whom the premises or any part thereof have been lawfully sub-let before proceedings for recovery of possession or ejectment were commenced to retain possession under this section or be in any way operative against any such sub-tenants

'(6) Where a landlord has obtained an order or judgment for possession or ejectment under this section on the ground that he requires a dwelling-house for his own occupation and it is subsequently made to appear to the court that the order or judgment was obtained by misrepresentation or the concealment of material facts the court may order the landlord to pay to the former tenant such sum as appears sufficient as compensation for damage or loss sustained by that tenant as the result of the order or judgment

(7) The provisions of the last preceding subsection shall apply in any case where the landlord has after the thirty-first day of July nineteen hundred and twenty-three obtained an order or judgment for possession or ejectment on any of the grounds specified in paragraph (d) of sub-section (1) of this section and it is subsequently made to appear to the court that the order or judgment was obtained by misrepresentation or concealment of material facts and in any such case the court may if it thinks fit in addition to making an order for payment of compensation by the landlord to the former tenant direct that the dwelling-house shall not be excluded from this Act by reason of the landlord having come into possession thereof under the said order or judgment and if such a direction is given this Act shall apply and be deemed to have applied to the dwelling-house as from the date mentioned in such direction

5.—(1) Where the tenant of a dwelling-house to which the principal Act applies has obtained from the sanitary

ground of
disrepair

authority a certificate that the house is not in a reasonable
state of repair and has served a copy of the certificate upon
the landlord it shall be a good defence to any claim against
the tenant for the payment of any increase of rent permitted
under paragraph (c) or paragraph (d) of subsection (1) of
section two of the principal Act in respect of any subsequent
rental period that the house was not in a reasonable state
of repair during that period and in any proceedings against
the tenant for the enforcement of such claim including
proceedings for recovery of possession or ejectment on the
ground of non-payment of rent so far as the rent unpaid
includes such increase the production of the said certificate
shall be sufficient evidence that the house was and continues
to be in the condition therein mentioned unless the contrary
is proved

Provided that this section shall not apply in any case
where and so far as the condition of the house is due to the
tenant's neglect or default or breach of express agreement

-(When after the issue of any such certificate the
landlord has executed to the satisfaction of the sanitary
authority the repairs which require to be executed in order
to put the dwelling-house into a reasonable state of repair
the authority shall on the application of the landlord and
upon payment of a fee of one shilling issue a report to
that effect

Notices
increase of
re

6 —(1) The county court if satisfied that any error or
omission in a notice of intention to increase rent whether
served before or after the passing of this Act is due to a
bona fide mistake on the part of the landlord shall have
power to amend such notice by correcting any errors and
supplying any omissions therein which if not corrected or
supplied would render the notice invalid on such terms
and conditions as respects arrears of rent or otherwise as
appear to the court to be just and reasonable and if the
court so directs the notice as so amended shall have effect
and be deemed to have had effect as a valid notice

—(2) The form of notice in the First Schedule to the principal Act shall be amended by the substitution of the words

date of service of this notice " for the words " date of
this notice "

Permitted
increases of
rent of sub-
tenancies

7.—(1) Where part of a dwelling-house to which the
principal Act applies is lawfully sub-let, and the part so
sub-let is also a dwelling-house to which the principal Act
applies, then, in addition to any increases permitted by
paragraphs (a) to (e) of sub-section (1) of section two of
the principal Act, an amount not exceeding ten per cent.
of the net rent of the dwelling-house comprised in the sub-
tenancy shall be deemed to be a permitted increase in the
case of that dwelling-house, and an amount equivalent to
five per cent. of the net rent of the dwelling-house comprised
in the sub-tenancy shall be deemed to be a permitted increase
in the case of the dwelling-house comprised in the tenancy.
Subsection (2) of section three of the principal Act shall
not apply as respects any increase permitted under this
sub-section.

(2) Where part of any such dwelling-house is so sub-let
the tenant shall, on being so requested in writing by the
landlord, supply him within fourteen days thereafter with
a statement in writing of any sub-letting, giving particulars
of occupancy including the rent charged, and should the
tenant without reasonable excuse fail to do so or supply a
statement which is false in any material particulars he shall
be liable on summary conviction to a fine not exceeding two
pounds.

(3) In subsection (6) of section two of the principal Act
the expression " landlord " shall in relation to a sub-tenancy
be taken to include not only the person who is immediate
landlord of the sub-tenant but also the landlord of that
person.

Limitation on
recovery of
overpayments
or arrears

8.—(1) No increase of rent which becomes payable by
reason of an amendment of a notice of increase made by
order of the county court under this Act shall be recovered in respect of any rental period which ended more than
six months before the date of the order.

(2) Any sum paid by a tenant or mortgagor which under
subsection (1) of section fourteen of the principal Act is

recoverable by the tenant or mortgagor shall be recoverable at any time within six months from the date of payment but not afterwards, or in the case of a payment made before the passing of this Act at any time within six months from the passing of this Act but not afterwards.

13 & 14
Geo 5 c 17

3 Nothing in this section shall affect the operation of the Rent Restriction (Notices of Increase) Act, 1923.

Excessive
charges for
furniture
&c taken
over in con-
nexion with
tenancies

9 (1) Where the purchase of any furniture or other articles is required as a condition of the grant, renewal or continuance of a tenancy or sub-tenancy of a dwelling-house to which the principal Act applies, the price demanded shall, at the request of the person on whom the demand is made, be stated in writing, and if the price exceeds the reasonable price of the articles, the excess shall be treated as if it were a fine or premium required to be paid as a condition of the grant, renewal or continuance, and the provisions of section eight of the principal Act, including penal provisions, shall apply accordingly.

(2) Where a tenant who by virtue of the principal Act retains possession of a dwelling-house to which that Act applies requires that furniture or other articles shall be purchased as a condition of giving up possession, the price demanded shall, at the request of the person on whom the demand is made, be stated in writing, and if the price exceeds the reasonable price of the articles, the excess shall be treated as a sum asked to be paid as a condition of giving up possession, and the provisions of subsection (2) of section fifteen of the principal Act, including penal provisions, shall apply accordingly.

Amendment
of provisions
of the
principal Act
as to houses
let with
furniture &c

10 (1) For the purposes of proviso (ii) to subsection (2) of section twelve of the principal Act, which relates to the exclusion of dwelling-houses from the principal Act in certain circumstances, a dwelling-house shall not be deemed to be bona fide let at a rent which includes payments in respect of attendance or the use of furniture unless the amount of rent which is fairly attributable to the attendance or the use of the furniture, regard being had to the value of the same to the tenant forms a substantial portion of the whole rent

(2) In sections nine and ten of the principal Act (which relate to limitation of rent of houses let with furniture and penalties for excessive charges for such lettings) the expressions 'landlord' and 'tenant' shall respectively be substituted for the expressions 'lessor' and 'lessee.'

11.—(1) The county court shall have power on the application of a landlord or a tenant to determine summarily any questions as to the amount of the rent, standard rent or net rent of any dwelling-house to which the principal Act applies or as to the increase of rent permitted under that Act or this Part of this Act

Power of county court to determine questions as to standard rent, &c

(2) The Lord Chancellor may by rules and directions made and given under section seventeen of the principal Act provide for any questions arising under or in connection with the principal Act or this Part of this Act being referred by consent of the parties interested for final determination by the judge or registrar of a county court sitting as an arbitrator or by an arbitrator appointed by such judge

PART II

RESTRICTIONS AFTER EXPIRY OF PRINCIPAL ACT

12.—(1) If proceedings are taken against the person who on the twenty-fourth day of June nineteen hundred and twenty-five is tenant of a dwelling-house to which the principal Act then applies (hereinafter referred to as the sitting tenant) for the recovery of possession of the dwelling-house or for the ejectment of the tenant therefrom at any time after that day should it appear to the court that the proceedings are harsh or oppressive or that exceptional hardship would be caused to the sitting tenant by the making or giving of an order or judgment for possession or ejectment the court may refuse to make or give such an order or judgment or may adjourn the application for or stay or suspend execution of any such order or judgment

Restriction on right to possession in certain cases after the expiry of the principal Act

11

or postpone the date of possession for such period or periods and subject to such conditions as it thinks proper; and if such conditions are complied with the court may, if it thinks fit, discharge or rescind any such order or judgment.

(2) For the purpose of the exercise of its jurisdiction under this section the court may direct that the tenancy of the sitting tenant shall be treated as a subsisting tenancy notwithstanding the determination of the same by any notice to quit or similar notice or otherwise and may set aside and annul any such notice accordingly, and shall have power to determine what increase of rent (if any) is fair and reasonable, regard being had to the character and condition of the dwelling-house and the rents of similar dwelling-houses in the locality.

(3) The court shall not exercise any of the powers given to it under the foregoing provisions of this section in any case where it is satisfied that greater hardship would be caused to the landlord by the exercise of the power than would be caused to the tenant by the refusal to exercise it.

(4) In any such proceedings an order or judgment for possession or ejectment against the sitting tenant of the dwelling-house shall not, unless the court otherwise directs, be operative against a sitting tenant of a part of the dwelling-house which, on the twenty-fourth day of June nineteen hundred and twenty-five, is lawfully sub-let to him and is a separate dwelling-house to which the principal Act applies; and the court shall, in relation to that part of the dwelling-house and the sitting tenant thereof, have all the like powers and jurisdiction as it has in relation to the whole dwelling-house and the sitting tenant thereof.

(5) In order to assist the court in the determination of questions arising under this Part of this Act in relation to the rent, character or condition of dwelling-houses, the Minister of Health may establish reference committees to whom such questions may be referred by the court for consideration and report.

(6) The foregoing provisions of this section shall not apply to proceedings against a sitting tenant under the Small

Tenements Recovery Act 1838 and any such proceedings shall, on the application of the sitting tenant be discontinued subject to any provision that may be made by rules under this Part of this Act for transfer to the county court

1 & 2 Vict
c 74

13 —(1) If the county court on the application of a sitting tenant is satisfied by the production of a certificate of the sanitary authority and such further evidence (if any) as may be adduced that the dwelling-house is not in a reasonable state of repair and that the condition of the dwelling-house is not due to the tenant's neglect or default or breach of express agreement the court may order that the rent shall be reduced until the court is satisfied on the report of the sanitary authority or otherwise that the necessary repairs (other than any repairs for which the tenant is liable) have been executed and subject to the terms of the order the rent shall be payable at such reduced rate as may be specified therein until the court is so satisfied

Reduction of
rent pending
the execution
of repairs

(2) The powers of the county court under this section may be exercised by the court in any proceedings against a sitting tenant to which the last preceding section of this Act applies

14 —(1) Where a dwelling-house in the occupation of a sitting tenant is subject to a mortgage to which the principal Act applied the county court may on the application of the landlord make an order restraining the mortgagee from calling in his mortgage or taking steps for enforcing his security or for recovering the principal money thereby secured if it is satisfied that such calling in enforcement or recovery would cause exceptional hardship to the landlord The county court may on the application of the mortgagee or landlord rescind or vary any order so made if satisfied that by reason of any material change in circumstances rescission or variation is necessary or proper

Restriction on
calling in of
mortgages

(2) The restrictions imposed on a mortgagee by an order under this section may be imposed subject to such conditions as regards increase of interest or otherwise and for such time as appears to the court to be proper but so

nevertheless that the restrictions shall cease to be operative
if at any time after the making of the order—

    (a) interest is more than twenty-one days in arrear; or

    (b) any covenant by the mortgagor (other than the
        covenant for the repayment of the principal money
        secured) is broken or not performed; or

    (c) the mortgagor fails to keep the property in a proper
        state of repair or to pay the interest and instal-
        ments of principal recoverable under any prior
        encumbrance; or

    (d) the sitting tenant ceases to be tenant of the dwelling-
        house

(3) This section shall not apply to a mortgage where the
principal money secured thereby is repayable by means of
periodical instalments extending over a term of not less
than ten years from the creation of the mortgage

**Regulations
as to reference
committees**

15.—(1) The constitution and procedure of reference committees established under this Part of this Act shall be
such as may be prescribed by regulations made by the
Minister of Health

(2) In addition to any questions that may be referred to
a reference committee by the county court under this Part
of this Act provision may be made by the regulations for
the reference to and determination by a reference committee
of any questions in relation to the rent payable or to be
paid by a sitting tenant which may be submitted to them
by the tenant and landlord

(3) Before any regulation under this section is made it
shall be laid in draft before both Houses of Parliament
and such regulation shall not be made unless both Houses
by resolution approve the draft, either without modification
or addition or with modifications or additions to which both
Houses agree but upon such approval being given the
Minister of Health may make the regulation in the form in
which it has been approved and the regulation on being
so made shall be of full force and effect

16 The Lord Chancellor may make such rules and give such directions as he thinks fit for the purpose of giving full effect to the provisions of this Part of this Act relative to legal proceedings

Rules as to procedure

17 This Part of this Act shall continue in force until the twenty-fourth day of June nineteen hundred and thirty

Duration of Part II

Provided that if a resolution is passed by both Houses of Parliament for the repeal of this Part of this Act on some earlier date it shall be lawful for His Majesty in Council to repeal this Part of this Act on such date as may be specified in that behalf in the resolution

PART III

GENERAL

18—(1) For the purposes of the principal Act and this Act a certificate of a sanitary authority as to the condition of a dwelling-house shall specify what works (if any) require to be executed in order to put the dwelling-house into a reasonable state of repair and on any application to a sanitary authority for a certificate or report for the purposes aforesaid a fee of one shilling shall be payable but if the authority as a result of such application issues a certificate to a tenant the tenant shall be entitled to deduct the fee from any subsequent payment of rent

Certificates of sanitary authorities and definition of repairs

(2) On any application to a county agricultural committee for a certificate for the purpose of paragraph (iii) of subsection (1) of section five of the principal Act a fee shall be payable by the applicant to the county agricultural committee of such amount as the Minister of Agriculture and Fisheries shall by regulation determine

(3) An instrument purporting to be a certificate or report of a sanitary authority or of a county agricultural committee and to be signed by an officer of the authority or committee shall without further proof be taken to be a certificate or report of the authority or committee unless the contrary is proved

(4) A sanitary authority may appoint a committee for

the purposes of the principal Act and this Act and may delegate with or without restrictions to such committee or to an existing committee of the authority all or any of the powers of the authority under the principal Act or this Act

(5) For the purposes of this Act the expression 'repairs' means any repairs required for the purpose of keeping premises in good and tenantable repair and any premises in such a state shall be deemed to be in a reasonable state of repair and the landlord shall be deemed to be responsible for any repairs for which the tenant is under no express liability

Application to Scotland

19 This Act shall apply to Scotland subject to the following modifications :—

(a) The twenty-eighth day of May shall be substituted for the twenty-fourth day of June the Scottish Board of Health shall be substituted for the Minister of Health references to the registrar of a county court shall not apply and 'exciseable liquor' shall be substituted for 'intoxicating liquor'

10 & 11 Geo 5 c 8

(b) For removing doubts it is hereby declared that nothing in the principal Act affects the operation of the House Letting and Rating (Scotland) Act 1920 and the reference in subsection (2) of section one of the last mentioned Act to the provisions of Acts repealed by the principal Act shall be construed as a reference to the provisions of section three of the principal Act

Short title construction and extent

13 & 14 Geo 5 c 7

20 This Act may be cited as the Rent and Mortgage Interest Restrictions Act 1923 and shall be construed as one with the principal Act save that this Act shall not apply to Ireland and the principal Act the Increase of Rent and Mortgage Interest Restrictions (Continuance) Act 1923 the Rent Restrictions (Notices of Increase) Act 1923 and this Act may be cited together as the Rent and Mortgage Interest Restrictions Acts 1920 and 1923

APPENDIX II.

TEXT OF THE INCREASE OF RENT (&c.) RULES

———◆———

A

STATUTORY RULES AND ORDERS
1920, No. $\frac{1261}{L37}$
INCREASE OF RENT AND MORTGAGE INTEREST (RESTRICTIONS) ENGLAND

County Court Procedure

THE INCREASE OF RENT AND MORTGAGE INTEREST (RESTRICTIONS) RULES 1920 DATED JULY 9 1920 MADE BY THE LORD CHANCELLOR UNDER THE INCREASE OF RENT AND MORTGAGE INTEREST (RESTRICTIONS) ACT 1920 (10 & 11 GEO 5 c 17)

Preliminary

The following Rules under the Increase of Rent and Mortgage Interest (Restrictions) Act 1920 (in these Rules referred to as the Act) shall apply to the County Courts and to the City of London Court which shall for the purposes of these Rules be deemed to be a county court **10 & 11 Geo 5. c 17**

Rule 3 of these Rules as to applications under the County (Emergency Powers) Act 1914 shall apply also to the High Court and the rules made under that Act shall have effect subject to that Rule **4 & 5 Geo 5, c 78**

These Rules may be cited as the Increase of Rent and Mortgage Interest (Restrictions) Rules 1920 and shall come into operation on the 15th day of July 1920

On the coming into operation of these Rules the following
Rules viz.:—

S. R. & O.
1916 No. 63
S. R. & O.
1919 No.
623

The Increase of Rent and Mortgage Interest (War
Restriction) Rules 1916 dated the 29th January 1916,
and the like Rules 1919 dated the 21st May 1919
shall be annulled without prejudice to anything done
thereunder and these Rules shall apply to all proceedings pending under the Rules hereby annulled on the
day when these Rules come into operation

*Applications under Section 2 Section 9 Section 12 sub-
section (1 g) or (3) Section 6 or Section 5
subsection (6)*

Applications
under 10 & 11
Geo 5 c 17
sec 2 sect 9
sect 12
subsect 1 and
3, sect 6 or
sect 5 sub-
sect 6

1   An application to the county court under the Act
   (a) to determine any question or make any order or
       declaration relating to increase of rent under
       section 2 or section 9 or
   (b) to apportion the rent or rateable value of the pro-
       perty under section 3 or section 12 or
   (c) for leave to distrain under section 5 or
   (d) by a member of the tenant's family under section 12
       subsection (1 g) or
   (e) for compensation under section 5 subsection (6)
may be made in the case of (e) to the court in which the order
or judgment complained of was obtained and in all other
cases to the court in the district of which the premises are
situate

Applications
under sect 7
proviso 2

2   (1) An application to the county court under the Act
for an order authorising a mortgagee to call in and enforce
a mortgage of a leasehold interest to which the Act applies
pursuant to the second proviso to section 7 may be made—
   (a) to the court in the district of which the mortgaged
       property is situate or
   (b) to the court in the district of which the mortgagor
       resides or carries on business or
   (c) if the mortgagee resides or carries on business in the
       district of any court mentioned in section 81 of the
       County Courts Act 1888 and the mortgagor resides

51 & 52 Vic
43, s 81

or carries on business in the district of any other court mentioned in the said section, either to the court in the district of which the mortgagee resides or carries on business, or to the court in the district of which the mortgagor resides or carries on business.

3.—(1) Subject to the provisions of this Rule, the Courts (Emergency Powers) Rules and the County Courts (Emergency Powers) Rules as to applications to the High Court or to the county court for leave to foreclose or realize any security to which the Courts (Emergency Powers) Act, 1914 applies, shall cease to apply to mortgages of leasehold interests to which the Increase of Rent and Mortgage Interest (Restrictions) Act, 1920 applies, and this Rule shall apply in lieu thereof.

Applications under Courts (Emergency Powers) Act 1914 (4 & 5 Geo 5 c 78), and Rules, how affected by these Rules

(2) An application under the last preceding Rule for an order authorizing a mortgagee to call in and enforce a mortgage of a leasehold interest shall, if and so far as an application for leave to foreclose or realize the security is required under the Courts (Emergency Powers) Act, 1914, be deemed to be also an application for leave to foreclose or realize the security under that Act, and no separate application under that Act shall be necessary.

(3) If during the progress of the proceedings on any such application it shall be made to appear to the court that the mortgage is one to which the Increase of Rent and Mortgage Interest (Restrictions) Act, 1920 does not apply, but that leave to realize or enforce the security is required under the Courts (Emergency Powers) Act, 1914, and that the amount of the principal sum secured by the mortgage does not exceed five hundred pounds, the application may proceed in the county court as an application for leave to foreclose or realize the security under the last mentioned Act and the County Courts (Emergency Powers) Rules, and those Rules shall apply accordingly; but if the amount of the principal sum secured by the mortgage exceeds five hundred pounds, the application shall not proceed under the last mentioned Act, unless the respondent consents to the county court having

jurisdiction in the matter in which case the court shall have jurisdiction to deal with the application as an application for leave to foreclose or realize the security under the last mentioned Act and Rules and those Rules shall apply accordingly

(4) If it shall be made to appear to the court that the mortgage is one to which neither of the above mentioned Acts applies, the application shall be struck out

Application by summons Forms 1 2 5 7 11 15 and 16

4 An application under these Rules (other than the applications referred to in rules 19 and 20) shall be made by means of a summons according to such one of the forms in the Appendix as shall be applicable to the case entitled

In the Matter of the Increase of Rent and Mortgage Interest (Restrictions) Act 1920

Preparation, Filing &c of Summonses

Preparation &c of summons and copies

5 The summons shall be prepared by the applicant and filed with the registrar with as many copies as there are parties to be served Provided that any summons with the necessary copies may if the registrar so thinks fit be prepared in his office and the registrar shall examine complete seal and sign the summons and copies and return the copies to the applicant for service

Service and Substituted Service

Time for service

6—(1) The summons shall be served on every person affected thereby four clear days at least before the day fixed for the hearing of the summons unless the judge or registrar gives leave for shorter service On an application by the Sanitary Authority under section 2 subsection (2) notice in writing of the summons shall be given to the tenant by the Sanitary Authority

Mode of service

(2) Service shall be effected in accordance with the provisions of Order LIV Rules 2 and 3 of the County Court Rules as to service of notice of an interlocutory application

Substituted service

(3) The practice of the courts as to substituted service of summonses and notices shall apply to summonses under these Rules

Applications to Registrar

7 Any application under these Rules may be made to the   Application
registrar subject to the following provisions —   to registrar

(a) The registrar may in any case and shall on the application of either party made on the hearing of the
application and before the registrar has given his
decision refer the matter to the judge

(b) The judge may vary or rescind any determination or
order made by the registrar and may make such
determination or order as may be just

(c) An application for such variation or rescission shall be
made on notice in writing in accordance with the
County Court Rules as to interlocutory applications, and the notice shall be filed within four
clear days from the date of the determination or
order of the registrar and if it is not so filed no
such application shall be allowed to be made without leave of the judge

Evidence in Support of Application

8 No affidavit in support of the application shall be used   Evidence in
except by leave of the court but the court shall hear oral   support of
evidence tendered by either party   application

Power to hear Cases in Private

9 The court may at any stage of the proceedings on an   Power to hear
application under the Act order that the case shall thence- cases in
forward be heard in private   private

Transfer of Proceedings

10 If during the progress of the proceedings on any   Transfer of
application it shall be made to appear to the judge that the proceedings
same could be more conveniently heard in some other court,
it shall be competent to the judge to transfer the same to
such other court and in any such case the provisions of
section 85 of the County Courts Act 1888 and section 10
of the County Courts Act, 1919 and of Order VIII Rule 9
of the County Court Rules shall apply

Decisions of Court

11. On the hearing of the application, or at any adjournment thereof, the court, on proof of the service of the summons, if the respondent does not appear shall—

(a) in the case of an application under section 2 or section 9 or section 5, subsection (6) determine the question raised or make or refuse the order or declaration asked for, or

(b) in the case of an application under subsection (3) of section 12 apportion the rent or rateable value, or

(c) in the case of an application under section 6 give or refuse leave, or

(d) in the case of an application under section 7 make or refuse an order authorising the mortgagee to call in or enforce the mortgage, or

(e) in the case of any application make such other determination order or declaration in the matter as the court shall think fit.

Power to impose Conditions

12 On an application for an order authorising a mortgagee to call in and enforce a mortgage the court may after considering all the circumstances of the case and the position of all the parties make or refuse to make the order subject to such conditions as the court may think fit

Certificates Orders or Declarations on Application

13 When the court has given its decision on any application a certificate of the determination of the court or an order or declaration in accordance with the decision of the court shall be prepared and sealed and signed by the registrar and duplicates thereof shall be delivered to the bailiff who shall within twenty-four hours send the same by post or otherwise to the parties but it shall not be necessary for the party in whose favour a certificate or order or declaration is made to prove, previously to taking proceedings thereon that it was posted or reached the opposite party

General Provisions as to Procedure on Applications

14 Subject to the provisions of the Act and these Rules **Ordinary** the practice and procedure of the court in an action and in **practice of** particular the practice and procedure with respect to the **the Court to** summoning of witnesses and with respect to discovery and **be followed** inspection of documents shall with the necessary modifications apply to proceedings on an application under the Act

15 — (1. The following fees shall be payable under **Fees** Schedule B Part I of the Treasury Order regulating Fees in the County Courts on applications under the Act and these Rules in lieu of all other fees on such proceedings viz —

On an application for an order or declaration or the determination of a question relating to the increase of rent of premises or for leave to distrain —

		s	d
6d in the £ or part of a £ calculated on 4 weeks standard rent (or on an application under section 9 of the actual rent of the premises or in the case of leave to distrain on the rent to be distrained for but not exceeding		2	6
On an application for the apportionment of rent or rateable value or for compensation under section 5 sub-section 6		10	0
On an application for an order authorising a mortgagee to call in and enforce a mortgage		20	0

The foregoing fees shall include drawing sealing and issuing the certificate or order (except in the case of an application for leave to distrain in which case there shall be payable for drawing sealing and issuing the order (a) a further fee of 6d in the £ or part of a £ on the rent to be distrained for not exceeding 2s 6d (a) and the fee prescribed by paragraph 12 of Part I of Schedule B or the Fees Order shall not be taken

(2) On summonses to witnesses the fees prescribed by Schedule A of the Fees Order shall be taken.

a Amended (11 Jan 1921 S R & O 1921 N

(3) On applications for discovery or inspection of documents and on applications for rescission or variation of orders or judgments under section 5 subsection 3 the fees prescribed by paragraphs 10 and 12 of Part I of Schedule B of the Fees Order shall be taken

(4) The court may remit or excuse in whole or in part any fee paid or payable under this Rule

Costs

16.—(1) The costs of any application under the Act and these Rules shall be in the absolute discretion of the court

(2) The court may either fix the amount of such costs or allow them on the scale applicable to an interlocutory application in an action for an amount equal to—

(a) in the case of an application for an order or declaration or determination of a question relating to the increase of rent or for leave to distrain the amount on which fees are payable under Rule 15 or

(b) in the case of an application to apportion rent or rateable value one-half of the annual rent or rateable value apportioned to the premises or

(c) in the case of an application for an order authorising a mortgagee to call in and enforce the mortgage the amount of the principal sum secured Provided that Column B of the Scale shall apply in all cases above twenty pounds to the exclusion of Column C

(3) Where the amount does not exceed ten pounds there may be allowed for all work done by a solicitor in relation to the application—   s. d.

If the amount exceeds £2 but does not exceed £5   6   8

If the amount exceeds £5 but does not exceed £10   10   0

(4) In the case of an application for compensation under section 5 subsection 6 the Court may either fix the amount of such costs or allow them on the scale applicable in an action

(5) In the case of any other application the Court shall fix the amount of such costs

(6) The court may direct that any costs allowed shall be

payable by the opposite party or in the case of an application for an order authorising a mortgagee to call in and enforce a mortgage that they shall be included in the security, and any order directing payment of costs shall be included in the certificate or order, and shall be enforceable in the same manner as an order for payment of costs made in an action

Forms

17.—(1) The forms in the Appendix hereto, with such modifications as may be necessary, shall be used for summonses, applications, certificates and orders under the Act and these Rules

(2) The registrar of any Court may apply to the Treasury for any of the said forms to be printed and supplied to him, and if the application is granted may obtain such forms and supply the same without charge for the use of parties requiring the same

Forms

Proceedings for the Recovery of Rent or Mortgage Interest, or for the Recovery of Possession of Tenements or Ejectment of Tenants

18 Where proceedings are taken in the county court for the recovery of rent of any premises to which the Act applies or of interest on a mortgage to which the Act applies, or for the recovery of possession of any premises to which the Act applies or for the ejectment of a tenant from any such premises the court shall, before making an order for the recovery of such rent or interest or for recovery of possession or ejectment, satisfy itself that such order may properly be made, regard being had to the provisions of the Act

On proceedings for recovery of rents or mortgage interest, or for recovery of possession or ejectment regard to be had to the Act

Death of Tenant Intestate

19 Where on the death of a tenant intestate a member of his family requires the decision of the Court under the latter part of section 12 subsection 1 (g) of the Act the judge shall give such directions as to the procedure to be followed and the notices to be given to and the attendance of all such persons as may be interested as he shall think fit and he (or the registrar if so directed by him) shall con-

Death of tenant intestate

sider what may be urged (either orally or in writing) by or on behalf of such persons, and thereupon give his decision, provided that the registrar's decision may be varied by the judge pursuant to Rule 7. Rule 13, relating to certificates of decisions, shall apply to a decision under this sub-section if so directed by the judge

Applications for Stay Rescission or Variation of Orders or Judgments

Applications for stay, rescission or variation of orders or judgments.

20 An application to the court for stay, suspension discharge, rescission or variation of orders or judgments under section 5 sub-section (2) or (3) may be made on notice in writing in accordance with the County Court Rules as to interlocutory applications

The 9th day of July 1920

APPENDIX

I.

Summons for Determination of Question or Declaration or Order relating to Increase of Rent under Section 2, subsections (1) or (3)

In the County Court of   holden at

In the Matter of the Increase of Rent and Mortgage Interest (Restrictions) Act 1920

No of Application

Between

A B
(address and
description)   Applicant
and

C D
(address and
description)   Respondent

To
of

TAKE NOTICE that you are hereby summoned to attend this Court on   the   day of   , at the hour of   in the   noon on the hearing of an application on the part of   of   for the determination pursuant to the above-mentioned Act of a question for for a declaration or order relating to the increase of rent of certain premises *or of part that is to say (here specify the part   of certain premises)* to which the said Act applies situate at   and known as   of which the applicant is the tenant and you the respondent are the landlord *or of which you the respondent are the tenant and the applicant is the landlord* the question being   in respect of the transfer to the tenant of certain burdens and liabilities previously borne by the landlord *or in respect of the transfer to the landlord of certain burdens and liabilities previously borne by the tenant   or here state the question to be determined in the declaration or order asked for*   and for an order providing for the costs of the application

AND FURTHER TAKE NOTICE that if you do not attend in person or by your solicitor at the time and place above mentioned such proceedings will be taken and determination or declaration or order made as the Court may think just

Dated this   day of   19

By the Court

Registrar

To (the respondent naming him)

2

Summons for Order authorising Mortgagee to call in and enforce Mortgage

In the County Court of   holden at

In the Matter of the Increase of Rent and Mortgage Interest (Restrictions) Act 1920

No of Application

Between

A B
(address and description)   Applicant

and

C D
(address and description)   Respondent

To
of

TAKE NOTICE that you are hereby summoned to attend this Court on   the   day of   at the hour

13

of   in the   noon, on the hearing of an application on the part of   of   , for an order that notwithstanding the provisions of the above-mentioned Act, the said   may be at liberty to call in and enforce a certain mortgage to which the said Act applies, dated the   day of   granted by you the respondent to the applicant [or to   and assigned by him to the applicant] on certain leasehold property situate at   , and known as   , on the ground that the security is seriously diminishing in value or is otherwise in jeopardy, and that for that reason it is reasonable that the mortgage should be called in and enforced,   , and for an order providing for the costs of the application

AND FURTHER TAKE NOTICE, that if you do not attend in person or by your solicitor at the time and place above mentioned such proceedings will be taken and determination made as the Court may think just

Dated this   day of   19

By the Court

Registrar

To (the respondent,
    naming him)

J

Certificate on Application for Determination of Question or Declaration or Order relating to Increase of Rent, under Section 2 subsections (1) or (3)

In the County Court of   holden at

In the Matter of the Increase of Rent and Mortgage Interest (Restrictions) Act, 1920

No of Application

Between

A B
(address and
    description)   Applicant,

and

C D
(address and
    description)   Respondent

On the application of   and upon hearing   ,

This Court doth pursuant to the above-mentioned Act determine and declare [or order] as follows:-

[(a) that as the result of the transfer to the applicant, A B., [or the respondent C D.,　　] the tenant　　certain premises [or of part, that is to say (*here specify the part*)　　of certain premises to which the said Act applies, situate at　　and known as　　of the following burdens and liabilities formerly borne by the respondent, C D. [or by the applicant, A B.　　] the landlord that is to say (*here specify the burdens and liabilities transferred*)　　the terms on which the said premises are held are on the whole less favourable to the tenant than the previous terms and that the rent of the said premises has thereby been increased for the purposes of the said Act by the sum of　　a week [or are on the whole not less favourable to the tenant than the previous terms and that the rent of the said premises has not been increased for the purposes of the said Act]

[or (b) that as the result of the transfer to the applicant A B　　[or the respondent, C D.,　　] the landlord of certain premises [or of part that is to say (*here specify the part*)　　of certain premises to which the said Act applies, situate at　　and known as　　of the following burdens and liabilities previously borne by the respondent C D.　　[or the applicant A B.　　] the tenant that is to say (*here specify the burdens and liabilities transferred*)　　and the increase of rent in respect of such transfer the terms on which the said premises are held are on the whole more favourable to the tenant than the previous terms, and that the increase of rent in respect of such transfer is to be deemed not to be an increase of rent for the purposes of the said Act [or are on the whole less favourable to the tenant than the previous terms and that the increased rent in respect of such transfer is to be deemed to be an increase of rent for the purposes of the said Act to the extent of　　a week

[or as the case may be]

[or (*here state the decision of the Court on the question or matter the subject of the application*)]

15 (2)

[Add, if so ordered,

And it is ordered that the respondent, C D , or the applicant A B do, on or before the day of , 19 , to pay to the applicant, A B [or to the respondent, C D ,] his costs of this application, which are hereby allowed at the sum of £

Dated this day of 19

By the Court

To *the applicant*
and respondent,
naming them)

Registrar

I

Order on Application for Order authorising Mortgagee to call in and enforce Mortgage

In the County Court of holden at

In the Matter of the Increase of Rent and Mortgage Interest (Restrictions) Act 1920

No of Application

Between

A B
(address and
description)
Applicant

and

C D
(address and
description)
Respondent

On the application of and upon hearing

This Court being satisfied that the security of the applicant on certain leasehold property situate at and known as under a certain mortgage to which the above-mentioned Act applies dated the day of granted by the respondent to the applicant [or to and assigned by him to the applicant] is seriously diminishing in value or is otherwise in jeopardy and that it is reasonable that the said mortgage should be called in and enforced doth pursuant to the above-mentioned Act order that notwithstanding the provisions of the said Act the applicant, A B be at liberty and he is hereby authorised to call in and enforce the said mortgage

[If any conditions imposed add subject to the following conditions that is to say —

(b) It is ordered that the application of the applicant A B
for an order authorising him to call in and enforce a
certain mortgage to which the above-mentioned Act applies,
on certain leasehold property situate at   and known
as   dated the   day of   19   granted by
the respondent C D, to the applicant A B   or to
          and assigned by him to the applicant A B
be and the same is hereby dismissed

Add, if so ordered.

And it is ordered that the applicant A B   be
allowed as against the respondent C D   his costs of
his application which are hereby allowed at the sum of
£

And it is ordered that the said sum of £   be added
to the security created by the said mortgage or that the
respondent C D   do pay the said sum of £   to
the applicant A B   on or before the   day of
          19

(b) And it is ordered that the applicant A B   do,
on or before the   day of   19   pay to the
respondent C D   his costs of this application which
are hereby allowed at the sum of £

Dated this   day of   19

By the Court

To (the applicant   Registrar
    and respondent
    naming them)

Summons for Apportionment of Rent or Rateable Value of
    Property under Section 12 subsection (3).

In the County Court of   holden at

In the Matter of the Increase of Rent and Mortgage
    Interest (Restrictions) Act 1920

No. of Application

Between

A B
    (address and
    description)   Applicant
                    and
C D
    (address and
    description)   Respondent
To
    of

TAKE NOTICE that you are hereby summoned to attend this Court on   the   day of   , at the hour of   in the   noon on the hearing of an application on the part of   , of   for the apportionment of the rent on the 3rd day of August, 1914 [*or (i) the property was last let before or first let after the 3rd August, 1914 insert the date at which it was so let, see Act Section 12, subsection 1 (a)*]   [*or the rateable value on the 3rd day of August, 1914 or (ii) the property was first assessed after that date insert the date at which it was first assessed*] of certain property situate at   and known as   and comprising certain premises [*or part, that is to say (here specify the part)*   *of certain premises*] situate at   and known as   for the purpose of determining the standard rent [*or the rateable value*] of the said premises [*or of the above-mentioned part of the said premises*] for the purposes of the above-mentioned Act   and for an order providing for the costs of the application

AND FURTHER TAKE NOTICE that if you do not attend in person or by your solicitor at the time and place above mentioned such proceedings will be taken and determination made as the Court may think just

Dated this   day of   19

By the Court

Registrar

To (*the respondent naming him*)

6

Certificate on Application for Apportionment of Rent or Rateable Value

In the Matter of the Increase of Rent and Mortgage Interest (Restrictions) Act 1920

No of Application

Between

A B
(*address and description*)   Applicant,

and

C D
(*address and description*)   Respondent
On the application of   and upon hearing

This Court for the purpose of determining the standard rent *or rateable value* of certain premises *or of part that is to say (here specify the part)* of certain premises to which the above-mentioned Act applies situate at and known as and comprised in a certain property known as doth pursuant to the above-mentioned Act declare that the rent at which the said property was let on the 3rd day of August 1914 *or if the property was last let before that date or first let after that date* on the day of 19 *(the date on which it was so let)* shall be apportioned between the said premises *or the said part of the said premises* and the rest of the said property as follows viz :—

£ to the said premises *or the said part of the said premises* and

£ to the remainder of the said property

or doth pursuant to the above-mentioned Act declare that the rateable value of the said property on the 3rd day of August 1914 *or if the property was first assessed after that date* on the day of 19 *(the date on which it was first assessed)* shall be apportioned between the said premises *or the said part of the premises* and the rest of the said property as follows viz :—

£ to the said premises *or the said part of the said premises* and

£ to the remainder of the said property

Add if so ordered

And it is ordered that the respondent C D *or the applicant A B* do on or before the day of 19 pay to the applicant A B *or to the respondent C D* his costs of this application which are hereby allowed at the sum of

Dated this day of 19

By the Court

Registrar

*To (the applicant
and respondent
naming them)*

7

*Summons for Order of Suspension and Declaration relating
to Increase of Rent under Section 2 subsection (2)*

In the County Court of   , holden at

In the Matter of the Increase of Rent and Mortgage
Interest (Restrictions) Act, 1920

No. of Application

Between

A B

*(address and
description)*   Applicant,

and

C D

*(address and
description)*   Respondent

To

of

TAKE NOTICE that you are hereby summoned to attend
this Court on the   day of   at the hour of   in
the   noon on the hearing of an application under
Section 2 subsection (2) of the said Act   on the part
of   of   for a declaration that certain premises (or
part, that is to say *here specify the part)*   of certain
premises to which the said Act applies situate at
and known as   of which the applicant (or where the
applicant is the Sanitary Authority state the name of the
tenant) is the tenant and you the respondent, are the landlord are not in all respects reasonably fit for human habitation (or are not in a reasonable state of repair) and that the
condition of the premises is not due to the tenant's neglect,
or default or breach of express agreement if any and
for an order suspending the increase of rent pursuant to
Section 2 subsection (2) of the said Act until further order
or for such other declaration and order in that behalf as
the Court may think fit   and for an order providing
for the costs of this application

AND FURTHER TAKE NOTICE that if you do not attend
in person or by your solicitor at the time and place above
mentioned such proceedings will be taken and declaration
and order made as the Court may think just

Dated this   day of   19

By the Court

To (*the respondent   Registrar
naming him)*

8

Order on Application for Order of Suspension and Declaration relating to Increase of Rent under Section 2 subsection (2)

In the County Court of   holden at

In the Matter of the Increase of Rent and Mortgage Interest (Restrictions) Act 1920

No. of Application

Between

A B
   (address and
      description)   Applicant,
                                    and
C D
   (address and
      description)   Respondent
On the application of   and upon hearing

The Court being satisfied that certain premises (or that part that is to say (*here specify the part*)   of certain premises to which the said Act applies situate at   and known as   of which the applicant (or where the Sanitary Authority is the applicant state the name of the tenant) is the tenant and the respondent is the landlord are not in all respects reasonably fit for human habitation (or are not in a reasonable state of repair) and that the condition of the premises is not due to the tenant's neglect or default or breach of express agreement doth declare accordingly and doth order pursuant to Section 2 subsection (2) of the said Act that the increase of rent of   be suspended until respondent upon notice of application in that behalf shall have satisfied the Court that the necessary repairs (other than the repairs if any for which the tenant is liable) have been executed (or such other declaration or order as the Court thinks fit)

(Or it is ordered that the application of the said   be and the same is hereby dismissed

(Add order as to costs if any see Form 6

Dated this   day of   19

By the Court

To the applicant   Registrar
   and respondent
      naming them

9

*Notice of the Application under Section 5, subsection (2) or
(3) for Stay, Suspension, Discharge, Rescission or
Variation of Order, or Judgment*

In the Matter of the Increase of Rent and Mortgage
Interest (Restrictions) Act 1920

In the County Court of   holden at

No. of Application

Between

A B
  *(address and
    description)*   Applicant,

and

C D
  *(address and
    description)*   Respondent

Take Notice that the applicant A B   [or the
respondent C D   intends to apply to the Judge of
this Court on   the   day of   19   at the hour
of   in the   noon to stay [suspend discharge
rescind or vary the order or judgment made or given]
in this matter on the   day of   19   whereby
it was ordered [or adjudged] that *(here recite order or
judgment)*

and for an order providing for the costs of this application.

And further take Notice that the grounds of my
intended application are that

(here set out circumstances)

Dated this   day of   19

(Signed)

Applicant [or Respondent]

or Applicants [or Respondents]
               Solicitor]

To the respondent or applicant
    naming him
and to Messrs
    his solicitors
and to the registrar of the Court

10

Order on Application under Section 5 subsection (2) or (3) for Stay Suspension Discharge Rescission, or Variation of Order or Judgment

In the Matter of the Increase of Rent and Mortgage Interest (Restrictions) Act 1920

In the County Court of   holden at

No of Application   .

Between

A. B
(address and
    description)   Applicant

and

C D
(address and
    description)   Respondent

On the application of   for the stay suspension [discharge rescission or variation] of the order made [or judgment given] in this matter on the   day of   19 whereby it was ordered [or adjudged] that

(here recite order or judgment)

and upon hearing

It is ordered that the said order [or judgment] be and the same is hereby stayed suspended [or discharged or rescinded or varied] as follows —

(here set out terms of order)

[Or It is ordered that the application of the said be and the same is hereby dismissed]

[Add order as to costs if any see Form 7]

Dated this   day of   19

By the Court

Registrar

To (the applicant
    and the respondent
        naming them)

H

*Summons on Application for Determination of Question or
Declaration and Order under Section 9.*

In the County Court of   , holden at

In the Matter of the Increase of Rent and Mortgage
Interest (Restrictions) Act, 1920

No. of Application

Between

A B
     (address and
          description)   Applicant

and

C D
     (address and
          description)   Respondent

TAKE NOTICE that you are hereby summoned to attend
this Court on   the   day of   19   at the hour
of   in the   noon on the hearing of an application
on the part of   of   the particulars of which are
hereunto annexed

AND FURTHER TAKE NOTICE that if you do not attend
in person or by your solicitor at the time and place above-
mentioned such proceedings will be taken and order made as
the Court may think just

Dated this   day of   19

By the Court

Registrar

To (the Respondent
     naming him)

PARTICULARS

*To be appended or annexed to summons and if on separate
paper with heading as in summons*

1 On or about the   day of   19   the
Respondent let certain premises or a part that is to say
[here specify the part] of certain premises] to which the

said Act applies situate at   and known as   to the Applicant at a rent of   a week *or a month or as the case may be]*   which rent includes payment in respect of furniture

2 The Applicant alleges that the rent charged for the premises so let to him is yielding or will yield to the Respondent a profit more than 25 per cent in excess of the profit which might reasonably have been obtained from a similar letting in the year ending on the 3rd day of August 1914

3 The Applicant therefore applies to the Court under section 9 of the Increase of Rent and Mortgage Interest (Restrictions) Act 1920—

(a) for a declaration that it is proved to the satisfaction of the Court that the rent charged on the letting of the said premises by the Respondent to the Applicant is yielding or will yield to the Respondent a profit more than 25 per cent in excess of the profit which might reasonably have been obtained from a similar letting in the year ending on the 3rd day of August 1914 and for an assessment by the Court of the amount of such last-mentioned profit and

(b) for an order that the said rent so far as it exceeds such sum as would yield such last-mentioned profit and 25 per cent thereon shall be irrecoverable and

(c) for an order that the amount of any payment of rent in excess of such sum made by the Applicant in respect of any period after the passing of the said Act shall be repaid to the Applicant and may without prejudice to any other mode of recovery be recovered by the Applicant by means of deductions from any subsequent payment of rent and

(d) for an order providing for the costs of this application

Dated this   day of   19

Applicant

or Applicant's Solicitor

12

Order on Application under Section 9

In the County Court of   holden at

In the Matter of the Increase of Rent and Mortgage
Interest (Restrictions) Act 1920

No. of Application

Between

A. B.
(address and
description)   Applicant

and

C. D.
(address and
description)   Respondent

On the application of   for an order under section 9
of the Increase of Rent and Mortgage Interest (Restrictions)
Act 1920 and upon hearing

The Court doth declare that it is proved to its satisfaction
that the rent charged on the letting by the Respondent to
the Applicant of certain premises *or a part that is to say
there specify the part*   of certain premises] to which
the said Act applies situate at   and known as   a
rent of   a week *or a month or as the case may be*
          which rent includes payment in respect of the use
of furniture is yielding *or will yield* to the Respondent
a profit more than 25 per cent. in excess of the profit which
might reasonably have been obtained from a similar letting
in the year ending on the 3rd day of August 1914 which
last-mentioned profit is hereby assessed by the Court at the
sum of   a week *or a month or as the case may be*

And it is ordered that the said rent to the extent of
a week *or as the case may be]*   being the amount by
which the said rent exceeds the sum of   per week *or
or as the case may be*   which would yield such last-
mentioned profit and 25 per cent. thereon shall be
irrecoverable

And it is further ordered that the sum of   being the
amount of the payments of rent in excess of the said sum
of   per week *or as the case may be]*   made by

the Applicant in respect of the period of the said letting after the passing of the Increase of Rent and Mortgage Interest (Restrictions) Act, 1920 shall be repaid to the Applicant and may without prejudice to any other method of recovery, be recovered by the Applicant by means of deductions from any subsequent payments of rent

Add if so ordered—

And it is ordered that the Respondent do pay the said sum of   to the Applicant on the   day of   [or by instalments of   for every   days, the first payment to be made on the   day of   ].

Add also if so ordered—

And it is ordered that the Respondent do on or before the   day of   pay to the Applicant his costs of this application which are hereby allowed at the sum of

Or, if application fails—

On the application of   for an order under section 9 of the Increase of Rent and Mortgage Interest (Restrictions) Act, 1920 and upon hearing

It is ordered that the said application be and the same is hereby dismissed

Add directions if any as to costs

Dated this   day of   19

By the Court

Registrar

*To (the applicant
and respondent
naming them)*

---

13 and 14

*For summons and order for leave to distrain adapt forms 5
and 6 and 7 the Consolidated County Courts (Emergency Powers) Rules 1918*

15

Summons for Declaration and Order relating to payment
of Compensation under Section 5 subsection (6)

In the County Court of   holden at

In the Matter of the Increase of Rent and Mortgage
Interest Restrictions Act 1920

No of Application

Between

A B
address and
description   Applicant
                              and
C D
address and
description   Respondent
To
        of

Take Notice that you are hereby summoned to attend
this Court on the   day of   at the hour of
in the   noon on the hearing of an application under
Section 5 subsection (6) of the said Act on the part of
        of   for a declaration that the order or judg-
ment dated the   day of   and made or given in
an action in this Court

                here give title of action

for possession of or ejectment from certain premises or of
part that is to say

                here specify the part

of certain premises
to which the said Act applies situate at   and known
as   of which the Applicant was the tenant and you
the Respondent were the landlord was obtained by misrepresentation or the concealment of material facts
and that the applicant is entitled to recover from you compensation for damage or loss sustained by him as the result
of the said order or judgment and for an order ordering
you to pay the sum of £   or such sum as shall appear
to the Court sufficient as compensation for such damage or
loss or for such other declaration and order in that behalf
as the Court may think fit and for an order providing for
the costs of this application

AND FURTHER TAKE NOTICE that if you do not attend in person or by your solicitor at the time and place above-mentioned such proceedings will be taken and declaration and order made as the Court may think just

Dated this   day of   19

By the Court

Registrar

To *the Respondent,*
naming him

16

Order on Application for Declaration and Order relating to Payment of Compensation under Section 5 subsection (6)

In the County Court of   holden at

In the Matter of the Increase of Rent and Mortgage Interest (Restrictions) Act 1920

No of Application

Between

A B
   (address and
      description)   Applicant

and

C D
   address and
      description)   Respondent

On the application of   and upon hearing

The Court doth declare and adjudge that the order or judgment dated the   day of   and made or given in an action in this Court *(here give title of action)* for possession of or ejectment from certain premises or or part that is to say *(here specify the part)* of certain premises to which the said Act applies situate at and known as   of which the applicant was the tenant and the respondent was the landlord was obtained by mis-representation or the concealment of material facts and that the applicant is entitled under Section 5 subsection (6) of the said Act to recover against the respondent the sum of £　　as compensation for damage or loss sustained by the applicant as the result of the said order (or judgment and it is ordered that the respondent do pay the said sum of £　　to the Registrar of this Court on the　　day of　　, or it is ordered that the application of the said be, and the same is hereby dismissed

(Add order as to costs if any, see Form 6)

Dated this　　day of　　　19

By the Court,

Registrar

To (the applicant
and respondent,
naming them)

B

STATUTORY RULES AND ORDERS, 1923, No. $\frac{101}{L\ 16}$.

LANDLORD AND TENANT, ENGLAND

Rent (Restrictions on Increase of)

County Court Procedure

The Rent (Restrictions) Rules 1923, dated August 7, 1923, made by the Lord Chancellor under the Rent and Mortgage Interest Restrictions Acts 1920 and 1923 (10 & 11 Geo 5, c 17 and 13 & 14 Geo 5, c 32)

1 The Increase of Rent and Mortgage Interest (Restrictions) Rules 1920 (S R & O 1920 No 1261), (hereinafter referred to as the principal Rules) other than Rules 2 3, 12, 19 and 20 shall be extended to include applications under Part I of the Rent and Mortgage Interest Restrictions Act, 1923 (hereinafter referred to as the 1923 Act) except under subsection (2) of section 11 and the forms

prescribed by the principal Rules shall be used with the necessary modifications accordingly

2.—(1) The fees payable in the case of any such original application under the 1923 Act shall if the same could not have been made under the principal Act be as directed by Rule 15 of the principal Rules in the case of an application under the principal Act for the apportionment of rent Where the application could have been made under the principal Act the fees shall be as directed by that Rule in the case of such an application

(2) The costs of any such original application under the 1923 Act whether the same could or could not have been made under the principal Act shall be in the absolute discretion of the Court and the Court in every such case shall fix the amount of such costs

3 The Court may exercise the power of amendment conferred by subsection (1) of section 6 of the 1923 Act either on an original application by landlord or tenant in that behalf as directed by the foregoing Rule 1 or where proceedings before the Court are pending in which the validity of any notice of increase is in question or is material on request by either party at any time in the course of those proceedings

4—(1) Where parties desire to have any questions arising under the principal Act or Part I of the 1923 Act settled by arbitration pursuant to the provisions of subsection (2) of section 11 of the 1923 Act they shall sign and deliver to the County Court of the district in which the demised premises are situate a request in writing in accordance with the form set out in the Appendix to these Rules which shall stand as Form 17 in the Appendix to the principal Rules

(2) On receipt of the application in the case where with the consent of the parties the arbitration is to be before a person nominated by the judge the judge shall proceed forthwith to nominate an arbitrator and notify the nomination to the parties

The arbitrator. whether the judge, registrar or other person, shall, after communication with the parties fix an early date convenient to the parties for the arbitration in the Court Buildings or some other place convenient to the parties. and after hearing the parties or their representatives and the evidence, he shall give his determination in writing either at the arbitration or afterwards as soon as may be and shall deliver the same to each of the parties or their representatives

(3) The Arbitration Act. 1889 (52 & 53 Vict c 49) shall not apply to an arbitration under subsection (2) of section 11 of the 1923 Act

(4) The only fee payable on such an arbitration shall be the sum of 1*l* 10*s* which should be sent to the Court with the application. Where a person other than the judge or registrar acts as arbitrator, the fee of 1*l* 10*s* shall be handed to him. Where the judge acts as arbitrator, the fee shall be deemed to be included in Schedule A of the Treasury Order regulating Fees in the County Courts. Where the registrar acts as arbitrator, the fee shall be deemed to be included as to half in Schedule A, and as to half in Schedule B Part I of that Fees Order

5 These Rules may be cited as the Rent (Restrictions) Rules, 1923

Dated the 7th day of August 1923

APPENDIX

17

FORM OF REQUEST FOR ARBITRATION UNDER SECTION 11 (2)

In the County Court of   holden at

In the Matter of the Rent and Mortgage Interest Restrictions Act, 1923

Whereas certain questions have arisen between us in relation to the tenancy of
under or in connection with the principal Act or Part I of the above-mentioned Act of 1923 that is to say

we hereby request the judge or registrar of the above court or some person to be nominated by the judge to act as arbitrator between us and determine the above questions under section 11 (2) of the Act of 1923 such determination to be final and conclusive and binding upon us for all purposes

Each of us is to bear and pay his own costs but the court or arbitrator's fee of 1/ 10s sent herewith is to be borne by us in equal shares

The arbitrator may view the premises before determining any question He may also at the request of either of us exercise the power of amending a notice of increase conferred on the court by section 6 (1) of the Act of 1923

Signature)

The words in brackets may be struck out if desired by the signatories

APPENDIX III.

TEXT OF THE REPEALED ACTS

———◆———

A

INCREASE OF RENT AND MORTGAGE INTEREST (WAR RESTRICTIONS) ACT 1915

5 & 6 Geo. 5. c. 97

23rd December 1915

Be it enacted &c.

Restriction
of increase
of rent or
rate of
mortgage
interest

1.—(1) Where the rent of a dwelling-house to which this Act applies, or the rate of interest on a mortgage to which this Act applies, has been, since the commencement of the present war, or is hereafter during the continuance of this Act, increased above the standard rent or the standard rate of interest as herein-after defined, the amount by which the rent or interest payable exceeds the amount which would have been payable had the increase not been made shall, notwithstanding any agreement to the contrary, be irrecoverable.

Provided that—

> (i) This subsection shall not apply to any rent or mortgage interest which accrued due before the twenty-fifth day of November nineteen hundred and fifteen; and

> (ii) Where the landlord has since the commencement of the present war incurred, or during the continuance of this Act incurs, expenditure on

the improvement or structural alteration of a
dwelling-house (not including expenditure on
decoration or repairs) an increase of rent at a
rate not exceeding six per cent per annum on
the amount so expended shall not be deemed to
be an increase for the purposes of this Act and

(iii) Any transfer to a tenant of any burden or liability
previously borne by the landlord shall for the
purposes of this Act be treated as an alteration
of rent and where as the result of such a
transfer the terms on which a dwelling-house is
held are on the whole less favourable to the
tenant than the previous terms the rent shall be
deemed to be increased whether or not the sum
periodically payable by way of rent is increased
and any increase of rent in respect of any
transfer to a landlord of any burden or liability
previously borne by the tenant where as the
result of such transfer the terms on which a
dwelling-house is held are on the whole more
favourable to the tenant than the previous terms
shall be deemed not to be an increase of rent for
the purposes of this Act and if any question
arises under this proviso the question shall be
determined by the county court whose decision
shall be final and conclusive and

(iv) Where the landlord pays the rates chargeable on or
which but for the enactments relating to compounding would be chargeable on the occupier
of any dwelling-house an increase of the rent
of the dwelling-house shall not be deemed to be
an increase for the purposes of this Act if the
amount of the increase does not exceed any increase in the amount for the time being payable
by the landlord in respect of such rates over
the corresponding amount paid in respect of the
yearly half-yearly or other period which included the third day of August nineteen hundred

and fourteen and for the purposes of this proviso the expression "rates" includes water rents and charges; and

(v) Where the rate of mortgage interest has been increased in compliance with or in consequence of a notice in writing demanding either repayment of the mortgage or an increased rate of interest given prior to the fourth day of August nineteen hundred and fourteen such increase shall not be deemed to be an increase for the purposes of this Act; and

(vi) Wherever an increase of rent is by this Act permitted no such increase shall be due or recoverable until the expiry of four clear weeks after the landlord has served upon the tenant a notice in writing of his intention to increase the rent accompanied

(a) where the increase of rent is on account of such expenditure as is mentioned in proviso (ii) to this subsection by a statement of the improvements or alterations effected and of their cost; and

(b) where the increase of rent is on account of an increase in rates by a statement showing particulars of the increased amount charged in respect of rates on the dwelling-house; and

(c) where such a notice has been served on any tenant the increase may be continued without service of any fresh notice on any subsequent tenant.

2. A person shall not in consideration of the grant renewal or continuance of a tenancy of any dwelling-house to which this Act applies require the payment of any fine premium or other like sum in addition to the rent and where any such payment has been made in respect of any such dwelling-house after the twenty-fifth day of November nineteen hundred and fifteen then the amount shall be re-

coverable by the tenant by whom it was made from the landlord, and may without prejudice to any other method of recovery be deducted from any rent payable by him to the landlord, but this provision shall not apply to any payment made in agreement entered into before the fourth day of August one thousand nine hundred and fourteen

(3) No order for the recovery of possession of a dwelling-house to which this Act applies or for the ejectment of a tenant therefrom shall be made so long as the tenant continues to pay rent at the agreed rate as modified by this Act and performs the other conditions of the tenancy, except on the ground that the tenant has committed waste or has been guilty of conduct which is a nuisance or an annoyance to adjoining or neighbouring occupiers, or that the premises are reasonably required by the landlord for the occupation of himself or some other person in his employ, or in the employ of some tenant from him, or on some other ground which may be deemed satisfactory by the court making such order, and where such order has been made but not executed before the passing of this Act the court by which the order was made may, if it is of opinion that the order would not have been made if this Act had been in operation at the date of the making of the order, rescind or vary the order in such manner as the court may think fit for the purpose of giving effect to this Act

(4) It shall not be lawful for any mortgagee under a mortgage to which this Act applies, during the continuance of this Act and so long as interest at the standard rate is paid and is not more than twenty-one days in arrear and the covenants by the mortgagor (other than the covenant for the repayment of the principal moneys secured) are performed and observed, and so long as the mortgagor keeps the property in a proper state of repair and pays all interest and instalments of principal recoverable under any prior encumbrance, to call in his mortgage or to take any steps for exercising any right of foreclosure or sale or for otherwise enforcing his security or for recovering the principal moneys thereby secured

Provided that this provision shall not apply to a mortgage where the principal money secured thereby is repayable by means of periodical instalments extending over a term of not less than ten years from the creation of the mortgage nor shall this provision affect any power of sale exerciseable by a mortgagee who was at the twenty-fifth day of November nineteen hundred and fifteen a mortgagee in possession, or in cases where the mortgagor consents to the exercise by the mortgagee of the powers conferred by the mortgage.

Provided also that if in the case of a mortgage of a leasehold interest the mortgagee satisfies the county court that his security is seriously diminishing in value or is otherwise in jeopardy, and that for that reason it is reasonable that the mortgage should be called in and enforced, the court may by order authorise him to call in and enforce the same, and thereupon this subsection shall not apply to such mortgage.

Interpreta-
tion and
application

2. — (1) For the purposes of this Act, except where the context otherwise requires —

    (a) The expression "standard rent" means the rent at which the dwelling-house was let on the third day of August nineteen hundred and fourteen, or where the dwelling-house was not let on that date, the rent at which it was last let before that date, or in the case of a dwelling-house which was first let after the said third day of August, the rent at which it was first let:

    (b) The expression "standard rate of interest" means in the case of a mortgage in force on the third day of August nineteen hundred and fourteen the rate of interest payable at that date, or in the case of a mortgage created since that date the original rate of interest:

    (c) The expression "rateable value" means the rateable value on the third day of August nineteen hundred and fourteen, or in the case of a house or part of a house first assessed after that date the rateable value at which it was first assessed:

(d) The expressions landlord tenant mortgagee and mortgagor include any person from time to time deriving title under the original landlord tenant mortgagee or mortgagor

(e) The expression mortgage includes a land charge under the Land Transfer Acts 1875 and 1897

38 & 39 Vic. c 87
60 & 61 Vic c 65

(2) This Act shall apply to a house or a part of a house let as a separate dwelling where such letting does not include any land other than the site of the dwelling-house and a garden or other premises within the curtilage of the dwelling-house and where either the annual amount of the standard rent or the rateable value of the house or part of the house does not exceed—

(a) in the case of a house situate in the metropolitan police district including therein the city of London, thirty-five pounds

(b) in the case of a house situate in Scotland thirty pounds and

(c) in the case of a house situate elsewhere twenty-six pounds

and every such house or part of a house shall be deemed to be a dwelling-house to which this Act applies Provided that this Act shall not apply to a dwelling-house let at a rent which includes payments in respect of board attendance or use of furniture

(3) Where for the purpose of determining the standard rent or rateable value of a dwelling-house to which this Act applies it is necessary to apportion the rent at the date in relation to which the standard rent is to be fixed or the rateable value of the property in which that dwelling-house is comprised a county court may on application by either party make such apportionment as seems just and the decision of the court as to the amount to be apportioned to the dwelling-house shall be final and conclusive

(4) Subject to the provisions of this Act this Act shall apply to every mortgage where the mortgaged property consists of or comprises one or more dwelling-houses to which

this Act applies or any interest therein except that it shall
not apply —

(a) to any mortgage comprising one or more dwelling-
houses to which this Act applies and other land if
the rateable value of such dwelling-houses is less
than one-tenth of the rateable value of the whole
of the land comprised in the mortgage; or

(b) to an equitable charge by deposit of title deeds or
otherwise.

(5) Where this Act has become applicable to any dwelling-
house or any mortgage thereon it shall continue to apply
thereto whether or not the dwelling-house continues to be a
dwelling-house to which this Act applies.

(6) Where the standard rent payable in respect of any
tenancy of a dwelling-house is less than two-thirds of the
rateable value thereof this Act shall not apply to that rent
or tenancy nor to any mortgage by the landlord from whom
the tenancy is held of his interest in the dwelling-house.

Rules as to
procedure

3 The Lord Chancellor may make such rules and give
such directions as he thinks fit for the purpose of giving
effect to this Act and may by those rules or directions provide for any proceedings for the purposes of this Act being
conducted so far as is desirable in private and for the remission
of any fees.

Application
to Scotland
and Ireland

4 (1) This Act shall apply to Scotland subject to the
following modifications—

"Mortgage" and "incumbrance" mean a heritable security;
"fine" means grassum or consideration other than
rent; "mortgagor" and "mortgagee" mean respectively the debtor and the creditor in a heritable
security; "covenant" means obligation; "mortgaged
property" means the heritable subject or subjects
included in a heritable security; "rateable value"
means yearly value according to the valuation roll;
"rateable value on the third day of August nineteen
hundred and fourteen" means yearly value according to the valuation roll for the year ending not with

day of May nineteen hundred and fifteen: "assessed" means entered in the valuation roll: "committed waste" means "wilfully destroyed the property"; "land" means lands and heritages; "enactments relating to compounding" include the House-letting and Rating (Scotland) Act 1911; "rate" means assessment as defined in the last-mentioned Act; "Lord Chancellor" means the Court of Session; "rules" means act of sederunt; and "county court" means the sheriff.

1 & 2 Geo. 5, c. 53.

(2) Application to Ireland.

5. (1) This Act may be cited as the Increase of Rent and Mortgage Interest (War Restrictions) Act, 1915.

Short title and duration.

(2) This Act shall continue in force during the continuance of the present war and for a period of six months thereafter and no longer, but the expiration of this Act shall not render recoverable any rent or interest which during the continuance thereof was irrecoverable or affect the right of a tenant to recover any sum which during the continuance thereof was under this Act recoverable by him.

B.

INCREASE OF RENT, &c. (AMENDMENT) ACT 1918.

(8 Geo 5 c 7.)

[2nd May 1918.]

Be it enacted, &c.

1 Subsection (3) of section one of the Increase of Rent and Mortgage Interest (War Restrictions) Act 1915, shall have effect as if at the end thereof the following provision was inserted —

Restriction of meaning of landlord in 5 & 6 Geo 5 c 97, s 1 (3).

"For the purposes of this subsection the expression 'landlord' shall not include any person who since the thirtieth day of September nineteen hundred and

seventeen has become landlord by the acquisition of
the dwelling-house or any interest therein otherwise
than by the devolution thereof to him under a settle-
ment made before the said date or under a testa-
ment or disposition on intestacy

and the provisions of the said subsection with respect to
orders made but not executed before the passing of that
Act shall apply to orders made but not executed before the
passing of this Act as if this Act had been substituted for
that Act in the said subsection

Provided that this enactment shall not apply in any case
where the court is satisfied by certificate given by or on
behalf of the Board of Agriculture and Fisheries or as
regards premises in Scotland by the Board of Agriculture
for Scotland or in Ireland the Department of Agriculture
and Technical Instruction for Ireland, that the premises
in question are required for the occupation of a person
engaged or employed in agricultural work of urgent national
importance

Short title　2 This Act may be cited as the Increase of Rent &c.
Amendment Act 1918

C

INCREASE OF RENT AND MORTGAGE
INTEREST RESTRICTIONS ACT 1919

9 Geo 5 c 7

2nd April 1919

Be it enacted &c.

Principal
Act and
Amending
Act

1 The Increase of Rent and Mortgage Interest (War
Restrictions) Act 1915 (hereinafter referred to as the principal Act) and the enactments amending that Act shall
continue in force until Lady Day nineteen hundred and
twenty-one (during the period hereinafter referred to
as the seventh period) as from the time when but for

this Act the principal Act would have expired and the said
Lady Day the principal Act shall have effect subject to the
modifications contained in the two next succeeding sections

2.—(1) An increase in the rent of a dwelling-house to
which the principal Act applies payable in respect of the
extended period or any part thereof which would but for
the principal Act be recoverable shall be recoverable if or
so far as the amount of the increase does not exceed ten
per centum of the standard rent

Provided that no such increase shall be due or recoverable
if the sanitary authority of the district in which the house
is situate on the application of the tenant certifies that the
house is not reasonably fit for human habitation or is not
kept in a reasonable state of repair nor in any case until or
in respect of any period prior to the expiry of four clear
weeks after the landlord has served upon the tenant a notice
in writing of his intention to increase the rent and informing the tenant of his right to apply to the sanitary authority
for such a certificate as aforesaid

(2) On any such application to a sanitary authority a fee
of one shilling shall be payable but if the authority as a
result of the application issues such a certificate as aforesaid
the tenant shall be entitled to deduct the amount of the fee
from any subsequent payment of rent

(3) The increase of rent permitted by this section shall be
in addition to any increase permitted by section one of the
principal Act

3. Nothing in the principal Act shall prevent an increase
in the rate of interest payable in respect of the extended
period on a mortgage to which the principal Act applies
if the increase does not exceed one half per centum per
annum and the rate when so increased does not exceed five
per centum per annum and subsection 4 of section one of
the principal Act shall apply as if the reference therein to
the standard rate included a reference to such increased rate

4. As from the passing of this Act the principal Act and
the enactments extending that Act shall have and be deemed

Margin notes (right column):

Limited
power of
increasing
rents during
the extended
period

Limited
power of
increasing
rate of
mortgage
interest

Extension of
principal Act

other- parts of houses let as separate dwellings where such letting
ed Houses does not include any land other than the site of the dwelling-
house and a garden or other premises within the curtilage
of the dwelling-house and where

   (a) in the case of a house situated in the metropolitan
police district including the City of London both
the annual amount of the standard rent and the
rateable value of the house or part of the house
exceed thirty-five pounds and neither exceeds
seventy pounds

   (b) in the case of a house situated in Scotland both the
annual amount of the standard rent and the rateable value of the house or part of the house exceed
thirty pounds and neither exceeds sixty pounds

   (c) in the case of a house situated elsewhere both the
annual amount of the standard rent and the rateable value of the house or part of the house exceed
twenty-six pounds and neither exceeds fifty-two
pounds

and shall also extend to mortgages not being mortgages to
which the principal Act as originally enacted applies where
the mortgaged property consists of or comprises one or more
of such dwelling-houses as aforesaid or any interest therein
subject however to the exceptions mentioned in subsection (1) of section two of the principal Act but in the
application to those houses and mortgages the principal Act
and the enactments amending that Act shall have effect
subject to the following modifications

   (1) for subsection (1) of section one of the principal Act
exclusive of the provisos to that subsection the
following provisions shall be substituted —

     Where the rent of a dwelling-house to which
this Act applies or the rate of interest on a mortgage to which this Act applies has been since the
twenty-fifth day of December nineteen hundred
and eighteen or is hereafter increased and such
increase would apart from this Act have been recoverable then if the increased rent exceeds by

more than ten per centum the standard rent, or the increased rate of interest exceeds by more than one half per centum per annum the standard rate the amount of such excess above the said ten per centum or one half per centum, as the case may be shall notwithstanding any agreement to the contrary be irrecoverable from the tenant or the mortgagor as the case may be and if paid may be recovered by the tenant or mortgagor in the manner and subject to the provisions of subsection (1) of section five of the Courts (Emergency Powers) Act 1917 7 & 8 Geo 5 c 25

(ii) in proviso (i) to subsection (1) and subsections (2) and (4) of section one of the principal Act the fourth day of March nineteen hundred and nineteen shall be substituted for the twenty-fifth day of November nineteen hundred and fifteen

(iii) in subsection (3) of section one of the principal Act references to the date of the passing of the principal Act shall be construed as references to the date of passing of this Act

(iv) in subsection (3) of section one of the principal Act for the reference to the standard rate there shall be substituted a reference to the rate permitted by this section

(v) at the end of paragraph (a) of subsection (1) of section two of the principal Act there shall be inserted the following proviso

Provided that if the rateable value of the dwelling-house on the said third day of August exceeds the standard rent as so defined that rateable value shall as respects that house be deemed to be the standard rent

5—(1) A landlord of a house to which the principal Act either is originally applied or is extended by this Act applies shall on being so requested by the tenant of the house furnish to him a statement as to what is the standard rent of the house and if he fails within fourteen days to do Minor amendments of the principal Act so or furnishes a statement which is false in any material particular he shall be guilty of an offence and liable on summary conviction to a fine not exceeding ten pounds

(2) Where a person who has since the thirtieth day of September nineteen hundred and seventeen purchased a house to which the principal Act either as originally enacted or as extended by this Act applies requires the house for his own occupation or that of some person in his employ or in the employ of some tenant from him nothing in the Increase of Rent &c. (Amendment) Act 1918 shall be construed as preventing the court from making an order for the recovery of possession of the house if after considering all the circumstances of the case including especially the alternative accommodation available for the tenant the court considers it reasonable to make such an order

(3) The principal Act both as originally enacted and as extended by this Act shall have effect as if in proviso (vi) of sub-section (1) of section one of that Act after the word "until" there were inserted the words "or in respect of any period prior to"

(4) Any rooms in a dwelling-house the subject of a separate letting as a dwelling shall for the purposes of the principal Act and this Act be treated as a part of a house let as a separate dwelling

Limitation on rent of houses let furnished

6.—(1) Where the occupier of a dwelling-house to which the principal Act either as originally enacted or as extended by this Act applies lets or has before the passing of this Act let the house or any part thereof at a rent which includes payment in respect of the use of furniture and it is proved to the satisfaction of the county court on the application of the lessee that the rent charged yields to the occupier a profit more than twenty-five per centum in excess of the normal profit as hereinafter defined the court may order that the rent so far as it exceeds such sum as would yield such normal profit and twenty-five per centum shall be irrecoverable and that the amount of any payment of rent in excess of such sum which may have been made in respect of any period after the passing of this Act shall be repaid to the lessee and without prejudice to any other method of recovery may be recovered by him by means of deductions from any subsequent payments of rent

(2) For the purpose of this section normal profit means the profit which might reasonably have been obtained from a similar letting in the year ending on the third day of August nineteen hundred and fourteen

7 At the end of paragraph (a) of subsection (1) of section two of the principal Act the following words shall be inserted —

> Provided that in the case of any dwelling-house let at a progressive rent payable under a tenancy agreement or lease the maximum rent payable under such tenancy agreement or lease shall be the standard rent

8 Neither the principal Act nor this Act shall apply to houses erected after or in course of erection at the passing of this Act

9 In the application of this Act to Scotland—

> (a) the twenty-eighth day of May shall be substituted for Lady Day and the local authority under the Public Health (Scotland) Act 1897 shall be substituted for the sanitary authority

> (b) as from the commencement of the extended period the principal Act shall be amended by the insertion in proviso (iv) of subsection (1) of section one after the word 'dwelling-house' where first occurring therein of the words 'or where by the law of Scotland owners rates are chargeable on the landlord of any dwelling-house'

10 Application of Act to Ireland

11 This Act may be cited as the Increase of Rent and Mortgage Interest (Restrictions) Act 1919 and shall be construed as one with the principal Act

Amendment of definition of standard rent.

Exception of new houses

Application of Act to Scotland 60 & 61 Vic c 38

Application of Act to Ireland

Short title and construction

17 2

D.

INCREASE OF RENT, &c. (AMENDMENT) ACT, 1919

(9 & 10 Geo. 5, c. 90)

[2nd December 1919]

Be it enacted, &c.

Orders for
possession

5 & 6 Geo. 5,
c. 97

1. (1) After the passing of this Act no order or judgment for the recovery of possession of a dwelling-house to which the Increase of Rent and Mortgage Interest (War Restrictions) Act, 1915 (hereinafter called the principal Act) or any of the Acts amending the same applies, or for the ejectment of a tenant therefrom, shall be made or given so long as the tenant continues to pay rent at the agreed rate as modified by the principal Act or any of the Acts amending the same and performs the other conditions of the tenancy, unless —

(a) the tenant has committed waste or has been guilty of conduct which is a nuisance or an annoyance to adjoining or neighbouring occupiers, and the court considers it reasonable to make such an order or give such judgment; or

(b) the tenant by sub-letting the dwelling-house or any part thereof or by taking in lodgers is making a profit which having regard to the rent paid by the tenant is unreasonable, and the court considers it reasonable to make such an order or give such judgment; or

(c) the premises are reasonably required by the landlord for the occupation of himself or some other person in his employ or in the employ of some tenant from him, and the court after considering all the circumstances of the case including especially the alternative accommodation available for the tenant considers it reasonable to make such an order or give such judgment;

(2) At the time of making any order or giving any judgment for the recovery of possession of any such dwelling-house or for the ejectment of a tenant therefrom, or in the case of any such order or judgment which has been made or given, whether before or after the passing of this Act and not executed, at any subsequent time the court may, if the order or judgment was made or given on the ground that the premises were reasonably required, rescind, stay or suspend execution thereof, or postpone the date of possession, for such period or periods as it shall think fit, either unconditionally or subject to such conditions in regard to payment by the tenant of rent or mesne profits and otherwise as the court shall think fit, and if such conditions are complied with, the court may, if it shall think fit, discharge or rescind such order or judgment.

(3) Where any order or judgment has been made or given before the passing of this Act but not executed, and in the opinion of the court the order or judgment would not have been made or given if this Act had been in force at the time when such order or judgment was made or given, the court may, on application by the tenant, rescind or vary such order or judgment in such manner as the court may think fit for the purpose of giving effect to this Act.

(4) Notwithstanding anything in section one hundred and forty-three of the County Courts Act, 1888, every warrant for delivery of possession of a dwelling-house to which the principal Act or any Act amending the same applies shall remain in force for three months from the day next after the last day named in the judgment or order for delivery of possession or ejectment, and for such other period or periods, if any, as the court shall from time to time, whether before or after the expiration of such three months, direct.

(5) This Act shall not apply to a dwelling-house let at a rent which includes payments in respect of board, attendance or use of furniture.

(6) In the application of this section to Scotland a reference to profits shall be substituted for the reference to mesne profits.

51 & 52 Vict. c. 3.

Short title,
construction
and repeal

2 (1) This Act may be cited as the Increase of Rent, &c. (Amendment) Act, 1919, and shall remain in force until the first day of July, nineteen hundred and twenty, and shall be construed as one with the principal Act

(2) The enactments set out in the schedule to this Act are hereby repealed to the extent specified in the third column of that schedule

Section 2.

SCHEDULE

Session and Chapter	Short Title	Extent of Repeal
5 & 6 Geo. 5, c. 97	Increase of Rent and Mortgage Interest (War Restrictions) Act, 1915	S. 1 (3)
8 Geo. 5, c. 7	Increase of Rent, &c. (Amendment) Act, 1918	The whole Act
9 Geo. 5, c. 7	Increase of Rent and Mortgage Interest (Restrictions) Act, 1919	S. 2 (2)

APPENDIX IV.

THE INTERPRETATION ACT, 1889

(52 & 53 Vict. c. 63.)

38.—(1.) Where this Act or any Act passed after the commencement of this Act repeals and re-enacts with or without modifications any provisions of a former Act, references in any other Act to the provisions so repealed shall unless the contrary intention appears be construed as references to the provisions so re-enacted.

(2.) Where this Act or any Act passed after the commencement of this Act repeals any other enactment, then unless the contrary intention appears the repeal shall not—

    (a.) revive anything not in force or existing at the time at which the repeal takes effect; or

    (b.) affect the previous operation of any enactment so repealed or anything duly done or suffered under any enactment so repealed; or

    (c.) affect any right, privilege, obligation, or liability acquired, accrued, or incurred under any enactment so repealed; or

    (d.) affect any penalty, forfeiture, or punishment incurred in respect of any offence committed against any enactment so repealed; or

    (e.) affect any investigation, legal proceeding, or remedy in respect of any such right, privilege, obligation, liability, penalty, forfeiture, or punishment as aforesaid;

and any such investigation, legal proceeding, or remedy may be instituted, continued, or enforced, and any such penalty, forfeiture, or punishment may be imposed, as if the repealing Act had not been passed.

×

INDEX.

———◆———

A

D

E

EXPIRY OF PRINCIPAL ACT,
business premises, in case of, 1, 21.
dwelling-house in case of
date of, 161
original 1, 3
effect of, on sums irrecoverable by landlord or mortgagee
149
restrictions after 161—166
mortgagee calling in of, 165, 166
rent, 164, 165
right to possession, 162—164
powers of Court, 163

F

FINE See Premium
FURNISHED HOUSES,
how affected 6
increase of rent of, 6, 75—76
whether contracting out of Act permissible, 76

FURNITURE See also Application of Principal Act.
amount necessary for purposes of sect 12 (2) (i), 33
letting of furnished house not necessary, 33 n
meaning of
fixtures 34
linoleum, 34
tools of trade 34

G

GRANT RENEWAL OR CONTINUANCE, 91, 92
GREATER HARDSHIP 113—115, 163

H

HOUSE
meaning of, in sect 12 (2) (iii) of the principal Act, 28, 29
may include adjoining premises, 28

I

INCLUDES,
meaning of in sect 12 (2) (i) of principal Act, 31, 32

V

SUPPLEMENT

TO

THE RENT RESTRICTIONS ACTS,

1920, 1923.

INCLUDING THE

Prevention of Eviction Act, 1924, and a consideration of all the English, Scotch and Irish Cases dealing with the subject, with an Appendix containing the text of the Prevention of Eviction Act, 1924

BY

THEODORE JOHN SOPHIAN. B.A. (Oxon.),

OF WADHAM COLLEGE, OXFORD, THE INNER TEMPLE AND SOUTH-EASTERN CIRCUIT,
BARRISTER-AT-LAW, PROXIMO PRIZEMAN, YARBOROUGH-ANDERSON SCHOLAR,
AND AUTHOR OF THE ' RENT RESTRICTIONS (NOTICES OF INCREASE) ACT, 1923 "

LONDON
STEVENS AND SONS. LIMITED,
119 & 120, CHANCERY LANE,
Law Publishers.

1924

PRINTED IN GREAT BRITAIN BY
C. F. ROWORTH, 88, FETTER LANE, LONDON, E.

PREFACE.

—◆—

SINCE the publication of the first edition of this work, there have been numerous decisions of considerable importance on the subject of Rent Restriction, and several Bills have been before Parliament with the object of altering the earlier Acts. Of these Bills, however, only one, the Prevention of Eviction Act, 1924, has so far found its way to the Statute Book. It seems probable that no further alteration in the law will be made for the present, with the exception, perhaps, that the period of full control may be extended.

In this supplement, I have noted every reported decision in the English, Scotch and Irish Courts, and I have also dealt with the Prevention of Eviction Act, 1924, the text of which will be found in the Appendix.

THEO. J. SOPHIAN.

2, HARCOURT BUILDINGS,
    TEMPLE
        31st July, 1924

(v)

INDEX TO THE SECTIONS OF THE ACTS.

———————

TABLE OF CASES.

W

SOPHIAN'S RENT RESTRICTIONS ACTS.

SUPPLEMENT, JULY, 1924.

Page 2, line 19

Lastly, the Rent and Mortgage Interest Restrictions Act 1923 has been amended by the **Prevention of Evictions Act 1924** which repeals paragraphs iv and v of sect 4 **(1) of that Act** and substitutes new provisions therefor

Page 2, line 29

After 'Amendment Act of 1923' add ' and the Prevention of Evictions Act, 1924 '

Page 2 line 31

After '1923' add " and the Prevention of Evictions Act, 1924 "

Page 5, note (r)

Add " *Michael v Phillips* ((1924 1 K B 16) "

Page 7 note (h)

For the liability of a landlord to his statutory tenant for breach of agreement to repair according to the original tenancy agreement see *Heath v Rowlands* 157 L T 473

Page 8, line 1

After "that" read "a statutory tenant may be entitled to the benefit of"

Page 8, lines 2 and 3

Delete lines 2 and 3 from "is" to "tenancy"

Page 8, lines 6—8

Instead of lines 6—8 read "It has, however, been held by the Court of Appeal in *Keeves v. Dean, Nunn v. Pellegrini* 40 T. L. R. p. 211, that the statutory tenant has no right to assign. The question however whether the statutory tenant had the right to sub-let was left open in those cases."

Page 8, note (k)

Add *Batchelor v. Murphy* (40 T. L. R. 642), *Sherwood v. Tucker* 158 L. T. 5

Page 12, line 6

Add "Although there has been a letting at a material date the Court may nevertheless disregard the letting if the rent at which the premises were let at such date cannot be ascertained (*Tarrant v. Barston* 59 L. J. at p. 279)"

Page 12, line 16

Add *Brakspear v. Barton* (40 T. L. R. 607)—discount for liquor supplied by landlord to tenant of licensed premises

Page 12, line 24

From a consideration of the above cases therefore it appears that, for the purpose of determining the standard rent at any rate if not for the purpose of the Rent Restrictions Acts in general, such matters as the incidence of the payment of rates and taxes or the existence of clauses or agreements allowing a discount for liquor supplied by the landlords to the tenants of licensed premises are to be disregarded

Page 12, line 34

Where the rent to be considered at the material date is less than the rateable value the rateable value will be the standard rent (sect 12 (1) (a), subject to this qualification viz that if such rent is less than two-thirds of the rateable value, it is to be ruled out of consideration entirely (sect 12 (7), and recourse must be had to an earlier tenancy (if any, in which the rent happens to be more than two-thirds of the rateable value. Thus in *Brakspear v Barton* (40 T L R 607), premises which had been let in 1910 at a rental of 75*l* were subsequently let in 1920 at a rental of 120*l* There were several intervening tenancies, in all of which the rental was less than two thirds of the rateable value which was 68*l* It was held that the standard rent was 75*l* and not the rateable value of 68*l* If in the above case the rent of all the tenancies previous to 1920 had happened to be less than two-thirds of the rateable value, the standard rent would apparently have been 120*l* the rent at which the premises were first let at a rental above two-thirds of the rateable value

In *Woods & Co, Ltd v City and West End Properties Ltd* 38 T L R 98, premises were let on August 3rd 1914 at a rental of 18*l* per annum, with an additional rent of 2s a week as the tenant's contribution towards the expenses of the housekeeper for cleaning the premises, such additional rent to be recoverable by distress It was held that inasmuch as the parties had agreed to treat the 2s per week as rent the standard rent was not 18*l* but that sum increased by the payment of 2s per week viz 23*l* 4s The correctness of this decision however may be called in question as according to the express finding of the Court the tenancy on which the determination of the standard rent was based was one which included the payment of sums on account of attendance, and such tenancies are expressly excluded from the provisions of the Act. **Sect 12, 2 (1)** of the Act of 1920.

Page 13, line 25

In *Ichyala* v *Peppercorn* (157 L. T. 492) a house had been let out in flats in August 1914, and it was sought to apportion the rent of a flat in the house, and consisting of four rooms. It was proved that the flat had been let as a whole in 1922 at a rental of 22s. 6d. per week, two of the rooms in the said flat having been occupied by the owner of the house in August 1914, and the other two having been let at that time at 10s. per week. It was held that as the house itself had never been let as a whole in August 1914, no case for apportionment arose, and that the standard rent of the flat was the rent at which it had been first let as a whole — in 1922.

Page 14, line 23

This section provides the tenant with a means of ascertaining the standard rent, but it is submitted that in any event the onus of proving the standard rent will fall on the tenant in cases where he is claiming overpayments of rent, or where he is otherwise alleging that the rent he has paid or is still paying is not recoverable by the landlord. See *Komm* v *Cohen* 40 T. L. R. 123. For somewhat similar provisions with regard to rates, see the **Statement of Rates Act, 1919**.

Page 16, line 26

It should also be observed that the effect of **sect 12, 8** of the Act of 1920 is not such as to put the rooms which are the subject of the separate letting in the same position as if they were a self-contained flat or tenement into which part of the house may have been converted within the purview of sect 12, 9. *Sutton* v *Boylen* 68 S. J. 82.

Page 17, note (s).

Add "See also *Sutton v Begley* (68 S J 88)"

Page 18, line 21

After "floors." Read "The Divisional Court however in *Ibrahim v Williams* 40 T L R 767 has taken a contrary view, and has held that there can be no apportionment of even that part of the premises which has not been affected by the conversion, since the whole of the premises considered as an unit is taken out of the Act by reason of the conversion (see sect 12 9). It is to be observed, however that Rowlatt J expressed the opinion that if an application for apportionment were made before the reconstruction the right to apportion might not thereby be taken away."

Page 18 note (t)

Add "*Marchbank v Campbell*, 1923 1 K B 245 *Sutton v Begley* (68 S J 82)"

Page 20 line 18

"An order for apportionment is retrospective and the tenants right to recover overpayments is not limited to such overpayments made by him subsequently to the order for apportionment. In other words the apportionment has retrospective effect (*Kamm v Cohen* 40 T L R 123)"

Page 21 line 1

"In considering whether a house is within the Acts or not the status of the premises must first be determined and for that purpose where there are several existing tenancies regard must be paid to the position of the occupying tenant and to his position alone. Thus in *Proud v Hunter* (*ante* 40 T L R 545 a

... This decision has been affirmed by the Court of Appeal *Time* 31st July 1924

landlord had let premises unfurnished. The tenant sub-let the premises furnished. The tenancy is between the tenant and the sub-tenant being clearly outside the Act, it was held in an action for possession by the landlord against the mesne tenant that the premises were not controlled, the protection they had originally enjoyed having been lost by reason of the sub-letting of the premises *furnished.*

Page 21, line 20

Add bb to *Duke of Richmond and Others v. Dewar and Others*

This case was distinguished in a somewhat similar case, *Hutton v. Coombes, L. J. 12 C. C. R. 83,* inasmuch as in the former case the tenant was obliged to provide sleeping accommodation for his servants.

Page 21, line 1

Add: The purpose for which the premises are structurally adapted must be taken into consideration. *Franklin v. Darby L. J. 13 C. C. R. p. 11 Barnes v. Radcliffe* 1923 2 I. R. 158

Page 22, line 2

Add: In *Hutton v. Coombes 12 L. J. C. C. R. p. 83* premises consisting of a lock-up shop with rooms over occupied by the tenant's manager which were let to the proprietor for the purposes of his business as a boot repairer were held to be business premises, there being nothing in the nature of the business which necessitated the residence of a manager over the shop or made it incumbent on the proprietor to provide any residence for his manager.

Where premises are let as business premises a tenant cannot alter their character by using them in breach of the conditions of his tenancy as a dwelling-house, and the fact that the landlord may have tacitly acquiesced in the breach would appear to be immaterial. *Epsom Grand Stand Assn. v. Clarke, per Bankes*

L J 35 T L R p 525 *Franklin v Darby* 13 L J
C C R 13 *Williams v Perry* 40 T L R 539 Furthermore the question at issue must be decided relatively to the
particular landlord and tenant and for this purpose the tenancy
in question itself must be looked at (*Ib*)

In *Burns v Radcliffe* (1923) 2 L R 158 premises which
were used as a temperance hotel—that being the purpose for which
they were let—were nevertheless held to be a dwelling-house
within the Act on the ground that the house at the time of the
letting was structurally a dwelling-house and the business that was
carried on was in itself not only not incompatible with but
actually required residence It was also pointed out by Andrews
L J (*ib* at p 163) that **sects 12 and 13** of the Act of 1920
were not mutually exclusive (*cc*) and that premises which were
protected by **sect 13** of the Act of 1920 might still be protected
after the expiry of that provision if the character of the business
was such that it might reasonably be said to be carried on in a
dwelling-house

In *Williams v Perry* 40 T L R 539 it was held by the
Divisional Court that a dwelling-house which hitherto might
notwithstanding **sect 12 (6)** of the Act of 1920 have enjoyed the
protection of the Rent Restriction Acts, might be converted into
business premises and thus be deprived of such protection just
as much by the agreement of the parties and the user of the
premises as by structural alteration

Page 23 line 6

After 'school-house' add *Brakspear v Barton* 40
T L R 607 —licensed hotels

Page 24 line 5

Add This provision (*cc*) **sect 12 (6)** of the Act of 1920
however does not prevent a house from being decontrolled in cases

(*cc*) See *per Salter J* and *J v Perry* 1921 2 K B 94 and *Cox
v Barbour* 1922 1 K B 325 and per Scrutton L J in *Brakspear v Barton*
(*cc*) 40 T L R at p 158 L T R at p 152

where the premises are converted into business premises whether by structural alteration or the mere agreement of the parties that the premises should be used for business purposes only, in the terms *Williams v. Perry*, 40 T. L. R. 539. The same observations would apply to premises that might be taken out of the operation of the Acts by reason of any of the matters contained in provisos I. and III. of sect. 12 (2) of the Act of 1920.

Page 25 line 30

Before *separate* read: The word dwelling-house must be construed in its ordinary sense as relating to the entire structure as a whole, *Abrahart v. Webster*, 40 T. L. R. 767.

Page 31 line 21

After *Heard v. Wallace* add: Note also Approved by Bankes L.J. in *Walker v. Jones and Goodwin* (129) L. T. R. at p. 51 *contra* Younger, L.J. *ib* at p. 51.

Page 31 line 29

After *Ltd* add: It should be observed however, that the point before the Court in this case was with reference to the standardisation of the premises the Court holding that the rent was the total rent payable including the rent on account of attendance. This decision moreover it seems cannot be supported since the tenancy on which the standard rent was based was one which included as the Act virtually held payments in respect of attendance. Such a tenancy it is submitted cannot be taken into consideration for the purpose of arriving at the standard rent, inasmuch as such tenancies are excluded from the operation of the Acts. Sect. 12 (2) of the Act of 1920.

Page 32 line 9

Where one rent is reserved but there is an apportionment between the rent proper and the charges on account of board &c.

the tenancy will undoubtedly be outside the protection of the Act. See *Dick v Duncan* (1923) W. N. 90, for an example of such a tenancy.

In *Nadler v Wilson* 40 T. L. R. 639, premises had been let at a rent of 7*l*. 4*s*. together with a sum of 5*s*. per week, payable for attendance. The total sum payable was 87*l*. 4*s*. per annum, and this was payable quarterly in one sum of 21*l*. 16*s*. the agreement stating that the rent was to include the charge for attendance. It was held that the tenancy was outside the Acts by virtue of sect. 12 (2) (i) of the Act of 1920. From this decision it is apparently to be inferred that the intention of the parties is the material factor to be considered and if it is intended that the total rent payable should include the payment for board &c the tenancy will not be protected by the Acts, it being immaterial in such a case that the total rent has been apportioned by the parties themselves as between the rent proper and the various payments for board, &c

Page 33 line 10

After the word "services" Read ' See also *Michael v Phillips* (1923) W. N. 337,'

Page 36, line 8

Add "See however, judgment of Rowlatt J. in *Jenkinson v Wright* Times 29th July 1924,'

Page 39 line 20

A tenant may lose the protection of the Acts if he ceases to occupy the premises himself and parts with their possession as for example by sub-letting them. *Hicks v Scandale Brewery Co* 157 L. T. 366. In any case the tenant loses the protection of the Acts if he lets the premises in such a way that the undertenancy so created is outside the provisions of the Acts as for example if he sub-lets the premises furnished. *Prout v Hunter* 40 T. L. R. 345 '

Page 10, lines 6—15.

Instead of lines 6—15, "would . . . . agreement," read: "is a matter of some doubt by reason of the decision of the C. of A. in *Keeves v. Dean, Nunn v. Pellegrini.*

"If a statutory tenant purports to assign or sub-let, the assignee will not be protected according to the decision in *Keeves v. Dean* (40 T. L. R. 214), nor, it is submitted, will the sub-lessee be protected, since, although the matter was left open in the above cases it seems difficult to draw any distinction for this purpose between assigning and sub-letting. It should be observed that in either case the statutory tenant himself loses the protection of the Act, since he parts with the possession of the premises (*Hicks v. Scandale Brewery,* 157 L. T. 366.'

On the death of the tenant of controlled premises the original tenancy, if not determined at the date of the death will pass either to the executor *Collis v. Flower,* 1921, 1 K. B. 409, or to the administrator *Mellows v. Low* 155 L. T. 90. If however, the tenant at the date of his death is a statutory tenant, the provisions of **sect. 12 1, (g)** will then apply *(Keeves v. Dean,* 130 L. T. R. at pp. 599, 600.)

Page 10, line 26

The better opinion would appear to be that a statutory tenant cannot dispose of his statutory tenancy by will. The true position of the statutory tenant has become increasingly difficult to unravel since the decisions in *Keeves v. Dean* and *Hicks v. Scandale Brewery, Ltd.*

Page 11, lines 9—11

Delete lines 9—11 and read instead. The Acts, it should be observed, are not binding on the Crown nor on any Government Departments founded on the Prerogative as for instance the War Department *Lord Advocate v. Barlow* 1924, Sc. L. T. (Sh. Ct., Rep. 72), though it would be otherwise in the case of such administrative bodies which have no connection with the

Prerogative as for instance the Prison Commissioners *Prison Commissioners for Scotland v Donaldson* '1922, Se L 7 Sh Ct Rep 91 It may be urged however that the provisions of sect 12 10 of the Act of 1920 indicate that the Crown is impliedly bound by the provisions of the Acts

Page 12 line 24

Furthermore by sect 2 2 of the **Prevention of Evictions Act 1921,** where a landlord has on or after the 15th April 1921 taken possession of a dwelling-house under a judgment or order rescinded by reason of the provisions of that Act the possession thus obtained is not to exclude the premises from the operation of the Rent Restrictions Acts

Page 13 line 5

After controlled add Note (bb See *Read v Drury* '88 J P 185) '

Page 13 lines 7—9

Delete the words and in this respect *Nunn v Pelligram*

Page 14 line 7

Add In *Read v Drury* 88 J P 185 however it has been held that the word landlord in sect 2 1 means the person who is the landlord *vis-a-vis,* the person who as against him seeks to invoke the Rent Acts

Again in *Jenkinson v Wright* Times 29th July 1921 the Divisional Court took a similar view in holding that a person who held a lease of 99 years with 5 years unexpired residue and who had sub-demised the premises by way of mortgage, and had attorned tenant to the mortgagee was to be regarded as a landlord for the purposes of sect 2 1 in an action for possession brought by him against his tenant

Page 11, line 14.

Delete the words "A or possibly B were in possession" and read instead "C subsequently obtained possession from D, in which case, it is submitted, all other subsisting tenancies in the premises would be decontrolled (See *King v York*, 35 T. L. R. 256 *Prout v Hunter*, 40 T. L. R. 541."

Page 18 note (a).

Add at end of note after '*Molloy v Thomson* ' *Glass v Crombie* (1921), Sc. L. T. (Sh. Ct.) Rep. 6

Page 49, line 1

Nor does the Act avoid *in toto* agreements containing provisions contrary to the Act Thus if a tenant agrees with his landlord to pay a rent to which the landlord is not entitled, the agreement for payment of rent will, nevertheless, stand to the extent allowed by the Act so, also, will any other provisions which are unaffected by or are not contrary to the Acts (*Brakspear v Barton*, 40 T L R at p 609)

Page 49, line 15.

By virtue of **sect 1 of the Notices of Increase Act, 1923,** a new method of determining a tenancy for the purposes of the Rent Acts has been introduced, *i e,* merely by the service of a valid notice of increase (*Aston v Smith*, 40 T L R 576.

Page 49, note (c)

Add "*Precious v Reedie* (40 T L R 578, deciding that in the case of a monthly tenancy the notice must terminate on the day of the month on which the tenancy began The same principle applies also to quarterly and weekly tenancies

Page 51, line 10

Delete words ' *Bridges* v *Chambers* and in '

After ' *Michael* v *Phillips* ' read ' which follows the earlier decisions of *Bridges* v *Chambers* ((1919) W N 54 and *Worthy* v *Mann* &c ((1916) W N 390 decided under the Act of 1915 '

Page 52 lines 4—16

Delete lines 4—16 and read instead " Where premises are let at a rent below the standard rent the landlord will not be entitled to increase the rent merely by terminating the tenancy and giving the tenant notice that his rent will be increased if he continues in possession This it is submitted is the true view of the decision of the Divisional Court in *Darby* v *Palmer* ((1924 W N 111 The Acts do not in any way prevent or render illegal the raising of rent to the amount of the standard rent Such an increase will be governed by the ordinary law relating to landlord and tenant whereas increases above the standard rent are statutory increases governed by the provisions of the Rent Restrictions Acts 1920 1923 It will be therefore essential for the landlord in claiming the former increase to show that there was an actual agreement to pay this increase and he will not discharge this burden merely by showing that the tenancy was duly determined and that the tenant continued in occupation thereafter notwithstanding a demand from the landlord claiming the increase See *Glossop* v *Ashley* per Atkin L J ,1922 1 K B at p 14

As regards increases above the standard rent in such a case such increases are to be based on the standard rent and not on the lower rent hitherto paid by the tenant The landlord will of course be entitled to these increases only on complying with the provisions of sect 3 of the Act of 1920

Page 54 line 10

This decision was followed though not without some hesitation by McCardie J in *Bradshaw* v *Baxter* 40 T L R

607, the learned judge holding that rent is to be deemed to have been increased since the 25th March, 1920, within the meaning of sect. 1 of the Rent Restrictions Act, 1920, where the increased rent begins to accrue on a subsequent date. The word "from" is apparently synonymous with the word "since" for the purpose (*ib.* at p. 609).

Page 54, line 29

After "wrong" add note (...) " See, however, *Michael* v. *Phillips*."

Page 55, line 20

Where a tenant of licensed premises was, on the execution of a subsequent lease, deprived of the benefit hitherto enjoyed by him of a 10 per cent. discount on all liquor supplied to him by his landlords, it was held that there was no alteration of the rent within the meaning of sect. 3 (2) of the Act of 1920, and that the tenant was not entitled to recover from the landlord the sums in excess of what he would have paid had the discount continued. *Brakspear* v. *Barton*, 40 T. L. R. 607. McCardie J., held that as the rent must be disregarded for the purposes of the Rent Acts it followed that the discount for goods supplied under the rent must also be disregarded (*ib.* at p. 611).

Page 55, line 28

So also it would seem, notwithstanding *Brakspear* v. *Barton*, 40 T. L. R. 607, *Westminster and General Properties and Investment Co.* v. *Simmons*, 35 T. L. R. 669, and the *dicta* of McCardie J. in *Glossop* v. *Ashley*, 37 T. L. R. at p. 566, that where a landlord transferred to himself the burden of the liability for rates hitherto borne by the tenants, he would be entitled to increase the rent hitherto paid by a corresponding amount. This would appear to follow from the proviso to sect. 2 (3) of the Act of 1920, although that proviso deals with the converse case.

Page 55, line 32

Where there is a notional increase of rent by the transfer of a burden previously borne by the landlord to the tenant, the landlord it is submitted, must in any event comply with the provisions of **sect. 3 (1) and (2)** of the Act of 1920 before he will be entitled to recover the increase from the tenant though it would appear that if the notional increase has been paid by the tenant as, for example by the payment of rates to the authorities the tenant cannot avail himself of **sect. 14 (1** of the Act of 1920, since that section refers to payments actually made to the landlord, and the tenant will be entirely without any remedy provided that the notional increase is within the permitted limits (see *O'Neill v. Bower* 58 I. L. T. R. 113 decided under sects. 8 (3) and 15 (1) of the Rent Restrictions (Ireland) Act 1923), otherwise it would appear the tenant might have a claim for money paid by him for or on behalf of the landlord

Page 56, line 1

Instead of the words increases of rent to which the landlord is entitled read suspension or reduction of rent under **sect. 2 (1 a** or as regards the lesser amount to be determined by the County Court under **sect. 2 (1) d (ii**

Page 56, line 27

Finally it is submitted that a landlord does not lose his right to recover rent to which he is otherwise entitled by reason of a failure on his part to comply with the provisions of **sect. 29 of the Housing Town Planning &c. Act, 1919**, in cases to which that section applies since that section merely provides for summary proceedings before the magistrate and does not otherwise affect the rights of the parties *Aaraway v. Bolster* Estates Gazette, 19th July 1924

Page 56, note a

Add *Brakspear v. Barton* 10 L. T. R. at pp 611, 612)

Page 58, note (o)

Add *Azulay v Matthews* (157 L T 366)

Page 59, line 20

It has been held by the Court of Appeal in *Bourne v Lytton* (40 T L R 390), that a notice claiming an increase under sect 2 1 para (d) 11 of the Act of 1920, is invalid unless the amount of the increase has been ascertained either by agreement or by the determination of the County Court in accordance with the provision and further, that an agreement between the parties after the date of the notice as to the amount of the increase would not have the effect of making the notice a valid one. In this case moreover, the question was expressly left open as to whether, in view of sect 2 (6) of the Act of 1920, the High Court had any jurisdiction to deal with the validity of a notice increasing rent under sect 2 (1) (d) of that Act

Page 59, line 22

Delete the words ' or (d)

Page 59 line 32

After the word Act read In *Bourne v Lytton* (40 T L R at p 393) however the decision in *Penfold v Newman* (1922, 1 K B 645) was approved of by the Court of Appeal but doubts were cast as to the correctness of the decision in the Irish case of *Elliot v Eills* (1923) 2 I R 45 by the majority of the Court (Bankes and Scrutton, L JJ Sargant L J *dissentiente,* '

Page 60 line 36

'The power of amendment given by sect 6 (1) of the 1923 Act is not confined to notices of increase which have been accompanied by a requisite notice to quit that power equally applies in cases where a notice of increase only has been served without any notice to quit. (*Williams v. Britannia Merthyr Steam Coal Co. Ltd.*, 40 T. L. R. 687.)

Page 61, line 9

Delete lines 9—13 from "on the other hand" to "landlord." Read instead: "The tenant, however, is not prevented by the amendment from recovering from his landlord (under **sect. 14 (1)** of the Act of 1920 as amended by **sect. 8 (2)** of the 1923 Act) increases of rent which have been paid in respect of a rental period which ended more than six months before the date of the amendment, since the effect of the amendment is to validate the notice as so amended only in respect of a period of six months before the date of the amendment and in respect of the future (*Williams v. Britannia Merthyr Steam Coal Co., Ltd.* 40 T. L. R. 687.) The correctness of this decision is, it is submitted, open to question."

Page 68, line 28

The view taken in this book has eventually been approved by the Court of Appeal in *Strickland v. Palmer*, 40 T. L. R. 649. Where there is a reduction in the amount of the rates, the rent is to be proportionately reduced. There can be no difficulty in making the necessary reduction since rent is regarded as accruing from day to day (*ib.* at p. 650.) Should there be a subsequent increase in the rates it would appear that the landlord will have to begin all over again and comply afresh with the provisions of **sect. 3 (1) and (2)** of the Act of 1920. (*Swan v. Britain*, 13 L. J. C. C. R. 18.)

Page 71, line 5

After "repairs" add note (*j*). "This increase is to be regarded as rent and is to be taken into consideration in order to arrive at the annual value of the premises for the purpose of Schedule A of the Income Tax Act 1918. *Biddle v. Mayo*, 40 T. L. R. 791.

Page 71 line 16

In the absence of agreement between the landlord and the tenant as to the amount of the increase where the landlord is responsible for part of the repairs, the landlord should apply to the County Court to determine the amount, since, until this is done, no notice of increase claiming an increase under this head can be valid (*Bourne v. Litton*, 1923, W. N. 301.)

Page 75 line 33

Add to "normal profit" note (*z*).

As to the method adopted for arriving at the normal profit in a Scotch case of *Langdon v. Elliott* (1924, Sc. L. T., Sh. Ct., Rep. 9.

Page 78 line 24

In *Landragan v. Simons* (40 T. L. R. 244) the Divisional Court held not only that the Act was retrospective but that it was applicable even in the case of an appeal from a judgment delivered at a time when the Act was not yet in force. (See also *Sturge v. Embrass*, 35 T. L. R. 659. *Scott v. Bamforth*, 13 I. J. C. C. R. 1.

Page 82 line 36

In *Landragan v. Simons* (40 T. L. R. p. 244) the Divisional Court expressly declared that the enacting first part of **sect 1 (1)** of the Notices of Increase Act which favours the landlord by validating the increase was not cut down by the concluding paragraph of proviso (c). *Ib.* at p. 245.

Page 83 line 1

If the landlord is otherwise entitled to the validated increase of rent, the fact that such rent has already been the subject of a judgment given in favour of the tenant necessarily on some date previous to the 7th June, 1923, date of the passing of the Acts, will not prevent the landlord, it is submitted, from subsequently recovering the validated increase, provided such judgment was delivered subsequently to the 15th February, 1923. The decision in *Landrigan v. Simons* (40 T. L. R. 244) though not expressly decided on this point appears to be in favour of this view.

Page 88, line 7.

The cessation of the benefit of a discount on all liquor supplied by the landlords to the tenants of a tied house was held not to be a fine premium or other like sum for the grant renewal or continuance of a tenancy within the meaning of **sect 8 (1) of the Act of 1920** (*Brakspear v. Barton* 40 T. L. R. 611.)

Page 92, line 26

So again in *Streatham v. Beaton* 1923, S. C. J., p 59 it was held that a premium exacted from his tenant by a landlord in return for the landlord's consent to the tenant's sub-letting the premises was not prohibited by **sect 8 (1)** of the Act of 1920.

Page. 93 line 7

After sect 5 (1), add *e.g.*, that the tenancy has been duly determined, and in this connection it should be noted that a valid notice of increase is to be regarded as a sufficient notice to quit by virtue of **sect 1 of the Notices of Increase Act 1923** (*Aston v. Smith*, 40 T. L. R. 576.)

Page 94, line 12

After sect 5 add The judge must consider *all* the circumstances of the tenancy those of the *tenant as well as the landlord* (*Shrimpton v. Rabbits* 40 T. L. R. 540.)

Page 94 line 22

After order add Whether on the original or any subsequent or renewed application. (*Scott v. Bamforth*, 13 L. J. C. C. R. 4.)

2 2

Page 94, line 26

Where an action for possession had been adjourned after
hearing, and the position of the parties had in the meantime
altered by the passing of the 1923 Act the Court held that on
the adjourned hearing the case had to be determined under the
provisions of the new Act. (*Scott v. Bamforth* 13 L. J. C. C. R.
4. See also *Landrigan v. Simons*, 40 T. L. R. 211.)

Page 95, line 2

This case further decided that the fact that the claim for
possession was in respect of part only of the demised premises
would not preclude the plaintiff from obtaining an order. (See
15 L. T. 502, 156 L. T. 337.

It should further be observed that proceedings under Ord. XIV
are not suitable to actions for possession under the Rent Acts.
(*Gill v. Luck* 40 T. L. R. 38.)

Page 95, line 18

Whether the words " rent lawfully due " refer to an agreement
between the parties as to the time of payment or whether to the
time when the matter is being investigated was considered an
open question by the C. of A. in *Gill v. Luck* 40 T. L. R. 38.
See also *infra*, pp. 96, 97.

Page 95, line 26

After " unfounded " add " It would be no defence however
to plead non-compliance with the provisions of sect. 29 of the
Housing &c. Act 1919 though that may be a factor to be taken
into consideration by the judge when exercising his discretion

As regards procedure it should be noted that the Rent Acts are not in
any way affected the right to raise an action of summary ejection at common
law in cases to which the Acts apply. *Pease v. Goalen* 1924 S. L. T. &c.
of Such decisions as *Haggerty v. Gormley* 1923 S. L. T. S. (1)
(p. 12) and *McIntosh v. Cockell* &c. (p. 130) cannot be regarded as correct

Page 96, note (n)

Add " *Bradspun v Barton* 40 T L R at pp 611, 612 '

Page 99, line 20

Add "And further, that the landlord will not be deprived of the benefit of this paragraph by a subsequent improvement in the conduct of the tenant though in any event the Court will retain its discretion in the matter *McIvor v Struthers* 1924, Sc L T (Sh Ct Rep 15)

Page 100, line 7

Where however, the condition of the tenant's premises is a nuisance to the tenant only and does not adversely affect the occupiers of other portions of the dwelling-house **para** b will not apply *McIvor v Struthers* 1924 Sc L T Sh Ct Rep 15)

Page 100, lines 12 and 13

As regards deterioration premises will not be regarded as having deteriorated because they have fallen into a greater state of disrepair by mere lapse of time (*McIvor v Struthers,*

Page 103, line 19

After '(Para (111)' read

D Where the dwelling-house is reasonably required by the landlord (not being a landlord who has become landlord by purchasing the dwelling-house or any interest therein after the 5th May, 1924) for occupation as a residence for himself or for any son or daughter of his over 18 years of age

and

the Court is satisfied after having regard to all the circumstances of the case *including any alternative accommodation available for the landlord or the tenant,* that greater hardship would be caused by refusing to grant an order or judgment for possession than by granting it   Sect 1 of the **Prevention of Evictions Act 1921** repealing paras iv and (v of sect 4 1 of the 1923 Act

The above paras iv and (v, of sect 4 of the Act of 1923 dispensed with the requirement of alternative accommodation in the following cases respectively viz —

Page 103 line 20

For "D" read (vi)

Page 103 line 28

For 1 read b

Page 111 line 32

After [ ] add but the landlord must in the first instance prove that the case falls within the provisions of para (d   *Edmunds v Jackson* 1923 Sc L L Sh Ct Rep 125

Page 112 line 17   Page 113 line 19

Delete from line 17 in page 112 to line 19 in page 113 and read instead —

Exception D — the passing of the **Prevention of Evictions Act 1921** was largely due to a failure on the part of judges, when making orders for possession under the now repealed para iv of the 1923 Act to consider all the circumstances of the case including those of the tenant as was eventually decided by the Divisional Court in *Shrimpton v Rabbits* H 157 L T 301 which overrules such cases as *Davis v Taylor* 42 L J C C R 76

Whereas under the above paragraphs of the 1923 Act a distinction was made between persons becoming landlords prior to

Cf also *Wilson v Porter* 157 L T 302 where it was held that the increased hardship of the tenant should have been taken into consideration and those becoming landlords subsequent to the 30th June, 1920, under the **Prevention of Evictions Act, 1924**, the 5th May, 1924, is made the crucial date. If the plaintiff seeking possession became the landlord after the 5th May, 1924, sect. 4 (1) (d) of the 1923 Act will strictly apply; but if the plaintiff became landlord prior to that date sect. 1 of the Prevention of Evictions Act, 1924, may enable him in the circumstance provided by that section to dispense with the provision of alternative accommodation.

Firstly, the landlord must not have become the landlord by purchase of the dwelling-house or any interest therein after the 5th May, 1924. In *Barrett v. Marshall* it was held that a purchaser is to be regarded as the landlord as from the date on which a binding agreement has been entered into. A tenant, moreover, may be regarded as becoming a landlord for the purpose of sect. 1 of the **Prevention of Evictions Act**, and in any claim for possession by him against a sub-tenant the date of the execution of the lease or tenancy agreement as between him and his superior landlord is to be regarded as the material date. *Hart v. Shrimpton*, 88 J. P. 672 (*see also* sect. 12 (1) (g), of the 1920 Act for the definition of "landlord").

Secondly, the premises must be reasonably required by the landlord for occupation as a residence for himself or for any son or daughter of his over 18 years of age. The landlord, therefore, cannot avail himself of this provision should he require the house for occupation as a residence for any other relative (*h*).

Thirdly, the Court must be satisfied, after a consideration of all the circumstances of the case including any alternative accommodation available for either the landlord or the tenant, that greater hardship would be caused by refusing to grant an order than by granting it.

Sect. 2 (1) of the Prevention of Evictions Act provides that where any order or judgment has been made or given before the passing of the Act but not executed, and in the opinion of the Court the order or judgment would not have been made or given if the Act had been in force at the time of the making of the order or the passing of the judgment, the Court may, on application by

(h) C. 88 J. P. 151.

... upon ... the order in such manner and subject ... conditions as the Court shall think fit for the purpose of ... the Act ... For a similar provision reference may ... sect. 5 (3) of the Act of 1920.

... ... *Neville v. Fisher* 12 ... ... *Webb v. Hurd* ab 91

... jurisdiction has to a considerable extent been created ... Court should refuse to exercise its discretion in ... *Neville v. Fisher* 12 I. L. C. C. R. ...

... reference is also made to the case of *City of Dublin* *Hospital v. Pleasants* 58 I. L. T. R. 91 decided under ... sect. 17 ... in the Irish Free State Rent ... Act 192.. where it was stated that ... a scheme to be ... public interest must partake of a public ... assistance is carried out in pursuance of ... municipal or similar authority or some ... construction on which the public ... country are citizens or inhabitants ... p. 92 ... It was accordingly held that ... ... cancer hospital was not such a ... 17 ... the Act contemplated.

... ... sect. 5 (1) ... of the Act of 1920 in ... ... person who ... ... now ... ... *Phillips v. ...*

Page 122, line 32

But was subsequently negatived by the Court of Appeal (40 T. L. R. 211). The decision of the Court of Appeal, however, expressly leaves open the question of the statutory tenant's right to sub-let as distinct from assign

Page 122, note (d)

Add "*Roberts v. Enlayde, Ltd.* ((1923) W. N. 313)"

Page 125, line 3

Add after the word "statutory" ' not even if such rent is paid and accepted after action brought (*Hall v. Loans* (1923) L. J. C. C. R. 68)

Page 118, line 13

After 'afterwards' add ' The last day for taking proceedings to recover overpayments made before the 31st July, 1923, is therefore the 31st January 1924 (*Tims v. Oliver*, 40 T. L. R. 588). The date of the commencement of the proceedings, whether by writ or summons, is the material date, and not the date of judgment (*Lewis v. Meehan; Ngole v. Tagle; Clark v. Potter*, 40 T. L. R. 579; *Damon v. Roberts*, Times, 24th July 1924)"

Page 151, lines 4, 5

Instead of the words 'It is in respect of such applications only it is submitted, that the ... This provision sect. 17 (2) ' further will apply to such actions as claims by tenants for overpayments of rent or claims by landlord for the recovery of controlled premises, and "

Page 151, line 9

This provision sect. 17 (2) however does not deprive the High Court of jurisdiction In dismiss or stay pending actions in the High Court (*Studd v. Peace*, 40 T. L. R. p. 315,

Page 151, note (r)

Add—"*Gill* v. *Lush*, 40 T. L. R. 38."

Page 152, line 31

Thus in *Strickland* v. *Palmer* (39 T. L. R. 315) the Divisional Court held that a right of appeal lay in an ordinary common law action for arrears of rent, although the actual point for the decision of the Court was whether the landlord was entitled to the increase by virtue of **sect. 2 (1) (b)** of the Act of 1920. In the same case in the Court of Appeal L. J. Bankes left open the question as to whether there would have been any right of appeal had the point been raised by application to the County Court under the Rent Restriction Rules (40 T. L. R. at p. 649), but it is submitted that there would have equally been a right of appeal had the matter been brought before the County Court in the form of an application under the Rules.

Page 153, line 16

Add—at end of line 16, note (*mm*)—
It would appear that it is only to such applications that the Scotch Act of Sederunt of 2nd December 1920 applies. (See *Paris* v. *Graham* (1924) S. L. T. 151, *contra* *White* v. *Gotcher*, 1923, S. L. T. (Sh. Ct.) R. 123, and *McArthur* v. *Cox*, ib. p. 130.)

APPENDIX.

PREVENTION OF EVICTION ACT, 1924
(14 & 15 Geo 5 c 18)

[14th July 1924]

Be it enacted, &c —

1 Paragraphs (iv) and (v) of subsection (1) of the section which by section four of the Rent and Mortgage Interest Restrictions Act, 1923, is substituted for section five of the Increase of Rent and Mortgage Interest (Restrictions) Act 1920, are hereby repealed as respects pending as well as future proceedings and the following paragraph shall be substituted therefor

Amendment of 13 & 14 Geo 5 c 32 s 4 ss (1 10 & 11 Geo 5 c 17

(iv) Where the dwelling-house is reasonably required by the landlord (not being a landlord who has become landlord by purchasing the dwelling-house or any interest therein after the fifth day of May nineteen hundred and twenty-four) for occupation as a residence for himself or for any son or daughter of his over eighteen years of age and the court is satisfied having regard to all the circumstances of the case including any alternative accommodation available for the landlord or the tenant that greater hardship would be caused by refusing to grant an order or judgment for possession than by granting it

2 —(1) Where any order or judgment has been made or given before the passing of this Act but not executed, and in the opinion of the court the order or judgment would not have been made or given if this Act had been in force at the time when such order or judgment was made or given

Application of Act to pending proceedings

the court on application by the tenant may rescind or vary the order or judgment in such manner and subject to such conditions as the court shall think fit for the purpose of giving effect to this Act

(2) Where a landlord has on or after the fifteenth day of April nineteen hundred and twenty-four taken possession of a dwelling-house under a judgment or order so rescinded as aforesaid such possession shall not in any case exclude the dwelling-house from the operation of the Rent and Mortgage Interest (Restrictions) Acts 1920 and 1923

3 This Act may be cited as the Prevention of Eviction Act 1924 and shall be construed as one with the Rent and Mortgage Interest (Restrictions) Acts 1920 and 1923 and those Acts and this Act may be cited together as the Rent and Mortgage Interest (Restrictions) Acts 1920 to 1924